HAROLD C. KNUTSON is a member of the Department of French at the University of British Columbia, Vancouver.

Although the last few years have witnessed the publication of many historical and interpretive studies on Molière, this book is the first to examine his total comic production in the light of archetypal criticism. It analyses the plays as a series of variations on a basic comic myth – a myth affirming organic and social vitality.

Using the methodology set forth in Northrop Frye's *Anatomy of Criticism* and Charles Mauron's *La Psychocritique du genre comique*, and with the aid of Susanne K. Langer's essay on 'The Comic Rhythm,' Professor Knutson establishes a basic archetypal approach to Molière and a working classification of his plays according to the various archetypal patterns used. He then devotes chapters to each group of plays.

As the book is arranged as a series of essays on specific plays, it will interest not only the scholar, but also the casual reader or theatre-goer who may wish to read a commentary on one particular work.

HAROLD C. KNUTSON

Molière: An Archetypal Approach

UNIVERSITY OF TORONTO PRESS
TORONTO AND BUFFALO

© University of Toronto Press 1976
Toronto and Buffalo
Printed in Canada

Library of Congress Cataloging in Publication Data

Knutson, Harold C.
Molière: an archetypal approach.

(University of Toronto romance series; 31)
Bibliography: p.
Includes index.
1. Molière, Jean Baptists Poquelin, 1622-1673
Criticism and interpretation. I. Series: Toronto.
University. University of Toronto romance series; 31.
PQ1860.K5   842'.4   76-15976
ISBN 0-8020-5348-3

This book has been published with the help of a grant from
the Humanities Research Council of Canada, using funds provided by
the Canada Council, and a grant from the Andrew W. Mellon Foundation
to the University of Toronto Press.

This book is gratefully dedicated to Simone,
who made it possible.

Contents

PREFACE ix

INTRODUCTION 3

1 Comedy: The Archetypal View 11

2 Buffoon 27

3 Exorcism: Theme and Variations 43

4 Exorcism: The Heavy Fathers 63

5 Romance 118

6 Irony: Beyond the Comic Myth 144

Conclusion 173

NOTES 180

APPENDIX A: Chronological List of Molière's Plays 192

APPENDIX B: Archetypal Criticism and *Structuralisme* 195

BIBLIOGRAPHY 200

INDEX 203

Preface

This book grew out of a graduate seminar on Molière which I taught at the University of British Columbia in 1968-9. To the students who composed this course I express my gratitude for the cheerfulness with which they allowed themselves to be subjected, along with Molière, to an unrelenting archetypal assault; and my thanks go to them as well for their fresh and stimulating insights, many of which have found their way into the following pages.

I must acknowledge the generous support of the Canada Council both in the form of a Short Term Research Grant for the summer of 1971 and a Leave Fellowship for the academic year 1972-3. I am indebted as well to the University of British Columbia for granting me a sabbatical year to complete this study.

May I single out for special mention a few of the many people who helped in one way or the other to bring this project to completion. A word of thanks, to begin with, to Larry Bongie of the Department of French at the University of British Columbia for his continuous support over the years. My research assistant, Mrs Ellen Humphrey, and my typist, Mrs Nancy Perri, both deserve a special tribute. Four colleagues read the manuscript before it went to the Press: Bernard Beugnot (University of Montreal), David Hayne (University of Toronto), as well as Helen Purkis and Donald Soule from the University of British Columbia. To all of them go my thanks for their judicious suggestions. My gratitude, too, to Jules Brody for his encouragement and invaluable editorial comments. Finally a word of praise for an efficient and courteous editor, Ron Schoeffel.

A FEW NOTES ON SCHOLARLY STYLE

Sources for quotations or basic supporting material will be identified in the text itself. Note references will therefore indicate only supplementary documentation intended to situate the text in a wider scholarly perspective.

All references to Molière's text are from Robert Jouanny's Classiques Garnier edition (Paris 1962, two volumes). Spelling is modernized where Jouanny keeps seventeenth-century orthography. Quotations are identified by act and scene (eg, IV, 3). Jouanny's own remarks are indicated by volume and page number.

All italics in quotations are in the original text.

This book has been published with the help of a grant from the Humanities Research Council of Canada, using funds provided by the Canada Council, and a grant from the Andrew W. Mellon Foundation to the University of Toronto Press.

AN ARCHETYPAL APPROACH TO MOLIÈRE

Introduction

A focal point of several related disciplines – psychology, anthropology, philosophy, criticism itself – the archetypal approach to literature comes at the crest of one of the great speculative surges of modern times and bears the mark of the boldest and most innovative minds of our era: Frazer, Freud, Jung, Cassirer, and many others. Much of their contribution to knowledge has of course become obsolete and discredited, but this relative disrepute should not prejudice us. Our concern here is not with the objective truth of a method's components, but with its suitability, the illumination it offers when we apply it to a work. The contribution of the various disciplines mentioned can be thought of as a scaffolding behind which the edifice of archetypal criticism can be built. Once construction is complete, the scaffolding can be done away with; the building must stand on its own merits and with its own justification.

The unifying principle on which archetypal criticism is posited and around which it seeks to organize its findings is that literature owes its ultimate appeal to recurrent conventions which enable the writer to communicate with the reader or onlooker. The 'communicable unit' through which literary meaning passes from producer to consumer is what Northrop Frye, the most distinguished theoretician and practitioner of this mode of analysis, calls an archetype: 'a symbol which connects one poem [in Frye's sense of literary work] with another and thereby helps to unify and integrate our literary experience. And as the archetype is the communicable symbol, archetypal criticism is primarily concerned with literature as a social fact and as a mode of communication. By the study of conventions and genres, it attempts to fit poems into the body of poetry as a whole' (*Anatomy of Criticism: Four Essays* [Princeton 1957] 99).

The fact of recurrence in literature cannot be disputed; symbols, character types, devices, and motifs have a tenacious life in widely differing areas and periods. The question naturally arises, why? Surely not mere coincidence, as Frye himself makes clear (*loc. cit.*). A more plausible but still spurious explanation of this recurrence is imitation. Authors do imitate, of course; but do they use consciously the stock-in-trade of their genre only because they are unable to invent new tools of expression? The important thing is that what they copy will appeal to their audience or readership. The reason for recurrence must then come from the audience's side; what makes it respond to devices and symbols that might seem so hackneyed and threadbare? To quote from Charles Mauron, the French scholar who has come closest to an archetypal view of comedy: 'l'imitation ou l'emprunt volontaire n'explique ni les types traditionnels, ni leur pouvoir maintenu de siècle en siècle, ni l'attachement que les créateurs leur portent. Les auteurs se copient, non les publics. Il faut donc invoquer des constantes psychologiques' (*La Psychocritique du genre comique* [Paris 1964] 15).

The hypothetical aspect of archetypal criticism lies not in the fact of literary convention but in the why of it. The explanation for the recurring elements goes back, ultimately, as Mauron concludes for comedy, to psychological factors. We must accept the hypothesis of some kind of psychological commonality in man, certain universals in the human psyche which resonate, so to speak, in contact with literary patterns.

What unifies the disciplines mentioned at the outset is that aspects of them have been used to provide the basis for this hypothetical construct. Freud's concept of the Oedipus complex has not only nurtured the archetypal theory of tragedy advanced by Maud Bodkin (*Archetypal Patterns in Poetry* [Oxford 1934] chapter 1), but forms the basis of a whole current of speculation about comedy culminating in Mauron's study of the comic genre. However, archetypal criticism is most at home with Carl Jung, the second great figure of traditional psychology, not only because of his more wide-ranging thought but because he promulgated the two hypotheses which actually form the underpinnings of archetypal theory. His concept of the collective unconscious furnishes a basis for the needed universal element noted earlier, namely, intrinsic psychological traits in man; and his coining of the word 'archetype' has been taken up by literary scholars in a wide variety of ways. While Jung applies this term to the latent image born in all of us and actualized by our own life experience, critics use it most often to describe the elements in literature which cause the Jungian archetype to stir under their stimulus and which therefore stabilize as literary conventions. The *anima*, for instance, is for Jung the female image inherent in all of us and actualized by our successive experience with real women. When it is objectified as a figure in literature it causes the original image to resonate. We can explain in this way the persistent recurrence of certain female images, particularly the splitting which betrays our ambivalence toward this figure: Frye's antithesis between the 'light' and 'dark' heroines of the Victorian novel comes immediately to mind, as does the contrast we find in French classical tragedy between viragos and gentle virgins, the Agrippine and Junie of Racine's *Britannicus.*

It is largely through Frazer's pioneer myth studies, so fruitfully elaborated upon by the Cambridge Hellenists, Gilbert Murray and Francis Cornford in particular, that archetypal criticism has acquired an important anthropological dimension. To summarize very schematically the complex thought evolved from this 'school':[1] the origin of myth, and therefore of the great re-enactments of mythological themes, is to be sought in ritual, in primitive religious observances like end-of-year ceremonies or fertility rites; these in turn give rise to narratives explaining or justifying them. Thus, recurrent features such as the death or sacrifice of a king in tragedy derive from ceremonies where kings were actually or symbolically put to death both as sacrificial figures and to enable renewed life to spring forth again in the person of a young ruler. Inasmuch as these ritual themes latent in myth are themselves recurrent, they give rise, naturally, to archetypes. Thus, we can speak of archetypes of sacrifice, of scapegoat expulsion, or death and resurrection, and the like.

Anthropology furnishes one more hypothesis, then, for literary recurrence – the appeal of fundamental ritual acts transformed into basic stories. This explanation, however, goes back to an assumed psychological one, for the rituals in question are attached to certain primitive desires and anxieties in the collectivity: fear of death, sterility, and disease, longing for life, health, and prosperity.

Implicit in this aspect of archetypal criticism is the view that myth itself is a recurrent element and that literary narratives can be reduced to basic stories which express, in their underlying ritual content, primitive human fears and aspirations. Here we rejoin Jung, who sees myth as a direct expression of the collective unconscious and therefore archetypal in nature. These ideas point forward as well to another great twentieth-century thinker, Ernst Cassirer, for whom myth 'sprouts forth from deep human emotions' (*The Myth of the State* [New Haven 1950] 43). But Cassirer does not view myth only in the customary narrative aspect; it expresses, for him, a fundamental mode of conceiving the world, a mode which antedates logical or scientific thinking. In 'mythic ideation,' 'all light is concentrated in one focal point of "meaning," while everything that lies outside these focal points of verbal or mythic conception remains practically invisible ... The part does not merely represent the whole, or the specimen its class; they are identical with the totality to which they belong; not merely as mediating aids to reflective thought, but as genuine presences which actually contain the power, significance and efficacy of the whole'

(*Language and Myth*, trans. Susanne Langer [New York 1946] 90-2). An aura of wonder, then, a quasi-religious mystery is a basic attribute of mythic thought; and language, Cassirer theorizes, comes into being from these moments of rapt contemplation. The human consciousness is able, through utterance, to objectify a particular mood, and set it on its course toward religious feeling. Even after the synthesizing and classifying function of the scientific mind has taken over, it is possible to recapture this particular, mysterious identity of word and feeling through another form of language, art; for 'there is one intellectual realm in which the word not only preserves its original creative power, but is ever renewing it; in which it undergoes a sort of constant palingenesis, at once a sensuous and a spiritual reincarnation. This regeneration is achieved as language becomes an avenue of artistic expression. Here it recovers the fullness of life; but it is no longer a life mythically bound and fettered, but an aesthetically liberated life' (*ibid*. 98). Art becomes a secularized form of religious utterance; but our awareness of symbolic function frees us from primitive dreads and puts our experience on the level of the aesthetic.

Cassirer's great admirer, Susanne Langer, has had much to do as well with providing a philosophical grounding for archetypal criticism. Her wide-ranging book on aesthetics, *Feeling and Form* (New York 1953), contains a stimulating discussion of what she calls the 'great dramatic forms': the comic rhythm and the tragic rhythm. 'As comedy presents the vital rhythm of self-preservation, tragedy exhibits that of self-consummation. The lilting advance of the eternal life process, indefinitely maintained or temporarily lost and restored, is the great general vital pattern that we exemplify from day to day. But creatures that are destined, sooner or later, to die ... hold the balance of life only precariously. ... Unlike the simple metabolic process, the forward advance of their individual lives has a series of stations that are not repeated; growth, maturity, decline. That is the tragic rhythm' (p 351).

Finally, the evolution of criticism itself – especially the great impulse of emancipation from the thraldom of literary history – has allowed archetypal methodology to emerge as a valid mode of literary analysis. Only with the general acceptance of the systematic internal study of texts could this species of it come into its own.

All of these currents of thought have been fused together in a brilliant and original synthesis: Frye's *Anatomy of Criticism*, by far the most complete and comprehensive statement on archetypal criticism ever published.[2] The two most important of the formative influences of archetypal criticism, psychology·and anthropology, become the two pillars of his archetypal vision. 'Poetry in its social or archetypal aspect ... not only tries to illustrate the fulfilment of desire, but to define the obstacles to it. Ritual is not only a recurrent act, but an act expressive of a dialectic of desire and repugnance: desire for fertility or victory, repugnance to drought or to enemies. We have rituals of social integration, and we have rituals of expulsion, execution, and punishment. ... Archetypal criticism, therefore, rests on two organizing rhythms or patterns, one cyclical, the other dialectic' (p 106). We recognize in the dialectic of desire and repugnance, of course, Mauron's 'constante psychologique,' expressed here as a kind of collective wish-fulfilment. But this dialectic dimension is by itself abstract and oscillatory; it expresses only a polarity, a to-and-fro rhythm. So the ritual, or recurrent element becomes equally important. As it is intimately associated with the great cycles of nature – the seasons of the year, the course of the day and night, lunar cycles, the tides – it is identified by Frye with the narrative side of literature. The recurrent conventions in literature are for him ritual forms, especially as they relate to nature symbolism derived from the cyclical phenomena mentioned.

'The union of ritual and dream in a form of verbal communication is myth' (*loc. cit.*). The two patterns fuse together in archetypal stories, and this ability to give narrative form to our deepest longings and fears and to embody the natural cycles in our narrative is uniquely and distinctively human. To quote Frye again, 'the most intelligent partridge cannot tell even the most absurd story explaining why it drums in the mating season' (p 107).

Literature, then, is seen as variations on recurrent stories associated with natural cycles and expressive of basic hopes and dreads. One of the archetypal critic's tasks is to isolate and classify these myths, reducing them to basic types. Taking his cue from the four seasons and the symbolic function they traditionally carry in literature, Frye argues for four *mythoi* or generic plots: comedy, romance, tragedy, and irony, attached respectively to spring, summer, fall, and winter. These in turn are reduced to 'a central unifying myth. *Agon* or conflict is the basis or archetypal theme of romance, the radical of romance being a sequence of marvellous adventures. *Pathos* or catastrophe, whether in triumph or in defeat, is the archetypal theme of tragedy. *Sparagmos*, or the sense that heroism and effective action are absent, disorganized or foredoomed to defeat, and that confusion and anarchy reign over the world, is the archetypal theme of irony and satire. *Anagnorisis*, or recognition of a newborn society rising in triumph around a still somewhat mysterious hero and his bride, is the archetypal theme of comedy' (p 192).

Curiously enough, the surge of 'new criticism' on Molière which has followed the publication in 1949 of Moore's now classic study[3] has not as yet led to a systematic study of archetypal devices or motifs in his theatre. The Anglo-Saxon reader familiar with Frye's fruitful methodology may express legitimate astonishment at this lacuna – all the more since Molière's plays, with their emphasis on the comic plot and strongly delineated obstacle figures, would seem a well-stocked hunting ground for this sort of approach. Certainly, the deeply rooted tradition of historical, supposedly objective scholarship in the field of French literature has inhibited systematic internal study of Molière, while archetypal criticism remains to this day a controversial subject.[4] Still, both Corneille and Racine have been studied from a boldly, almost provocatively archetypal standpoint in two works which have had a strong impact on scholarship: Serge Doubrovsky's *Corneille et la dialectique du héros* (Paris 1963), a thoroughgoing analysis of the hero archetype in Corneille, and Roland Barthes' controversial *Sur Racine* (Paris 1963), one of the outstanding examples of myth criticism in French scholarship.[5]

Only in Mauron's *Psychocritique du genre comique* do we come anywhere near to an archetypal view of comedy in Molière. Enlarging upon his attempt to discern Molière's 'mythe personnel' through his works ('L'Evolution créatrice de Molière,' in *Des Métaphores obsédantes au mythe personnel* [Paris 1962] 270-98), Mauron is here concerned with the impact of a 'mythe générique' on the audience. In that he speculates on the psychological basis of dramatic convention within the spectator, his approach is very much in the archetypal tradition. It is, however, only partially and fragmentarily concerned with Molière himself; and, as we shall see, Mauron's dogmatic Freudianism puts limits on his methodological usefulness.

This is not to say that the ground has not been broken in other ways. Although primarily concerned with the history of ideas, Paul Bénichou's perceptive chapter on Molière in *Morales du grand siècle* (Paris 1948) touches occasionally on various archetypal concepts, especially that of wish-fulfilment. Certain Molière comedies, particularly *Amphitryon* and *Don Juan*, give expression, in Bénichou's view, to a desire for omnipotence and pleasure-seeking in 'un monde plus brillant, plus irresponsable, plus libre d'entraves que le monde réel' (p 162). His analysis of Jupiter and Mercure and their persecution of their respective twins, Amphitryon and Sosie, is a genuine example of *psychocritique ante litteram*: 'le double, par son caractère de surnaturelle puissance, incarne les ambitions du moi, et son hostilité écrasante reflète l'incapacité de ce moi à s'élever réellement au niveau de ses désirs' (p 163).

Jacques Schérer's monumental *La Dramaturgie classique en France* (Paris, nd [1951]) draws attention as well to several archetypal features of comedy: among others, the function of parental obstacles (pp 63ff.),[6] the comic dénouement (p 137), and especially the custom, to be underlined later by Frye (p 165), of bringing together 'le plus grand nombre de personnages possible pour la fin d'une pièce' (p 141). To be sure, Schérer does not propose the usual archetypal explanations for these recurrent traits, nor does he clearly and systematically differentiate between the conventions of comedy and those of tragedy; thus, the tradition of the large final tableau is described as 'commune à tous les genres' (*loc. cit.*) notwithstanding its far greater and more characteristic use in comedy.

In a more recent publication, however, Schérer alludes to the polarity among characters in Molière in a way that brings him remarkably close to the archetypal idea of a social norm in comedy: 'les uns, approuvés par les spectateurs, incarnent l'aspiration normale aux plaisirs du monde. Les autres opposent à ces plaisirs un refus bourru, fondé sur une attitude rigoriste que le public de Molière ne peut pas admettre' ('Aventures des précieuses,' *RHLF* 72 [Sept.-Oct. 1972], 861).

Among books specifically on Molière, three in particular anticipate to one degree or another the approach to be used in the following pages: Guicharnaud's *Molière: une aventure théâtrale*, Gutwirth's *Molière ou l'invention comique*, and Lawrence's *Molière: The Comedy of Unreason*. To this list of full-length studies should be added two outstanding articles by Jules Brody, both of which treat of comic convention in a way often very close to the archetypal view: 'Esthétique et société chez Molière,' *Dramaturgie et Société*, ed. J. Jacquot (Paris 1968) I, 307-26; and '*Don Juan* and *Le Misanthrope*, or the Esthetics of Individualism in Molière,' *PMLA* 84 (1969) 559-76. Finally, special mention should be made of Francis Baumal's prophetic little book *Molière auteur précieux* (Paris, nd [1925]) which anticipated fifty years ago the rehabilitation of the romantic or 'chimérique' Molière which has taken place in recent criticism.[7]

Guicharnaud's sensitive and probing analysis of *Tartuffe, Don Juan*, and *Le Misanthrope* has been rightly described by Brody as 'a landmark in Molière studies' ('*Don Juan* and *Le Misanthrope*' n 5). Although not specifically archetypal in method, *Molière: une aventure théâtrale* shows an extraordinary intuitive understanding of the central tenets of this critical mode. Frye's dialectic of desire and repugnance finds a parallel in Guicharnaud's 'postulat fondamental de la comédie' in which order triumphs over corruption (p 143). In *Tartuffe*, for instance, 'l'intrigue peut déboucher dans une solution, sous la forme d'une victoire d'ordre stratégique qui assure, non le rachat des âmes corrompues, mais le rétablissement d'un order viable' (p 521). In emphasizing the importance of fantasy and convention in Molière's dramatic art, especially in the dénouement (cf. p 41), the author comes close to the basic archetypal concept of wish-fulfilment: 'On a affaire ... à une mise en ordre de la réalité, destinée à satisfaire un vœu de l'esprit' (p 143). Indeed, Guicharnaud's grasp of the true role of dramatic convention leads him to the idea of myth itself: 'le mythe ... de *l'aménagement*' which appears in the marvellous turnabout of the dénouement to show us 'ce qui *pourrait arriver* si le poète avait l'occasion d'organiser l'univers' (pp 143-4), a concept of poetic invention startlingly close to that of Frye, for whom 'one of the poet's functions is to visualize the goals of human work' (p 115).

While Guicharnaud anticipates archetypal methodology, Gutwirth's study of the development and elaboration of basic comic types in Molière prefigures to a degree its systematic application. Character typology constitutes a key component in the archetypal approach, but Gutwirth's preoccupation with categories of types causes him to attach comparatively little importance to the intrigue as such or to its resolution. A case in point is the statement that 'l'effondrement du cinquième acte de *Tartuffe* [qui] permet de reconnaître les bons des méchants ... n'ajoute rien à la comédie' (p 114). For the archetypal critic, this reversal is the key event in the play. Even when the unfolding of his thought brings him toward myth criticism, Gutwirth's remarks are tinged with value judgements. The romantic marriage of comedy 'n'est que formule rituelle de l'ordre de "et ils vécurent heureux le reste de leurs jours" ' (p 90). Clearly, such fairy-tale clichés deserve little attention in Gutwirth's view, although through them we reach the profound meaning of ritual, its relevance in terms of social renewal, and the basic archetypal function of *invraisemblance* in comedy. Not surprisingly, Gutwirth gives the *romanesque* in Molière short shrift; 'on a parlé d'un Molière précieux' is his disdainful allusion to the unnamed Baumal (p 83).

Chapter 1 of Lawrence's *Molière: The Comedy of Unreason* contains, finally, an explicit call for an archetypal analysis: 'It is curious that the concept of comic structure as rooted in ancient cyclic rites, so long an operative factor in criticism of English literature, has not been applied to Molière' (p 13). Lawrence does little more than sketch in the picture during the remaining part of the chapter and is concerned only with the first years of Molière's career – the last play studied is *La Princesse d'Elide* (1664). But he has the merit of being one of the first to appreciate explicitly the validity of the archetypal approach toward comedy and to envisage its application to Molière. It is his call that the following chapters attempt to answer.

1

Comedy: The Archetypal View

In the context of neo-classical European comedy, no element recurs more frequently, perhaps, than the familiar love plot we find so often in Molière: the boy-meets-girl theme culminating almost invariably in prospective marriage. In such varied forms as Italian erudite comedy, the *commedia dell'arte*, certain varieties of the Spanish *comedia*, or the whole tradition of French comedy from Corneille and Rotrou through such varied authors as Molière, Marivaux, and Beaumarchais, we find ourselves face to face with an astoundingly durable and adaptable comic plot. And far from fading out with the advent of Romanticism, it has survived until the present day in literature, both sophisticated and popular, as well as in television and the cinema. It is quite natural that archetypal criticism should be attracted to this recurrent feature and should propose a hypothetical explanation for it.

Practitioners of both the Anglo-Saxon approach to comedy and its approximate counterpart in French criticism have been so struck by the durability of this comic plot that they have abstracted it into a myth: the '*mythos* of spring' in Frye's quadripartite system, 'le mythe comique' in Mauron's *psychocritique*. 'What normally happens is that a young man wants a young woman, that his desire is resisted by some opposition, usually paternal, and that near the end of the play some twist in the plot enables the hero to have his will' (Frye 163). Mauron condenses this basic conflict and its resolution into a memorable formula: 'le blondin berne le barbon' (*Psychocritique* 57).

The fact of recurrence is incontrovertible. What is conjectural is the theoretical basis that each thinker has proposed for the comic myth. Their hypotheses can be seen as extensions and elaborations of the commonplace of comic theory found from Donatus on: that comedy is a celebration of life and of vital energy. '[Vita] capessenda exprimitur' as Donatus himself put it,[1] words of which the following paraphrase of Cassirer can be considered a modern echo:

'mythical thought is especially concerned to deny the fact of death and to affirm the unbroken unity and continuity of life' (D. Bidney, 'Myth, Symbolism, and Truth' in *Myth: A Symposium*, ed. T. A. Sebeok [Philadelphia 1955] 7). As death is man's basic anxiety, the feeling of his own vitality furnishes the highest sense of euphoria he can experience; comedy provides us with an opportunity to experience these vital impulses on the imaginative level.

Mauron resorts to two familiar Freudian concepts to postulate the 'constantes psychologiques' that for him underlie the appeal of the comic plot: the tripartite image of the psyche (id, superego, and ego), and, expectedly, the Oedipus complex. As concerns the first now classic view of the ego as mediating a conflict between instinct and moral imperative, Mauron seems to be on sure ground. The vital energy celebrated by comedy is analogous to the id; the impetuosity with which Molière's young lover is driven to possess his beloved suggests the power of instinctual drives. On the other hand, the *barbon* seems a superego figure; his opposition is usually unreasonable, inflexible, and supported by imperatives supposedly drawn from social norms. Molière's parents and parental surrogates can be considered in a way as projections of this moral censor, always alleging their authority founded in custom, always preaching blind obedience, and always threatening to impose their will with a heavy hand if contradicted.

In real life, the pleasure principle motivating the id is gradually subdued and controlled by the reality principle resident in the ego. The impulse to immediate gratification tends to be asocial while the sense of practical limits endeavours in part to put the ego in tune with social realities. Curiously enough, however, we witness in comedy a kind of moral reversal. The superego, usually a voice of guilt, anxiety, even terror, is embodied in a ludicrous 'barbon' whose authority is so diminished that he can be 'berné' without a second thought. By the same token, the unruly id is shown in a favourable light. We cannot but like the impulsive young hero of comedy and side with him in his struggle. The fundamental legitimacy of his impulses is confirmed by his victory at the end of the play, and by the unfavourable light in which his opponent is shown.

Mauron explains that apparent contradiction by another notion of traditional psychology: wish-fulfilment or what the Frenchman calls 'une fantaisie de triomphe.' To quote one of the fundamental tenets of his comic theory: 'la grande loi du genre comique, c'est que le principe de plaisir l'emporte' (*Psychocritique* 86). Mauron, however, is not content with this rather vague, but plausible notion of instinctual, vital forces legitimized vicariously by fantasy – the comic fantasy which becomes a sort of collective dream. The emotional content of comedy is at once deeper and more specific: the genre allows fulfilment, through imaginative projection, of the Oedipus complex. Thus, the two terrifying components of this classic disorder – desire for the mother and hatred for the father — are transformed through the operation of fantasy provided by the comic myth. Incest is made legitimate: the mother is transformed into the young girl of comedy, unrelated, a proper object for the son's love; the son becomes, in turn, the handsome, likeable young man of comedy. Parricide, the impulse to kill the hated father-rival, is carried out symbolically as the father figure is deflated by caricature into a bumbling and infantile fool who is shown as coveting a youthful creature he cannot satisfy and does not deserve. In short, the id impulse satisfied by the young man is desire for the mother and hostility for the father; the latter finds further expression in the other comic butts of comedy, all degraded father surrogates.

This thesis is eloquently and convincingly presented, and Mauron's fine literary sense mitigates the schematization of his thought. Yet, the Oedipal theory of comedy has serious deficiencies as a hypothetical construct. It compels Mauron to exaggerate the importance of *L'Avare* (p 61), the only play in a large and varied canon where father-son rivalry actually exists. More seriously, Mauron's attempt to extend the scope of *psychocritique* from author to genre, from the 'mythe personnel' to a 'mythe collectif' leaves us with nagging doubts. It is possible that Racine, Corneille, and other authors projected a personal Oedipus myth into their work; but can we assume that the dialectic of desire and repugnance which successive *audiences* have projected into comedy is founded on an Oedipal relationship? The concept seems a narrow and insecure base on which to build a theory suitable for an author of Molière's complexity.

A broader and more comprehensive psychological view of comedy obtains if we fall back upon Mauron's general notion of a conflict between the pleasure principle and the reality principle, and the victory, through fantasy transformation, of the former. At the same time, we come closer to Frye's own distinction between the two organizing patterns of literature, the dialectical and the cyclical, which combine in narrative form as myth. The former dimension in comedy we can easily envisage as a particularly explicit expression of the dialectic of desire and repugnance symbolized by the polarity between the young man and the father. The young man corresponds to the wish-fulfilment dream both in the idealized way in which he is depicted and in the improbable and miraculous way in which he usually gets what he wants. The father undergoes an opposite schematization in the form of caricature which at once expresses and neutralizes the anxieties normally attached to this superego symbol, and in the equally improbable and miraculous way in which he is normally defeated.

An overview of Molière's theatre confirms readily that this basic conflict between generations operates on several symbolic levels. If comedy is an act of faith in organic vitality, the triumph of youth means the victory of health, physical energy, good looks. All of Molière's *jeunes premiers* and *jeunes premières* embody a vague ideal of beauty and energy; they are analogous to the *adulescens* described by Frye, who has 'the neutrality that enables him to represent a wish-fulfilment' (p 167). The comic plot, moreover, and the majority of Molière's plays, end in prospective marriage; here organic and social vitality intersect; a new family, a miniature society, is about to be founded, symbolic both of bodily continuity and social renewal. Finally, in the most general sense, the family becomes a metaphor for society as a whole; comedy, with its final vision of reconciliation and youthful enthusiasm, gives vent to our longing for social harmony and order, a renewed faith in man and his society. The significance of comedy is 'ultimately social significance, the establishing of a desirable society' (Frye 286). We need go no farther than Moore for a confirmation of this principle as it concerns Molière: when we see examples of characters who would sunder themselves from society, 'the esthetic result of such pictures, upon an audience who share this view, is ... liberation and reassurance, as the poet unravels before them the strength and legitimacy of the social bond' (*Molière* 123).

The sense of euphoria obtained from wish-fulfilment in this way is all the more heightened when it results in part from the removal of a threat. Each of the affirmations just mentioned has a corresponding anxiety, an image of something which must be exorcized. Physical vitality implies our basic dread not only of death but also of all the symbolic forms of death that may occur in comedy: illness, physical degradation, and the ugliness resulting from it. The disease-bearing bogeyman in Molière is of course the doctor, and we shall have ample opportunity to comment on this archetypal role, so characteristically *moliéresque*. On the other hand, Molière does not usually dwell explicitly on physical deformity, except in *L'Avare* where we find the oldest of Molière's *barbons*. But even the younger ones, Arnolphe for instance, can be readily imagined as physically repulsive and utterly unsuited to rival with a handsome young man.

More importantly, I think, paternal figures represent a loss of social vitality. If the young stride self-assuredly toward marriage, the old enshroud themselves in excessive caution and peevishness; their energies are directed at clutching petulantly what they have: daughter, wife, ward, money; no longer able to win by love they rule by capricious tyranny, senseless interdicts. Thus they embody the opposite of the happy society of youth and its fellow travellers – a divisive and joyless world of bondage.

Molière drives this opposition home in his very *dramatis personae*. As Guicharnaud shows with *Tartuffe* (*Aventure* 19), the list of characters prepares us for a moral response to the action even before the play begins. While any sweeping generalization would be quickly demolished, such Greek-sounding names as Clitandre, Léonor, or the elegant ones inherited from the *romanesque* element of the *commedia* (Valère, Horace, Isabelle, Angélique) point to the romantic pole of the plot (Agnès seems the significant exception to this rule); the representatives of what Frye calls the 'humorous society' (the world of the blocking character) tend on the other hand to bear 'real' names (Monsieur Jourdain) or grotesque and clownlike ones such as Arnolphe, Tartuffe, Orgon, Argan.

The above points are more implied than explicit in Frye's dialectical view of comedy. He is actually more concerned with its ritual or cyclical aspect, the element which combines with desire and repulsion to produce, in this case, the *mythos* of spring. There are two ritual vestiges of seasonal renewal in comedy, the marriage ceremony and the expulsion of a scapegoat, both going back to the single fertility ritual hypothesized by Francis Cornford in his *The Origin of Attic Comedy* (London 1914). To quote Lawrence's summary, 'the complete ancient drama required four elements: an *agon* or contest between the old and new fertility principles; a sacrificial death; an *anagnorisis*, the discovery or recognition of the king followed by his initiation, resurrection or reincarnation; a feast and a marriage celebrating the epiphany of the young god and ending with a *kômos*, a procession with songs of joy' (p 14). All four elements have their counterparts in the comic story as utilized by Molière. We might say that the play itself is the contest, while the catharsis operated by the death or expulsion of the scapegoat corresponds to the defeat of the father; the recognition of the young victor and the norms he symbolizes, the feast and procession about to take place around the forthcoming nuptials highlight in turn the intensely euphoric tone of the dénouement.

Not only is the father figure defeated, but he is often tricked, ridiculed, and humiliated. Indeed, some plays are little more than scapegoat ceremonies – one thinks of the fury with which Monsieur de Pourceaugnac is repeatedly baited; often the defeated hero is made painfully aware of having been foiled, as in the striking case of Arnolphe's 'Ouf!' Exorcism is obviously a very important function in Molière's theatre and more space will be devoted to it than to any other aspect. But the other ritual function, euphoric wish-fulfilment in the comic reversal, has been all too often neglected in Molière, and one of my main tasks will be to re-establish what is, in my view, the correct balance.

One of Frye's most suggestive ideas is that the full meaning of comedy goes far beyond what we see on stage. 'The total *mythos* of comedy, only a small part of which is ordinarily presented, has regularly what in music is called a ternary form: the hero's society rebels against the society of the *senex* and triumphs, but the hero's society is a Saturnalia, a reversal of social standards which recalls a golden age in the past before the main action of the play begins' (p 171). In a wider mythical sense comedy is an unending recurrence of usurpation and liberation, each phase of liberation attempting to re-establish the harmonious and healthy society of an imagined golden age. This function of the genre brings us close to one of Mircea Eliade's basic ideas, the role of ritual in recapturing for the moment the spirit and power of an ancient, mythic past, in reliving events which occurred *in illo tempore* before the world began its slow process of depletion and corruption. Ritual constitutes a way of facing 'un problème fondamental de l'existence humaine,' namely 'la chute de l'ordre de l'existence et le retour de cet ordre' (*Aspects du mythe* [Paris 1963] 67). The final vision of comedy allows us to return in our imagination to a kind of 'temps fort,' a primitive time of happiness and perfection before it was corrupted by chronological time, the time of the life cycle, of birth, ageing, and death. In the same way, on a more individual level, it allows us to escape from 'le temps vécu' to the 'temps mythique paradisiaque' of childhood (Eliade 97).

We understand now why, from an archetypal standpoint, the all-important event in comedy is the sudden shift from the domination of the *senex*, 'the grotesque, monomaniacal intruder, standard in Molière's comedies, who would impose his private vision of the world on a reluctant majority' (Brody, '*Don Juan* and *Le Misanthrope*' 570), to that of the hero: the moment at which the hold of the usurper is broken (although the other characters may not, of course, have that foreknowledge), and where a 'kind of moral norm, or pragmatically free society' (Frye 169) emerges.

In the ritual view of comedy, then, the genre celebrates social renewal, a deliverance from life-negating or corrupting forces. 'The appearance of this new society is frequently signalized by some kind of party or festive ritual, which either appears at the end of the play or is assumed to take place immediately afterward' (Frye 163). This promise of festivity in Molière is usually linked to the marriage (or marriages) in prospect; the power and inclusiveness of this new society, now that the blocking figure has been disposed of, are symbolized by the final tableau which brings together the greatest number of actors possible in a general mood of reconciliation and euphoria. The *barbon* is physically or symbolically expelled; the principle of bondage and corruption that threatens any society is exorcized by the humiliation of its embodiment. The cyclical aspect of comedy, like the dialectical one, imposes an essential polarity which reaches its ultimate schematization in what Frye calls 'naive melodrama' (p 47). The radical opposition of norm and derogation of it suggests a kind of primitive social manicheanism bringing with it a contrast in audience attitude: reward and punishment, sentimentality and cruelty, sympathy and dislike, inclusion and rejection – such are the antinomies aroused by the comic myth in the spectator.

While it is not within the scope of this study to promulgate a theory of the risible, the polarity of our relationship to the comic myth does obviously impinge on that complex problem. As criticism has generally concentrated on the scapegoat figure in Molière, it is not surprising that laughter has been primarily considered, in Bergson's word, a 'correction' — that is, a form of punishment through ridicule. Indeed, classical and neo-classical comic theories (Molière's own possibly) have stressed the concept of derisive laughter implicit in the *castigat ridendo mores* commonplace, a laughter by which we show our contempt for abnormal behaviour and, by implication, our comfortable moral distance from the object of our mirth.[2] However, as I have sought to suggest elsewhere (*The Ironic Game: A Study of Rotrou's Comic Theater* [Berkeley 1966] 63), seventeenth-century comic theory is in its broadest sense dualistic, although not codified as such. There is a whole gamut of words which convey a non-derisive idea of mirth: *plaisant, agréable, enjoué,* etc. Just as the *castigat ridendo mores* theory has been perpetuated by Hobbes and Bergson, such theorists as Baudelaire and Freud have advanced a more comprehensive view of laughter as situated on two levels, one not directly related to moral norms.[3] Following the modern dualistic theory of Elie Aubouin (*Les Genres du risible* [Marseilles 1948]), I would advance for Molière what I believe to be true of Rotrou: that along with derisive laughter directed at comic butts, we experience a more indulgent mirth for the young heroes and heroines of comedy. They are our moral equals and we share their vision of society; our only superiority over them is in our total knowledge of the situation and their partial awareness as they struggle against the machinations of the obstacle figure. This laughter, arising essentially from dramatic irony, is indulgent, sympathetic, even tinged with pathos.

The archetypal view of comedy imposes a third kind of laughter, the exultation we experience when the young are in control, when evil has been symbolically banished, and a happy, reconciled society stands before us reflecting our own ideals. We might call this euphoric laughter the pure expression of well-being. When we feel it, comedy has fulfilled its purpose.[4]

Partaking of the ambiguity of all literature, comedy admits of several, complementary levels of interpretation. From the perspective of individual psychology, the spectator undoubtedly enjoys the triumph of instinctual vitality over constraint and limitation; to this is added, in the conventional plot, the pleasure of sharing the ardour of young love and organic dynamism symbolized by the founding of a new family; finally, on a social level, the emergence of a young, vital, and harmonious unit feeds our longing for a kind of utopia where corruption, conflict, and anxiety are far away. In the case of Molière, this social meaning is predominant; it accounts for the extraordinary richness of his theatre and the complex transformations and elaborations which the simple comic myth undergoes in his plays.

When we give imaginative form to a wish, a double transformation takes place. The elements of reality contained in the vision are purified and idealized, while the negative side of experience – what we want to expunge from our ideal world – is exorcized or devalued. An antithesis of idealization and caricature underlies comedy and parallels the two opposing ritual vestiges, marriage and expulsion. Yet, instinctual behaviour is more often than not the expression of anti- or a-social impulses, potentially disruptive and often dangerous. Alongside sexual vitality there are other impulses that lead to assault and murder. And sexuality, of course, has its own forms of violence and cruelty. When this instinct is incorporated by Molière into comedy, however, it is usually legitimized and socialized. Desire is decent and honourable, no matter how impetuous, and is made doubly acceptable by the implicit promise of marriage. When Molière depicts desire as gross and immediate, it is lust, a derogation of the norm. One has only to compare the passionate but respectful way Horace caresses Agnès with Tartuffe's panting ferocity toward Elmire.

On the other hand, moral constraints – the legitimate means society has elaborated to order its existence – are flayed and derided, their representatives hounded and humiliated. All authority figures – parents, teachers, doctors, priests, and their surrogates – become in Molière tyrants, pedants, hypocrites, monsters. We need only remember that in *Tartuffe* the paternal principle is embodied in Orgon, and the august *directeur de conscience* in Tartuffe himself. It is as if, in the comic fantasy, the asocial elements of instinct are transferred to the social order itself.

The problem becomes more specific and complex when we approach the comic dénouement in Molière. 'The resolution of comedy,' notes Frye, 'comes, so to speak, from the audience's side of the stage' (p 164). It assumes a communion between comedy and audience, an affirmation that both belong to the same world and share the same values. An individual who sets himself against the play's society must stand opposed to the audience as well. This social conformity of Molière's theatre has bothered many scholars. In his 'Esthétique et société chez Molière,' Jules Brody suggests that only the great, domineering, self-affirming characters of Molière's comedies are completely 'comic': 'l'intérêt le plus immédiat d'une comédie de Molière consiste en la rencontre entre une majorité non-comique qui se dévoue au principe même du compromis et un personnage comique qui n'admet aucun obstacle à son bonheur' (p 310). Yet, whatever regret we feel over their defeat, these 'comic' heroes symbolize a view of society which devalues their claim to authority and power. They articulate opinions about all manner of social problems: the relationship between child and parent, man and wife, the role of social games, the significance of religion in personal behaviour. Whatever surface plausibility their precepts may hold, they stand fundamentally for authoritarianism and austerity; they embody a joyless, despotic vision of man's relationship to man. Molière presents this demonic vision with complexity and subtlety from one play to another, but most often it is seen as an aberration from or an alien intrusion into normalcy. In *Tartuffe*, for instance, the dour, cruel, repressive world implanted by Orgon and Tartuffe threatens the normal social life around Elmire; the imprisoned characters can only observe helplessly the effects of this harsh and hypocritical ethic of self-mortification.

This impression of intrusion is quite expected if we remember that the second phase in the archetypal myth of comedy is usurpation, ritual bondage. This threat must be exorcized, and a new society – in fact, the restoration of the old – must be formed. This society in Molière is founded on the precept of married love and a certain confident self-indulgence. Again, 'reality' has been doubly transfigured. In the highly ritualized and hierarchical society of seventeenth-century France, the authority of the father and of the husband held absolute sway. Marriages were imposed on both parties, and the wife passed from one form of subjection to another. Such was reality marriage; its pathetic and often tragic results found ample expression in the novel of the time starting with Madame de La Fayette. Yet, these painful facts are abolished in Molière's comedy. Wife and husband freely choose each other in utter disregard of parental directives; the married relationship which awaits them shows no taint of subordination. It is, in Gutwirth's suggestive oxymoron, *'une obligation libre'* (p 90). Hence the comic dénouement is, even in seventeenth-century terms, a collective wish-fulfilment. The principle of authority is suspended and we celebrate a dream of a free, unfettered, harmonious existence based on mutual love projected unchanging into time.

That the values generally celebrated by Molière's theatre are ultimately conformist cannot be doubted; we share in a vision, a collective statement that 'this should be' and 'that should not be.' The comic reversal allows reality to be transfigured into dream, for until then, what we want to exorcize seems on the verge of triumphing. But miracle and exorcism admit of two interpretations. We can admire the social idealism and generosity expressed in the vision, but we must recognize the deep pessimism inherent in the fact that this idealism can be expressed only in the imagination. Brody is quite correct in insisting on the feeling of despair and impotence which underlies fantasy. 'Par des procédés qui tiennent quelque peu de l'exorcisme, Molière fait tomber le rideau sur un monde épuré, délivré de l'emprise du mal' ('Esthétique et société' 309). But what can man do about the evil which vitiates real life beyond the theatre? A century so at home with the idea of original sin could only shrug its shoulders.

Besides exemplifying the social meaning of comedy in its broadest sense, Molière's comedies were intended for a particular audience; if the dramatist was successful, as we know he was, he was able to respond to the demands of a *Weltanschauung*, to give his spectators the myths they wanted.[5] Paul Bénichou, in his seminal *Morales du grand siècle*, has propounded so convincing an interpretation of this world view that it has changed our whole outlook on the playwright. Bénichou's thesis, simply stated, is that the social ideal reflected in Molière's theatre is fundamentally aristocratic. He reacts vigorously and with heavy irony against those who held that Molière embodied 'les idées moyennes du bourgeois. Que de fois,' he reminds us, 'ce mot a été écrit, surtout depuis soixante ans, pour définir ses personnages ou sa philosophie! Bon sens et bourgeoisie sont deux notions à tel point confondues dans les esprits, que tout ce qui dans Molière raille la démesure passe aujourd'hui pour bourgeois' (p 159). Quite the contrary, insists Bénichou, Molière reflects rather the spirit of pleasure and amusement for which courtly *divertissements* like ballets, carousels, tournaments provided a vehicle: 'le côté facile et détendu de la chevalerie' (p 161).

We are reminded of the whole courtly atmosphere of the seventeenth century. Having shown his prowess in the *nobles travaux* for which Louis XIV, for instance, is eulogized in the prologue to *Les Fâcheux*, the perfect knight can indulge himself in well-deserved enjoyment. Licence is thus seen in the favourable context of the familiar courtly myth. The same pleasure-loving ethic finds form, on a less heroic level, in what Bénichou calls the 'libéralisme élégant des honnêtes gens' (p 194). 'La belle galanterie' was the ideal of the time: 'réunions galantes, bals, promenades et "cadeaux," sérénades, lectures de poèmes et de lettres, discussions sur l'amour, divertissements de danse et de chant' (p 191). In all these amusements men and women associated freely with a minimum of constraint. We recognize here the twofold aspect of aristocratic liberalism: freedom of thought and action legitimized by the inherent moral excellence of the aristocrat. In this sense this social ideal derives from the same tradition exemplified in the Abbaye de Thélème: 'fay ce que voudras' has meaning only because well-born people, if allowed to act freely, can do no wrong.

An ideal of play in a world of golden idleness, play made permissible by its own refinement and elegance – such is the moral tone of Molière's comedy. In some works, of course, this ideal of self-indulgence reaches an extreme of uninhibited licence. Self-seeking takes the form of amorous pursuit and all is governed by 'la loi toute-puissante du plaisir' (Bénichou 165). We shall come back to these ideas later when we reach the two works by Molière that best reflect what the same critic calls this 'surhumanité heureuse, libre, facile, païenne en un mot' (p 164); in *Amphitryon* and *Don Juan* the pleasure principle is taken to such lengths that it questions itself.

The 'pragmatically free society' which Frye sees as emerging from the comic reversal and this seventeenth-century aristocratic ideal founded on untrammelled pleasure-seeking and self-indulgence have obvious points in common. Indeed, the congruence between the general archetypal pattern and a specific embodiment of it could not be more striking, especially when we consider the role of the bourgeois in Molière's theatre. Bénichou demonstrates that, far from exemplifying an ideal of *bon sens*, the bourgeois in Molière 'est presque toujours médiocre ou ridicule' (p 172). In fact, he is seen point for point as the antithesis of the 'honnêtes gens.' His avarice, cowardice, tyranny, possessiveness, jealousy, and fear of cuckoldry contrast forcefully with the liberality, courage, tolerance, and trust shown by the enlightened. Here, too, we are in the presence of the tradition, active from the Middle Ages on, of dour, domineering misogyny that saw woman as an evil creature to be sequestered and subjugated.

Thus, the phase in comedy of ritual bondage, of usurped power and authority seems to take the form of a social class in Molière's own time. The bourgeois becomes in a sense a scapegoat figure; he appears to assume in the comic fantasy the guilt for the heavy imperatives that pressed down the century, thus making possible the unconstrained revels of the 'beau monde.'

In terms of the comic myth, these social implications lead us inevitably to the reversal, that central event which allows aristocratic pleasure-seeking to triumph over bourgeois constraint, an enlightened social order to win out over corruption. The traditional attitude toward this device in Molière needs no elaboration; critics were long ill at ease with such *invraisemblable* and gratuitous endings as we find in *L'Ecole des femmes, Tartuffe,* and *L'Avare.* It is essential for the purposes of this study that we free ourselves from such prejudices. For if we accept Frye's basic premise that the real meaning of comedy is *in* the comic reversal, in the passage from ritual bondage to pragmatic freedom, and if, at the same time, we condemn Molière's dénouements as defective, we are then led to the unacceptable conclusion that Molière's comedies are flawed in their very essence.[6]

Rather, we should reverse the proposition and ask: is there something in the essence of comedy which dictates reversals of the type we find in Molière? Only since Moore have critics really attempted to come to grips with this question. 'If such endings act well, should they not be regarded as the work of fancy rather than of logic?' (*Molière* 83). Bray enlarges upon the same idea in his own ringing defence of Molière's dénouements (pp 215-21). The keynote of these and later vindications of Molière's reversals is essentially the same: the very nature of comedy dictates that its ending be fortuitous: fantasy, not inevitability is its mainspring. The genre, in Frye's words, 'illustrates a victory of arbitrary plot over consistency of character. Thus, in striking contrast to tragedy, there can hardly be such a thing as inevitable comedy, as far as the action of the individual play is concerned' (p 170). Guicharnaud confirms how completely Molière's theatre fits the archetypal model: 'tension profonde du théâtre de Molière, le rapport entre la permanence des caractères et les aménagements possibles du monde représente en quelque sorte le contraire de "l'absurde" des visions modernes, où la liberté des hommes vient se briser contre des déterminismes' (*Aventure* 143).

The notion of the fortuitous leads us to the very heart of the genre; scholars of such varying persuasions as Frye, Langer, and Mauron agree on this point. Frye's 'victory of arbitrary plot' finds an echo in Langer for whom the comic rhythm creates the impression of 'a world that is forever taking new uncalculated turns' (p 342). Mauron, however, provides the clearest explanation of what he in turn calls 'cette insouciance des causes et des effets' (*Psychocritique* 32). Because of the ludic nature of comedy, the spectator is able to dismiss the ordinary canons of probability and admit in the comic form 'une incohérence contraire à son expérience réelle des actions humaines' (*ibid.* 29). Indeed, this change of vision is absolutely necessary if comedy is to arouse the impression of euphoria that is one of its hallmarks. Determinism of any kind, but especially temporal determinism, arouses anxiety; our imprisonment in time brings with it the inevitable concomitants of ageing and depleted energy. The arbitrariness of the events of comedy thus allows us to reverse this process in our imagination; by denying causality, the comic writer gives us another form of wish-fulfilment and thus contributes in one more way to the celebration of vital energy. Comedy allows one to forget that one is 'embarqué.'

Mauron is thus quite correct in taking Bergson to task for making of reversibility an automatic device opposed to life; quite the contrary: 'la physique tient un mouvement réversible pour idéal, parce qu'il échapperait à la dégradation de l'énergie, donc à la détermination temporelle. Dans l'univers réel, c'est cette dégradation qui est automatique et la vie cherche sans cesse à lui échapper en conservant et en créant. Vue sous cet angle, l'acquisition de la réversibilité constitue un triomphe' (*loc. cit.*).

In this context, tragedy, not comedy (as Frye has already hinted) is the image of 'reality.' To quote Mauron's illuminating paradox: 'la plus mythique des tragédies a moins de droits à l'irréalité que la comédie la plus quotidienne' (*ibid.* 29). This fundamental contrast between the two genres is developed at length by Frye and Langer as well and summarized by Langer in a perceptive antithesis between Fortune and Fate: 'Tragedy is the image of Fate, as comedy is of Fortune. Their basic structures are different; comedy is essentially contingent, episodic, and ethnic ... tragedy is a fulfillment, and its form therefore is closed, final and passional' (pp 333-4). This opposition is still more sharply focused in another context: 'Destiny conceived as Fate is, therefore, not capricious, like Fortune, but is predetermined' (p 352).

Tragedy, then, mirrors our life as a chain of causes and effects from which we cannot break free. We are at once the unwilling victims of the causes that precede us and the answerable cause of effects that follow from us; whence the curious and apparently contradictory blend in tragedy of inescapable fate and personal responsibility. It is no accident that the great tragic figures, like Phèdre, are obsessed by their paradoxical status as guilty victims.

Comedy, on the other hand, doubly neutralizes the anguish we experience as aware participants in the human condition. By presenting an image of contingency in a world unbound by causality but directed by a kind of providential comic destiny, the genre reinforces our sense of vitality. And as things happen by pure chance in this comic world, we need not be troubled by guilt or responsibility. Freed from these adult preoccupations, we can reach a state of untrammelled, child-like spontaneity that gives rise to the euphoria associated with the genre.[7]

The one point, of course, where plausibility must especially be banished is the dénouement. The comic reversal not only symbolizes reversibility in general; it is the magic door through which we pass from usurpation to freedom. The more implausible and extreme the resolution of plot the greater will be our sense of marvel and triumph. It is worth noting that Molière takes pains to accentuate the spectator's wonderment. He takes us first to a point of absolute despair where regeneration seems impossible, a downturn in the plot which Frye aptly calls the point of ritual death (p 179).[8] In some plays the threat of death may be explicit (L'Avare), presented symbolically in the guise, say, of imprisonment in a nunnery, or more vaguely as a living death of unhappy marriage, parental tyranny, or family misfortune as in the case of Tartuffe.

After this pause fraught with dread we are brought to the pinnacle of euphoria through the action of what Mauron calls 'la pensée magique,' the wish, realized in our imagination, to suspend normal expectations, to create an imaginary world different from the real one over which we have no control. In a startling anticipation of Mauron, Henri Gouhier applies this idea to the end of Tartuffe: 'formule non de piété mais de magie, de magie banale et prosaïque qui fait tomber le rideau au bon moment' (Théâtre et existence [Paris 1952] 216). A pointed rhetorical question by the same critic puts an end to all criticism of Molière's dénouements: 'à quoi bon ruser avec la loi du genre? ' (loc. cit.).[9]

The final and most characteristic operation of 'la pensée magique' is to bring time to a stop at curtainfall. The turbulent comic rhythm comes suddenly to an end; a final 'still' shows us the young lovers projected into a future where time will not age them, where marriage will not become jaded – what Gouhier calls 'ces situations au beau fixe' (p 209). Our vision of a stable, untroubled future is really a return to the golden age, a 'temps fort' in Eliade's terms, where beauty, health, and harmony reign supreme.

Those critics who scorned in the name of 'realism' and verisimilitude the gratuitousness of Molière's comic structures have done him a grave disservice; the 'invraisemblances' in his theatre, far from being flaws, underline and confirm Molière's profound, intuitive understanding of his chosen genre and its enduring spirit.

Such are, for the moment, the main elements in the working hypothesis on which my study of Molière's theatre will be based. Other methodological details will emerge during the course of our travels through a rich and varied canon of plays, details that at this point would appear, perhaps, as needless complexities. Yet the reader probably wonders how the abstract and generalizing nature of archetypal theory can have any relevance to particular plays, especially those expressing, as do Molière's, a profound and original vision. It should be said, first of all, that the rather schematic polarities we have just examined admit of considerable complication and subtlety. Few comedies adhere to the simple love triangle implied in the 'blondin-berne-barbon' myth. Two main devices in particular serve to broaden the dramatic interest of the generic story: figure splitting and extensions. The love interest may be based on two couples, sometimes more: the double plot, as it is called, obviously allows a far greater range of ironic effect, as there are more vantage points from which events can be seen. Occasionally a moral polarity intrudes. There is often a 'bon fils' nominally submissive to the father, and a 'mauvais fils' in open, aggressive hostility: Valère and Cléante in *L'Avare* provide a significant example. The father figure often divides as well into a 'good' father and a 'bad' one. The latter tends to be, naturally, the blocking figure, while his opposite appears as the long-lost father, affectionate, indulgent, and generous (eg, Harpagon-Anselme in *L'Avare*, Arnolphe-Oronte in *L'Ecole des femmes*). A mother figure may enter the action, usually on the side of the lovers; the Elmire of *Tartuffe* is one of the more obvious examples. Sometimes, however, the mother figure may appear as a Jungian witch, as with the perfidious Béline of *Le Malade imaginaire*.

Extensions take the form of auxiliaries, usually prolongations of the lovers and their interests (although the blocking character may have his valet, too). As avatars of the tricky slave of antiquity, they clearly have an important functional role. The wrong society, the one in control during most of the play, has authority and legality on its side, so that the only weapons against it are dissimulation and deception. True, Molière's young heroes and heroines are sometimes no strangers to these devices – one has only to think of Agnès and her innocent but inventive contrivances against Arnolphe. But as lovers tend to be impetuous and giddy, they need cooler heads to think for them, and as their decorum is fairly high – they are usually portrayed as well born – it is more fitting for social inferiors to do the dirty work of comedy. Finally, there may be moral contrasts among the auxiliaries, the most characteristic being the clever *serviteur* opposed to a stupid, bumbling one. We recognize, of course, the traditional opposition in the *commedia* between the first *zanno* – 'rusé, vif, amusant, spirituel,' and the second – 'sot, balourd' (cf. Gustave Attinger, *L'Esprit de la commedia dell'arte dans le théâtre français* [Neuchâtel 1950] 41-2).

However complex and varied the pattern of characters, function still remains all important: 'What a character is follows from what he has to do in the play' (Frye 171). Or, to apply here Barthes' remark about Racinian characters: 'il s'agit au fond de masques, de figures qui reçoivent leur différences, non de leur état civil, mais de leur place dans la configuration générale qui les tient enfermés' (p 21). That is why the only *vraisemblance* required in comedy is decorum, the consistency of character and conformity to type thrust upon form by function. And as function can finally be reduced to *agon* – the contest of the young man against an unreasonable adversary – the ultimate polarity of comedy is the traditional one redefined both by Frye and Sypher[10]: the struggle of *eiron* against *alazon*, each with his allies and spokesmen.

Multiple and extended functions only accentuate the complexity of Molière's theatre. The problem of coping with a large number of archetype clusters remains and seems to defy any attempt at working classifications. Yet, one criterion at least seems obvious: there are plays that adhere to the comic myth and those which do not. We find that the great majority of the comedies, including such masterpieces as *L'Ecole des femmes*, *Tartuffe*, and *L'Avare*, belong in the former category; they are founded on a love plot resolved typically by prospective matrimony. Only six plays (apart from the two 'treatise comedies,' *La Critique de L'Ecole des femmes* and *L'Impromptu de Versailles*) depart from this rule: *Les Précieuses ridicules*, *Le Mariage forcé*, *George Dandin*, *Amphitryon*, *Le Misanthrope*, and *Don Juan*. One might even argue that *Le Misanthrope* is a conventional comedy in this respect, with the marriage of Philinte and Eliante in the offing at the end; but as the primary dynamism pits Alceste against Célimène in a relationship which terminates in dissolution, we are entitled to place this comedy – problematical, like the others, not only in its use of comic convention but in its commentary on social norms – among Molière's exceptional works which go beyond the comic myth.

The twenty-odd comedies united by their adherence to the *mythe comique* do not lend themselves easily to sub-classification; such varied works as

L'Etourdi, Monsieur de Pourceaugnac, L'Avare, Les Amants magnifiques bespeak the existence of vast differences in dynamic principles, tone, social meaning. On close examination, though, the love-interest comedies can be conveniently separated into three rough categories. First of all, we may borrow Frye's basic distinction between the 'two ways of developing the form of comedy: one is to throw the main emphasis on the blocking characters; the other is to throw it forward on the scenes of discovery and reconciliation. One is the general tendency of comic irony, satire, realism, and studies of manners; the other is the tendency of Shakespearean and other types of romantic comedy' (pp 166-7). Tradition, of course, places Molière's typical work in the first category – what we shall call 'exorcism comedies' – and his most memorable plays do indeed provide us with unforgettable examples of strong blocking figures. But there are five plays in Molière's canon in which the conventional obstacle type is non-existent or barely suggested, and the tone of romance pronounced: *Le Dépit amoureux, Don Garcie de Navarre, La Princesse d'Elide, Les Amants magnifiques,* and *Psyché*. (Although surviving in incomplete or fragmentary form, *Mélicerte* and *Pastorale comique* show clear signs of belonging to this category as well.) Here the impediments to true love stem, in the romantic tradition, from the lovers themselves; false appearances and misunderstanding become the main vehicles for plot development.

Finally Langer's concept of comic rhythm suggests, as we shall presently see, a third category, where the buffoon, in the guise of a helpful auxiliary, provides the comedy with an irresistible *élan*, an indefatigable energy which make the plot itself recede into the background.

2

Buffoon

For Susanne Langer, 'the pure sense of life is the underlying feeling of comedy' (p 327). By 'pure sense of life' she means, essentially, the delight we take in our own adaptability, adroitness, and capacity for self-renewal. Comedy becomes 'an image of human vitality holding its own in the world amid the surprises of unplanned coincidence' (p 331). Once again we recognize the basic attitudes, if not the explicit tenets, of archetypal criticism: her comment about the origin of the genre could well have been written by Frye: 'what justifies the term "Comedy" is ... that the Comus was a fertility rite, and the god it celebrated a fertility god, a symbol of perpetual rebirth, eternal life' (*loc. cit.*).

Langer attaches great importance to the buffoon in symbolizing and expressing this pure sense of life. Here is 'the indomitable living creature fending for itself, tumbling and stumbling (as the clown physically illustrates) from one situation into another, getting into scrape after scrape and getting out again, with or without a thrashing. He is the personified *élan vital* ... His whole improvised existence has the rhythm of primitive, savage, if not animalian life, coping with a world that is forever taking new uncalculated turns, frustrating, but exciting. He is neither a good man nor a bad one, but is genuinely amoral – now triumphant, now worsted and rueful, but in his ruefulness and dismay he is funny, because his energy is really unimpaired and each failure prepares the situation for a new fantastic move' (p 342).

This eloquent portrait applies to Molière's most endearing clown figures. What distinguishes them, and the more general archetype drawn by Langer, is their repeated *élans* of energy. The contest between buffoon and the world takes place in a series of affirmations and denials. The protagonist pushes ahead, using his wit and energy time and again to overcome or bypass the obstacles that surge up incessantly in his path. The clown figure might thus be seen as the systolic phase in the pulsation of life. The diastolic phase would include all the events and forces that negate or neutralize the buffoon's strength and optimism. Implicit in Langer's ideas on comedy is a linear movement, an affirmation followed by an ebb or a resistance. The role Gutwirth attributes to the 'fâcheux' makes of this favourite comic type another form of the diastolic agent: he symbolizes 'le *retard* infligé à l'action, par lequel elle se complique de façon exaspérante pour le protagoniste' (p 131). Here, too, the image of pulsation is clearly suggested: 'il y a un art de ralentissement qui se conjure délicieusement avec le brio comique pour faire durer notre plaisir' (*loc. cit.*).

Simple though these general ideas may be, their application to Molière gives rise to unexpected complications. There are a good many clowns in his theatre: alongside Scapin there are such figures as Monsieur de Pourceaugnac, Monsieur Jourdain, Argan; beside the Sganarelle of *Le Médecin malgré lui* we may place the other Sganarelles, including the comic butt of *L'Ecole des maris*. A polarity of comic function confronts us again: there are clowns on the side of the lovers; some, on the other hand, embody or support the humorous society. In the latter case, he becomes a scapegoat and our laughter is derisive. Periodicity takes on a negative value which removes it completely from the sense of pure life.

In a word, buffoons, too, divide up along the lines of the classic *eiron-alazon* conflict of comedy. As the *alazon*-clown belongs to the exorcism function of the genre he will be studied in the chapters devoted to this subject. Here we shall consider buffoons in the *eiron* class, those who, in Langer's perspective, embody the 'right' energy of comedy.

One must make still another distinction in Molière's theatre between purely episodic clowns (eg, La Flèche in *L'Avare*) and those that dominate the action. And even in the latter case, the linear movement of pulsation suggested by Langer exists nowhere in its pure state. As she points out in her discussion of later, more sophisticated forms of comedy, the buffoon 'does not remain the central figure that he was in the folk theatre; the lilt and balance of life which he introduced, once it has been grasped, is rendered in more subtle poetic inventions involving plausible characters and an *intrigue* (as the French call it) that makes for a coherent, over-all dramatic action' (p 344). We return, then, to the comic *mythos*, the narrative by which archetypes become elements in a story. Clown figures thus constitute auxiliary sources of energy and add resourcefulness, wit, and common sense to the primary *élan* furnished by the young lover.

In rare cases in Molière, however, the role played by the buffoon is so considerable and the pulsation he produces so pronounced that the linear movement prevails over the comic dialectic. Heavy fathers, the lovers themselves, fade into the background as we are spellbound by the vitality, drive, and wit of the buffoon.

LE MÉDECIN MALGRÉ LUI

For Robert Jouanny, the Sganarelle of *Le Médecin malgré lui* is a 'canaille sympathique' (vol. II, p 4), an apt oxymoron that highlights our ambiguous attitude toward him. He has shortcomings that would normally place him on the 'wrong' side of comedy: coarse, greedy, lustful, pretentious, flippant, yet he succeeds in earning our affection. This is partly because he moves in a fanciful world from which we can be at a distance; the incongruity of Sganarelle's buffoon costume in his woodland setting – 'c'est un homme qui a une large barbe noire, et qui porte une fraise, avec un habit jaune et vert' (I, 4) – is ample evidence of this point. We are in the realm of farce where domestic acrimony is tempered by repartee: in the opening scenes, Martine is less the aggrieved wife here than the 'straight man' of twentieth-century comedy, feeding opportunities for one-liners. The play impulse is so strong that when M. Robert interrupts their quarrel the game continues against the intruder with hardly a break in stride. This mood of lightness and banter runs throughout the play. At the end, when Sganarelle is threatened with hanging, Martine laments: 'Encore si tu avais achevé de couper notre bois je prendrais quelque consolation' (III, 9).[1]

Even after making allowance for this atmosphere of fancy, one may wonder why this slow-witted drunkard is so endearing a creation. The reason is, I think, that we are in the presence of the true archetypal buffoon, 'all motion, whim, and impulse – the "libido" itself' (Langer 343). He is the only clown in Molière who harks unmistakeably back to an ancient, mythic past full of pan-gods, bacchanales, and fertility figures. Hubert hits the mark squarely when he describes Sganarelle as 'an uninhibited force of nature, as an undiluted Id who simply revels in all the creature comforts' (p 156).

Sganarelle's physical side is the most obvious link with the orgiastic tradition. His love for drink bursts out in a song of praise to his bottle (I, 5), and a kind of primitive dance is even suggested by the amusing physical gestures which punctuate this whole scene. This *lazzo* of the bottle makes, as Molière says in his stage directions, '*un grand jeu de théâtre*' (*loc. cit.*). The tradition of scatological humour which Sganarelle exemplifies – his query as to whether Lucinde's 'matière' is 'louable' for instance (II, 4)[2] – is closely linked as well to creatural man. But the key area where Sganarelle's uninhibited physical vitality imposes a definite periodicity on the play – the kind of pulsation that makes this a buffoon comedy – is sexual desire. Molière's theatre is not generally ribald; sex belongs to word, not action. The one exception to this rule is *Le Médecin malgré lui*. Sganarelle embodies sex in its crudest, most spontaneous form; his instinct springs into life with animal-like immediacy and automatism. Indeed, Sganarelle's unreflecting desire overwhelms him to the point where he is the plaything of a force far beyond him: the force of life itself. We must agree with Gutwirth that he represents 'la comédie dans l'épanouissement de sa bonne humeur, la comédie telle que nous la devons à Molière et à Molière seulement, enjouée en diable, ne ménageant ni les dos ni les derrières, lorgnant les seins' (p 50). But rather than generalize from this play, as does Gutwirth, to a somewhat dubious priapic view of Molière's comedy as a whole, we would be better advised to underline the extraordinary singularity of Le Médecin malgré lui itself. The fact is that Sganarelle is the only winning character in Molière who is priapic.

What triggers Sganarelle's impulses of raw desire is the nourrice Jacqueline, a figure whose earthy vitality and household function make of her a symbol of life-giving and life-nurturing strength. This well-endowed woman brings out in him a veritable mammary fixation for which medicine furnishes a convenient cover: 'C'est l'office du médecin de voir les tétons des nourrices' (II, 3). He offers, in an obvious bit of comic innuendo, to administer to Jacqueline 'quelque petit clystère dulcifiant' (II, 4). The same mood of play as underlies domestic strife between Martine and Sganarelle influences the portrayal of sex. Neither truly violent nor passionate, instinct is shown as a kind of delightful pagan gambol. The humour of the situation is driven home by Sganarelle's grotesque and parodic galanterie: 'Ah! Nourrice, charmante Nourrice, ma médecine est la très humble esclave de votre nourricerie, et je voudrais bien être le petit poupon fortuné qui tétât le lait ... de vos bonnes grâces' (II, 2).

The dialectic of pulsation implies ebb, a counter-force necessary to provide a contest for the buffoon. In the case of Sganarelle, the resistance is, appropriately enough, Jacqueline's husband. This kill-joy figure is always lurking in the background, ready to interpose himself between his wife and her ardent suitor. This rhythm of desire, coyness, and jealousy is a dominant one in the play and is repeatedly underscored by gesture. In III, 5, for instance, Sganarelle's courtship of Jacqueline comes to an abrupt end as they discover Lucas behind them: 'Chacun se retire de son côté,' the stage directions tell us, 'mais le Médecin d'une manière fort plaisante' (III, 3). These gestures and movements impart to the play a ballet-like atmosphere of fancy and airiness, even in the most farcical situations.

If at times slow-witted, the archetypal clown is infinitely adaptable. He manages in his stumbling, lurching way to make the best of the situation, even to convert obstacle into opportunity. He may thus grow with the events that befall him; instead of merely reacting in a rather mechanical and animalistic way, he may try to control the forces around him and turn them to his advantage. Greed may furnish him a stimulus to manipulate; profiteering is a more calculated form of creatural self-interest. A clown who succumbs to the lure of food and drink is not likely to disdain the offer of money or miss an opportunity to use the *commedia dell'arte* 'lazzo de la bourse.' The promise of wealth is clearly a catalyst in Sganarelle's transformation. A rudimentary common sense, more self-protection than anything else, turns into a kind of basic shrewdness and awareness. There is a greater metamorphosis in *Le Médecin malgré lui* than that of woodcutter into doctor, and one that passes through clearly defined phases.

The world of the unexpected, of comic Fortune, intrudes into Sganarelle's comfortable rustic and conjugal life in the guise of Valère and Lucas (I, 5). He is forthwith thrust into medical practice. Fortunately he still has a patchwork of memories from his 'rudiments' and his six years of medical apprenticeship; that slender baggage helps his survival instinct to improvise desperately – and to succeed against all expectations. His growing self-confidence reaches a high point during the consultation scene (II, 4). At first Sganarelle can only paraphrase the obvious:

GÉRONTE
La cause, s'il vous plait, qui fait qu'elle a
perdu la parole?

SGANARELLE
Tous nos meilleurs auteurs vous diront que
c'est l'empêchement de l'action de sa langue.

Questioned further, he tries the next line of deception, jargon, but his verve quickly peters out: 'venant ... pour ainsi dire ... à ... ' He falls back upon Latin and gathers strength with a few fragments from his rudiments, '*singulariter, nominativo*,' etc. A second foray into jargon proves more successful; after gaining time by repeating 'Ecoutez bien ceci' he convinces his 'audience' of his learning and his ability, and he is able to gloss over his celebrated misplacing of the heart and the liver.

At the end of II, Léandre, the young lover, intercepts the 'doctor' and implores his help. Sganarelle now assumes the role of comic auxiliary and is thus fully integrated into the comic myth. In III we find him completely transformed. The delight of serving Léandre and the discovery of the material advantages of medicine have given him a new perception of the world. His sardonic eulogy of medicine (III, 1) makes the lazy, dull-witted drunkard of the first scenes seem very remote. After making perceptive comparisons with the tailor's and the shoemaker's craft, he concludes: 'Le bon de cette profession est qu'il y a parmi les morts une honnêteté, une discrétion la plus grande du monde; et jamais on n'en voit se plaindre du médecin qui l'a tué.' This is not a *mot d'auteur*, but a perfectly plausible statement by a man who has realized that the world is divided into fools and knaves and that circumstances have made him a minority knave in a majority of fools. The ease with which *galimatias* succeeds makes him articulate; he now can pronounce reasoned discourses on whether or not women are more easily cured than men (III, 6), especially when he can thereby afford the lovers a chance to converse on their own. This ability to make jargon serve a double purpose reaches its culmination later in the same scene with the cleverly ironical remedy Sganarelle prescribes to Léandre while Géronte is within earshot: 'une prise de fuite purgative, que vous mêlerez comme il faut avec deux drachmes de matrimonium en pilules.'

An indication of this transformation, and another key perhaps to our ambiguous reaction to Sganarelle, lies in the change that occurs in our comic relationship to him. At the beginning he was the dupe of Martine's stratagem; we enjoyed seeing him perplexed by a situation that was perfectly clear to us. But as he gains control over the situation, we laugh with him, not at him; we are on his side in his game against the world of fools.

As a corollary of Sganarelle's dominant presence, the love plot is appropriately schematic, little more than a frame in which Géronte is a simplistic heavy father driven by greed to force an unhappy marriage on Lucinde. The daughter and Léandre are rather shadowy characters, too. The dialectic between lovers and obstacle is clearly subdued in order that Sganarelle may remain always in the foreground. Yet, the two rhythms are so much in phase that at the dénouement we are left with a sense of unity. The point of ritual death, that moment when the happy resolution seems impossible, when the 'real' world seems to triumph, is a good example. That element in the plot is often highlighted in Molière by actual allusions to death, as is the case here. Lucinde refuses to accept Valère: 'J'épouserai plutôt la mort' (III, 6). A moment later Sganarelle's complicity in the flight of the lovers is discovered. Events seem to turn against the fledgling doctor now in danger of dangling at the end of a rope. 'Ah! par ma fi!' exults Lucas, 'Monsieur le Médecin, vous serez pendu' (III, 8). The world of crime and punishment and moral responsibility lurks ominously nearby. But the 'pensée magique' intervenes to suspend the realities of forced marriage and capital punishment. The unexpected occurs and, appropriately, in the most gratuitous way: Léandre returns with the news that his rich uncle has died (a death so distant and so opportune that it carries no anxiety) and that he is now as rich as his rival. Géronte forgives lovers and doctor to bring about harmony and reconciliation. Sganarelle's 'optimisme spontané' (Jouanny, vol. II, p 3) is underscored in a dénouement which needs no scapegoats or exorcism to bring about the final miracle.

LES FOURBERIES DE SCAPIN

With Scapin we move into a more typical class of buffoon in Molière. Sganarelle is a lumbering clown driven by libidinal energy and thrust into circumstances to which he adjusts willynilly. Scapin, on the other hand, embodies one of Molière's most characteristic types, the resourceful valet (or *servante*) whose self-confidence and imagination are put to the service of youthful affection and the society which will emerge from it. Like Toinette in *Le Malade imaginaire*, he exemplifies wit in the broadest sense, inventiveness, repartee and play. But Scapin is unique in the way these qualities dominate the whole action. The typical *servus* figure in Molière has only an episodic role directly attached to the love plot. As an ally of the young, his imagination is directed to undoing what has been done, to planning ways of righting situations that are going wrong. Only rarely does he, like Scapin, direct the course of events; he merges rather into the dynamics of opposition between the new and the old societies. When the lovers get their way, their auxiliaries, no longer of use, fade into the background.

Scapin's exceptional trait is his virtuosity in intrigue, his love of challenge for challenge's sake. 'Je hais ces cœurs pusillanimes qui, pour trop prévoir les suites des choses, n'osent rien entreprendre' (III, 1). This proud *profession de foi* bears witness to Scapin's yearning for heroism and his faith in his abilities to achieve it within the limits of his 'condition.' The phrase 'cœurs pusillanimes' expresses genuine contempt and breaks with Scapin's usual practice (common to all valets and indicative of their good-humoured and detached view of themselves) of parodying noble words (eg, 'trois ans de galère de plus ou de moins ne sont pas pour arrêter un noble coeur' [I, 5]). This ambivalence of tone suggests a contradictory attitude in Scapin himself whose goal is aristocratic self-surpassing, but whose means are the base ones of his class, deceit and trickery.

Now he accepts a new challenge, an opportunity to end his career in a glorious apotheosis. Out of humanity, it is true, Scapin yields to the entreaties of the beleaguered young men, Octave and Léandre, who have both wedded secretly their beloveds and are on the verge of being married off in the normal way by their fathers. The imbroglio in which they are caught up is thus so hopelessly involved that it would challenge Scapin even if he were emotionally detached. The boldness and intricacy of his contrivances, a certain gratuitous detail and love of improvisation all confirm the impression of wit for wit's sake, the desire to outdo oneself. Each trick is more ingenious and complex than the preceding one and at the end success is literally a matter of life or death. Scapin's domination of the action, the impetus he provides to the phases of the plot, the impression of periodicity given by his tricks all point to the inclusion of this comedy in the 'buffoon' category. Our attention is held by the rhythm of the 'fourberies,' and the other components of this play fade into the background. The young lovers furnish the motivation for Scapin's virtuosity and the fathers are less obstacles than foils for the master trickster.

'Le rideau tombera quand Scapin jugera bon de clore le divertissement, ou plutôt la démonstration.' Jouanny's apt observation (vol. II, p 588) underlines the valet's hold over the plot and the complex role he plays. He is the *meneur de jeu* not only in its general, modern meaning but in its archaic sense of play-overseer; Scapin is more than the *primum movens* of the play, he is a stage director orchestrating movements, distributing roles (especially to himself), and pacing the action.[3]

Scapin's very first self-affirmation is as *metteur en scène* and actor (I, 3). He wants Octave to be resolute before his father and provides the young man with a dress rehearsal of the impending meeting. First the appropriate pose:

SCAPIN
Allons. La mine résolue, la tête haute, les
regards assurés.

OCTAVE
Comme cela?

Then the proper dialogue: Scapin plays the irate father, while exhorting Octave in his own voice to improvise an effective role:

SCAPIN
"Comment, pendard, vaurien, infâme, fils indigne
d'un père comme moi ... Est-ce là ... le respect que tu
me conserves? " Allons donc.

Scapin's own acting abilities cow the young man into silence and the arrival of Argante in person sends him scurrying off in terror.

The second pulsation of the play, directly after this scene, takes the form of Scapin's first *fourberie*, a futile effort to mollify Argante by pretending that his son was forced into an offending marriage. At the beginning of II this tone of defeat is accentuated, Molière's way, no doubt, of highlighting the brilliance of the two great purse-stealing *fourberies* which are the main substance of the act. The challenge of extracting large sums of money from miserly and suspicious old men is not to be taken lightly. In both tricks Scapin uses the full range of his imagination, orchestrates his presentation of the situation carefully, and exploits shrewdly the psychological mainsprings of his victims. His inventiveness is especially noteworthy in the second of these tricks, the well-known kidnapping and ransom story with its now proverbial refrain: 'Que diable allait-il faire dans cette galère?' (II, 7). Whatever its debt to Cyrano de Bergerac, it is perfectly in place both in the setting and the spirit of the play.

Scapin gives three impulsions to the comic rhythm in III — a mild effect of acceleration which points ahead to the final reversal. With the famous 'sac' scene, Scapin's powers of imagination and execution reach their apogee. Every meaning of the word *jouer* comes out here: game, dupery, and impersonation. The sack deemed so unworthy by Boileau[4] is but a stage prop: the comic energy of the scene surges out in Scapin's brio and self-assurance as he plays upon Géronte's terror, and in his unforgettable mimicry. This is unalloyed virtuosity, play for the sake of play. One senses that Scapin's self-professed motive to avenge himself for Géronte's 'imposture' is little more than a pretext for this elaborate 'gag'; Scapin's attention to detail, his exuberant delight in impersonation betray a certain gratuitousness; effect here goes far beyond cause.

This *fourberie* is the apotheosis of Scapin the role-player. He prepares his scene by situating it: Géronte, convinced that a whole gang of 'spadassins' intends to kill him, seeks a hiding place in the large sack provided by Scapin. The valet imitates the bravado of a 'Gascon,' then a 'Suisse,' while adding two versions of his own *persona*: the Scapin that discourses with the imaginary 'brave' and the equally theatrical Scapin who tosses asides to Géronte in order to reassure him:

SCAPIN
"Quoi? je n'aurai pas l'abantage dé tuer cé Géronte,
et quelqu'un par charité né m'enseignera pas où il
est? " (*A Géronte de sa voix ordinaire.*) Ne branlez pas ...
"Oh, l'homme au sac!" Monsieur.....

The scene reaches a climax when Scapin imitates a whole band of soldiers. So carried away is he by this feat that he fails to notice that the tables have been turned. We have enjoyed the contrast between Géronte's partial perception of the situation which seems 'real' to him, and our own complicity with the *meneur de jeu* who shows us the power of theatrical illusion. When Géronte emerges from the sack to realize that the 'army' is but one valet, the game is played against Scapin.

This fall from supremacy heralds the low ebb that Scapin's fortunes reach presently. Géronte swears that he will be 'envoyé au gibet avant qu'il soit demain' (III, 3). The world is on the verge of triumphing over the buffoon, whose impending defeat is highlighted, as with 'le médecin malgré lui,' by a point of ritual death. But once again, a wish-fulfilment pulls the plot back into the sphere of imagination. Opportune recognitions put an end to the comic imbroglio and the passage from bondage to freedom brings the fathers into the new society.

By minimizing at the dénouement the traditional opposition between young love and parental tyranny, Molière gives Scapin's central role in the play even more emphasis. But if the romantic plot has been properly resolved, the valet's safety is by no means assured. His is not the ordinary contest between buffoon and the world. Scapin's instinctive rashness carries with it its own obstacle, the punishment for overreaching himself, a kind of comic nemesis. Faced with a fittingly disastrous fall, he has no other recourse but to throw himself upon the mercy of the court. To improve his chances he calls once again upon his acting ability. The result is the delightful last scene in which Scapin, head swathed in bandages, is carried on stage apparently dying from a wound caused by a falling hammer. Both aggrieved fathers forgive the penitent valet. In order not to undermine the comic mood, the presence of death is made less ominous by a sense of irony, of play:

GÉRONTE
Je te pardonne tout, voilà qui est fait.

SCAPIN
Ah! Monsieur, je me sens tout soulagé depuis cette parole.

GÉRONTE
Oui; mais je te pardonne à la charge que tu mourras.

SCAPIN
Comment, Monsieur?

For someone so cruelly and so often duped, Géronte readily pardons Scapin unconditionally. The archetypal image of the festive banquet proposed by Argante ends the play: 'Allons souper ensemble, pour mieux goûter notre plaisir.' And the resurgent and victorious Scapin brings down the curtain with a wink to all: 'Et moi, qu'on me porte au bout de la table, en attendant que je meure.' This turnabout is a comic version of the death-and-resurrection archetype: the 'real' menace of capital punishment, the feigned mortal wound are forgotten as the invincible Scapin is carried off in triumph.

L'ETOURDI

Mascarille is the buffoon type who perhaps best illustrates our notion of comic rhythm. His ten stratagems, the ten pulsations he gives to the action, are so regular and so evenly spaced that the ensuing rhythm would seem at first glance contrived, too stylized for a real comic effect. But there are other dimensions to *L'Etourdi* and to Mascarille that mitigate this impression of a clockwork movement.

By temperament and by choice, Mascarille is, like Sganarelle and Scapin, on the side of love. His advice to his master carries with it a social ideal:

> D'un censeur de plaisirs ai-je fort l'encolure,
> Et Mascarille est-il ennemi de nature?
> Vous savez le contraire, et qu'il est très certain
> Qu'on ne peut me taxer que d'être trop humain.
> Moquez-vous des sermons d'un vieux barbon de père,
> Poussez votre bidet, vous dis-je, et laissez faire.
> Ma foi, j'en suis d'avis, que ces penards chagrins
> Nous viennent étourdir de leurs contes badins,
> Et vertueux par force, espèrent par envie
> Oter aux jeunes gens les plaisirs de la vie! (I, 2)

Mascarille refuses to be cast in the most un-comic role of all, the kill-joy, the 'censeur de plaisirs.' Instead he makes himself the spokesman for the comic spirit in condemning its opposite, the spirit of censoriousness ('sermons,' 'penards chagrins') associated with old age, religious exhortation, impotence ('vertueux par force') and paternal authority. Pleasure is seen on the other hand in the context of natural propensity ('nature'), humanity, youth. This message recalls and seems to confirm Mauron's dictum that the pleasure principle wins out in comedy. By implying that the young should be free to seek pleasure, that it is unnatural and inhumane to inhibit these spontaneous impulses, Mascarille expresses the wish-fulfilment function of the comic myth; at the same time he deflates by his sarcasm and well-chosen epithets those who oppose the pleasure principle.

Mascarille, in short, is not only on the side of the lovers; he knows *why* he is. But to act on their behalf is no small problem in *L'Etourdi*. The situation in which he and the characters find themselves is a complicated affair involving three young men, three fathers, and, at the dénouement, three young ladies. Imposed upon this romantic imbroglio is another principle of confusion: the ten stratagems of Mascarille, neutralized by the ten *contretemps* due mainly to Lélie. The plot itself is basically static until the recognitions at the end of the play. The premises of the plot, once stated, recede into secondary importance. Mascarille himself is the dynamic principle of *L'Etourdi*.

Like Scapin, Mascarille is a *meneur de jeu*, an indefatigable author of 'ruses, détours, fourbes, inventions' (I, 2) to advance the amorous fortunes of his master, Lélie. The decorum of the young lover calls of course for impetuosity, boldness, ardour; we find in Lélie all the attributes of irresistible desire, even if their verbal expression is subdued and respectable. A functional relationship exists between the master's ardour and the valet's inventiveness – the more carried away the lover is, the more practical and resourceful the auxiliary must be. But if Mascarille's powers of invention are so extraordinary in this play, it is because Lélie brings passion and impetuosity to its comic extreme – he is an unthinking, awkward, giddy fool, an 'étourdi.' Nowhere in Molière is a *jeune premier* cast in this role; nowhere is he so disrespectfully treated by his valet. Only Mascarille allows himself the luxury of telling his master: 'Vous avez la caboche un peu dure' (IV, 1) and of beating him (IV, 6). The fact that decorum has been so forced here puts both characters almost on the same level and allows an extraordinary exchange of roles. Lélie is at the same time a blessing and a curse for his valet; his 'étourderies' force Mascarille to attain new heights and to fail.

Knowing that his own master is his worst enemy, Mascarille must be especially vigilant, like the pilot to whom he compares himself: 'de peur de trouver dans le port un écueil, / Conduisons le vaisseau de la main et de l'œil' (II, 2). His optimism comes out in the same image: his ship is almost berthed, he needs just one more moment of attention to avoid the last reef. To his continual irritation, however, another hand seems to seize the wheel and direct the vessel towards the rocks. Fortune, the force of contingency against which the buffoon must struggle, seems perversely intent on converting imminent victory into crushing failure. Ironically, this force inhabits Lélie, the very person who stands to gain from Mascarille's success; in his frustration, the valet can think in no other terms but possession: he rails against his master's 'démon brouillon' (V, 1) and doggedly seeks to 'dessus son lutin obtenir la victoire' (V, 6).

Mascarille's feeling of impotence before his fate finds quintessential expression in his bitter and prophetic remark at the end of the first act and his third *contretemps*: 'Quand nous serons à dix, nous ferons une croix' (I, 9). Ten *contretemps* form the backbone of *L'Etourdi* and the curtain falls after the last. Mascarille does not give up in defeat; nor is victory his own work either. Comic providence alone overcomes the 'lutin,' and the love interest is resolved in the usual miraculous way. Not only will the three couples of the love plot be united, but Mascarille's own 'démangeaisons de mariage' will be satisfied as well.

The impression of triumph and joy we experience at the end of this comedy, however, is somewhat clouded by a sense of the ultimate ineffectuality of human invention. Destiny, an ally of Scapin, becomes a relentless obstacle for Mascarille.[5] This is no doubt why both the title and the subtitle of this play refer to the counterforce: *L'Etourdi, Les Contretemps*. Even if the title of the Italian original (*L'Inavvertito*) had suggested such a possibility, we could not imagine this play being called *Les Fourberies de Mascarille*. Yet, if Mascarille's tricks come to naught, so do the *contretemps* — proof that, in the final analysis a comic providence shapes our ends. Indeed, the impression of a miraculous, benevolent power would be lessened if the resolution were obtained by purely human means. Mascarille does not have to be effective. He embodies the high spirits of the buffoon and can carry in himself the energy that urges the action relentlessly onward.

Molière does give Mascarille sound motives for persevering when ever-new and more absurd 'étourderies' bedevil him. First, he is genuinely dedicated to his master and capable of great fellow-feeling in his regard: 'Allez, je vous fais grâce; / Je jette encore un œil pitoyable sur vous' (II, 7). Even in his most frustrated moments, he is able to dissociate the 'lutin' from the man, the demon from the possessed. And Mascarille does experience elation: not from execution, a pleasure usually denied him, but at least from anticipation ('j'avais médité tantôt un coup de maître, / Dont tout présentement je veux voir les effets' [I, 6]), and from his self-image, best exemplified in his mock-heroic mental picture of himself as a Roman hero covered with laurels:

> Je veux que l'on s'apprête
> A me peindre en héros un laurier sur la tête,
> Et qu'au bas du portrait on mette en lettres d'or:
> *Vivat Mascarillus, fourbum imperator!* (II, 8)

There is engaging self-mockery in this portrait of the artist with its macaronic Latin inscription. As with Scapin, Mascarille's basic buoyancy and good humour come out in parody of noble language. But the most entertaining and memorable example of parody is found, of course, in the well-known mock-heroic monologue at the beginning of Act III ('Taisez-vous, ma bonté, cessez votre entretien' [III, 1], vv. 901ff.). Here Mascarille pokes fun not only at heroic language, but at one of the basic conventions of tragedy: the high-serious inner struggle with its basic rhetorical conventions: symmetry, exclamations, apostrophes, and the like. The misfortunes of a valet who can inflate so wittily his *contretemps* cannot be totally dismaying.

Mascarille shares Scapin's delight in being a *meneur de jeu* — another reason why he perseveres in adversity. A trickster must of course be an actor ('Qu'un fourbe est contraint de prendre de figures!' [V, 1]), and like Scapin, Lélie's valet carries off his roles with brio. There is, however, less gratuitous exhibitionism on Mascarille's part; none of the one-man orchestra virtuosity of the 'sac' scene, for instance. Mascarille is forced by the situation to be more stage director than player; he is not on his own, as was Scapin; some of his ruses demand Lélie's participation, or collaboration at any rate, and Mascarille must rehearse with particular care any scene in which his muddle-headed master is to share a part. In II, 1, after spreading the story that Lélie's father is dead, he warns Lélie: 'Jouez bien votre rôle.' The master obediently counterfeits bottomless grief.

Role playing within a play suggests by analogy the role playing that *is* the play and, more generally, the conventions that underlie theatre. We are not surprised when Mascarille, in V, returns on stage with his *récit* of the key event in the dénouement, or what he calls 'la fin d'une vraie et pure comédie' (V, 9). The slight undertone of parody that accompanies the comic reversal becomes explicit here. The line between story and imitation, between action and representation, never very firm in comedy, dissolves momentarily to allow reality and convention to mix.

Whereas in the two previous plays the buffoon is made to endure a moment of ritual death, a threatening downturn in the action just before the happy ending, in *L'Etourdi* no such clearly defined moment exists. Mascarille's perennial failures probably insulate him against reprisals. The only explicit threat against him occurs fairly early in the play. In II, 4, Pandolfe, in an outburst of rage, exclaims: 'Quoi qu'il puisse coûter, je veux le faire pendre.' The closest one gets to a true 'point of ritual death' is in the discouraged lines, not of Mascarille, but his master, just before the reversal: 'Après tant de malheurs, après mon imprudence, / Le trépas me doit seul prêter son assistance' (V, 6).

The spectre of death is exorcized in a more general and diffuse way in *L'Etourdi*. There are touches of black humour, especially in the consequences of Mascarille's fourth trick. Here the valet has told Anselme that Lélie's father had suddenly died, but the terrifying aspect of death is quickly softened by caricature. First, Anselme's sententiousness is played off against Mascarille's straight-man quips:

ANSELME
Etre mort de la sorte!

MASCARILLE
                Il a certes grand tort:
Je lui sais mauvais gré d'une telle incartade. (II, 2)

Then Lélie wails in a grotesque counterpoint to Anselme's trite phrases of consolation:

ANSELME
Mais quoi? cher Lélie, enfin il était homme:
On n'a point pour la mort de dispense de Rome.

LÉLIE
Ah! (II, 3)

Finally, the whole subject is reduced to the level of farce with the dead man's return and Anselme's abject terror of what he construes to be a ghost.

The rhythm of *L'Etourdi* is not, then, a crescendo of energy reaching a climax, dipping suddenly to despair, and returning with a renewed and final thrust. It is a sustained, regular pulsation against a plot with few new developments. As a result, *L'Etourdi* represents the triumph of the comic rhythm in Molière. But at the same time the buffoon figure who embodies this rhythm appears as a rather forlorn character, whatever his momentary elation, for the comic pulsation is based on his failure: the next beat comes about only because the preceding stratagem has come to naught. Hence we leave the play with a curiously ambiguous attitude: elation and frustration, optimism and despair. For an ingenious valet on the right side of comedy, Mascarille's lot has been a hard one.

In these plays, the plot is only an organizing principle; the dynamic structure lies not in the struggle between fathers and lovers but in the periodicity which each buffoon figure gives to his comedy. A joyous, buoyant mood characterizes *Les Fourberies de Scapin* because the dominant forward motion is strong and resistance almost ineffectual. Sganarelle's earthy common sense and compassion for youthful love, combined with the free and easy rustic setting of *Le Médecin malgré lui*, give us a less euphoric but firmly established sense of security. In *L'Etourdi* the prevailing mood is somewhat different. As the strong counterforce neutralizes each of Mascarille's inventions, a tone of mounting irritation sets in. The impression of well-being created by Mascarille's mental and verbal resourcefulness is effectively counterweighted by the exacerbating intrusions of an alien and contrary force, all the more ironic in that the 'lutin' dwells in the young man who normally furnishes the primary energy of comedy. Here an impression of persecution arises from periodicity, an effect that Molière was to exploit masterfully in such works as *L'Ecole des femmes*, *George Dandin*, and *Le*

Misanthrope. Were he in the humorous society, Mascarille would make us think of Arnolphe. The world is hostile, and only Mascarille's extraordinary staying power makes us forget his implacable enemy.

'The clown is Life, he is the Will, he is the Brain.' No buffoon figures could be better characterized by Langer's three nouns (p 344) than Sganarelle, Mascarille, and Scapin – vitality, tenacity, and invention. Each is on the right side, carried by and contributing to the dominant movement of the play. Each endeavours to serve the cause of true love, even if in the final analysis only comic providence can right the situation.

3

Exorcism: Theme and Variations

We recall Frye's convenient distinction between the two ways of developing the comic form, by emphasizing the blocking character or by stressing the romantic resolution of the plot. 'One is the general tendency of comic irony, satire, realism and studies of manners; the other is the tendency of Shakespearean and other types of romantic comedy' (pp 166-7). Mindful of the traditional contrast between Elizabethan and French Classical comedy, we are tempted to set Molière opposite Shakespeare as exemplifying the first tendency. From Molière's own pronouncements about comedy to Bergson and beyond, the satirical function of comedy, and of Molière's comedy in particular, has been deemed the pre-eminent, if not the sole concern of the spectator and the scholar.

Only in fairly recent times has the full range of Molière's comic genius come to be appreciated, from the grossest, most vital farce to the most refined comedy. The simplistic opposition between Shakespeare and Molière rapidly breaks down as we realize that the Frenchman too had his romantic side, exemplified most characteristically in the courtly entertainments he produced for Louis XIV. It must quickly be added, to avoid another kind of oversimplification, that not all of Molière's plays created for the King are 'romantic.' The Court had the same broad range of tastes as the City; alongside such high-flown works as *Les Amants magnifiques* and *La Princesse d'Elide* we must place farces like the first *Tartuffe* and *Le Bourgeois gentilhomme*.

Romantic elements abound as well in his most realistic comedies. Exorcism in comedy occurs, after all, through the action of romance, for the blocking character is ultimately defeated by the familiar *romanesque* devices of reconciliation and discovery. What characterizes the group of plays we shall be analysing in this and the following chapters is not the presence of realism and the absence of romance, but the tension between the two – the tension which results from the basic dialectic of comedy. The greater the threat posed by the obstacle character, the more intense and miraculous will seem the triumph of young love. Molière's exorcism comedies must therefore be studied not only in the light of the initial dynamism of the blocking character but in the way this force is overcome by the operation of 'la pensée magique.' As in all vital dialectics these two elements are both antithetical and complementary.

Within these 'blondin-berne-barbon' comedies, a group of major plays stand out. Here a fully developed action (usually in five acts) centres upon an authoritarian figure and his efforts to impose his will on the world around him. Taking my cue from classical typology, I shall call these works heavy father comedies and study them in the following chapter.

There is another category of fairly short plays (one or three acts) with rather schematic plots. These will be the subject of the present chapter. Le Sicilien, for example, embodies our formula in its simplest form. The remaining plays in this group — Sganarelle, L'Amour médecin, La Comtesse d'Escarbagnas, Monsieur de Pourceaugnac, and Les Fâcheux — may be seen as variations and extensions of the basic pattern. While the initial situation arises from the love plot, other material fills out the action: themes like cuckoldry, medical charlatanism, class pretentiousness, or, in the last-named play, a plague of importunate people. All these additional elaborations are objects of exorcism function, although in a broader and more diffuse way than in the heavy father comedies. While not always directly connected with the plot, they belong to the same world of ridicule as the heavy father and therefore stand in moral contrast with the thrust of the emerging new society.

LE SICILIEN OU L'AMOUR PEINTRE

The spare plot of this one-act comedy-ballet can be reduced to the familiar triangle: Adraste, 'gentilhomme françois' (thus an outsider in the Sicilian setting), loves Isidore, a Greek slave owned by Don Pèdre who intends to make her his wife. Only one additional function is added to the basic schema: Hali, the comic auxiliary who, like the Mascarille of L'Etourdi, is undaunted by failure and sensitive about his reputation as a trickster. We find the same mildly parodic expression of these traits: 'Le courroux du point d'honneur me prend; il ne sera pas dit qu'on triomphe de mon adresse; ma qualité de fourbe s'indigne de tous ces obstacles, et je prétends faire éclater les talents que j'ai eus du Ciel' (4). Hali fails to live up to his promise, however, and becomes only a counterpoint to the main action. It is Adraste himself who seizes upon the trick that explains the subtitle of the play: by replacing his painter friend, Damon, who is doing Isidore's portrait, he gains access to the girl and quickly wins her affection. We may assume as well that he invents the final stratagem which fulfils his hopes and proves Don Pèdre's undoing: the substitution of another woman for Isidore who is quickly spirited away.

Le Sicilien illustrates simply, but forcefully, the link between the comic myth and dramatic irony. As trickery is one of the few weapons young people have when the blocking character is all-powerful, disguise and dissimulation contribute greatly to the dynamism of the plot. And, as the game is played by aware conspirators against unaware victims, two kinds of relationship are built up with the spectator: second-person irony where the viewer is an accomplice to the trick, a kind of irony symbolized by the wink to the audience; and third-person irony where we laugh from a standpoint of superior knowledge over the stage character.[1]

As *fourberie* is the sole dynamic principle of *Le Sicilien*, dramatic irony sustains the whole development. Fairly early on, relationships are still blurred. In 5 Don Pèdre overhears Adraste and Hali describe him as a 'fâcheux,' a 'bourreau,' a 'brutal' – one can imagine in his facial expressions the same hurt and anger as experienced by the Arnolphe of *L'Ecole des femmes* when he hears himself described in similar terms (III, 4). But at the same time Adraste and Hali are unaware that they are being overheard. At the end of the play the polarity is strong and complete. Don Pèdre declares with gloating satisfaction as he unwittingly gives Adraste the hand of the beloved Isidore in disguise: 'Trouvez bon qu'en ce lieu je vous fasse toucher dans la main l'un de l'autre, et que tous deux je vous conjure de vivre, pour l'amour de moi, dans une parfaite union.' Adraste picks up the cue to reinforce this unconscious irony and to affirm at the same time his solidarity with the spectator: 'Oui, je vous le promets, que, pour l'amour de vous, je m'en vais, avec elle, vivre le mieux du monde' (17).

From this pinnacle of apparent triumph Don Pèdre is toppled suddenly and mercilessly. Not only must he face the fact of being duped but he must also endure the harsh words Clímène metes out to him after the lovers have departed: 'Ce que cela veut dire? Qu'un jaloux est un monstre haï de tout le monde, et qu'il n'y a personne qui ne soit ravi de lui nuire, n'y eût-il point d'autre intérêt' (18).

In comedy 'the punishment always fits the crime' (Eustis 145); or, to put it another way, if there is punishment, there must be crime. Again *Le Sicilien* is schematic and explicit. Don Pèdre's jealousy is underlined repeatedly, even by himself: 'jaloux comme un tigre,' in his own words to Isidore, 'et, si vous voulez: comme un diable. Mon amour vous veut toute à moi' (6). He thus exposes his egoism and possessiveness, of which watchdog attention and sequestration are the futile consequences. The right to enforce such 'servitude' can in no way be legitimized; Don Pèdre is neither father nor guardian. The authority relationship here is the most spurious and inhumane of all: master and slave. Don Pèdre, it is true, intends to marry Isidore, but as the young lady rightly protests, this step would change 'mon esclavage en un autre beaucoup plus rude' (6).

Other traits somewhat fill out this rather flat character, particularly that other form of possessiveness, avarice. If he so imprudently welcomes under his roof Adraste disguised as a painter, it is because Adraste, as a 'gentilhomme françois,' will work only for 'gloire' and 'réputation' (10). We also note a subdued kind of comic inconsistency. Don Pèdre is unaware of his own shortcomings when he stigmatizes Adraste's feigned outburst of jealousy (15).

The positive aspect of the comic polarity – civility, confidence, freedom – is equally explicit. Isidore fails to understand her master's possessive character. 'Si j'aimais quelqu'un,' she declares, 'je n'aurais point de plus grand plaisir que de le voir aimé de tout le monde' (6). She also gives him the traditional warning so often repeated in Molière: 'L'on ne tarde guère à profiter du chagrin et de la colère que donne à l'esprit d'une femme la contrainte et la servitude' (6). Adraste's refinement and civility charm the girl: 'Messieurs les Français ont un fonds de galanterie qui se répand partout' (11), a trait underscored by the serenades addressed to Isidore which comprise the principal musical elements of the play.[2] Don Pèdre is depicted, on the other hand, as an embodiment of alien values, a kind of oriental despot with which the enlightened attitude of the Frenchman towards 'le beau sexe' can be flatteringly compared. This is the only example in Molière where the moral contrasts of comedy are seen in nationalistic terms.[3]

At the outset, the right world, interestingly enough, is the intruder's; Adraste bears the standard and gives the example of free and confident relations between men and women in a world of domestic bondage. But this latter world melts into air with Don Pèdre's defeat and the exorcism of the values he has embodied; his alienation and solitude receive telling emphasis in the curious last scene of the play. Outraged at the 'injure mortelle' he has suffered, the victim rouses up a *sénateur* in order to have 'l'appui de la justice.' But the festive ending of comedy has transformed the normally grave embodiment of equity and civic virtue. The senator turns out to be a master of revels who proceeds to invite Don Pèdre to 'une mascarade la plus belle du monde.' Don Pèdre protests the perfidy of the 'traître de Français' and the two talk at cross-purposes:

DON PÈDRE
Comment? de quoi parlez-vous là?

LE SÉNATEUR
Je parle de ma mascarade.

DON PÈDRE
Je vous parle de mon affaire.

LE SÉNATEUR
Je ne veux point aujourd'hui d'autres affaires
que de plaisir.

Far from being 'a strong discordant note' (Hubert 161), this charming little scene underlines the points already made. First, the *dialogue de sourds* emphasizes the irreconcilability of the two systems of values: Don Pèdre cannot understand festivity nor can the Sénateur comprehend retributive justice in a world dedicated to pleasure. The victory of the pleasure principle is heightened by its proclaimer, a respected public servant. The exotic setting is transmuted by the spirit of 'divertissement' emanating from this courtly entertainment. Louis XIV and his Court behold, in this episode of the 'Ballet des Muses,' a world of 'turcs et maures' freed from despotism by the power of French *galanterie*.

SGANARELLE OU LE COCU IMAGINAIRE

Like *Le Sicilien*, this one-act play is founded on the basic tension of comedy, presented again with rudimentary simplicity. Lélie and Célie are the functional equivalents of Adraste and Isidore; in this work, however, not only have they been in love for some time, but their affection has been sponsored by Célie's father, Gorgibus, who has promised his daughter to the young man. Gorgibus, however, has had a change of heart; the great wealth of another suitor, Valère, makes him a much more desirable son-in-law. This cavalier decision to go back on his word to Lélie and impose Valère upon his daughter puts Gorgibus into Don Pèdre's role as blocking character, although in the more customary form of the domineering father.

We would normally expect the pattern of guile and trickery found in *Le Sicilien* to fill out the actual development of this situation. But Molière chooses to unfold his action in a totally different way. The fortuitous, always an important element in comedy, is raised here to the level of the informing principle of the play; chance will be the mainspring of the action. The playwright builds up a delightful imbroglio out of a series of false appearances which accumulate in a totally gratuitous way. When Sganarelle bends solicitously over Célie, who has fainted at the prospect of a forced marriage with Valère, his wife imagines the worst. Similarly, when Sganarelle chances upon his wife in rapture before Lélie's portrait (which Célie had dropped during her faint), he also jumps to conclusions. The suppositions become more and more preposterous as the false impressions multiply. Finally, Célie's *suivante* asks a few business-like questions, the answers to which set things aright for the happy dénouement.

The basic lovers-father opposition with which the comedy began is quickly pushed into the background. In fact, the overwhelming importance of chance blurs all the functional relationships of *Sganarelle*. The lovers are more concerned with their *dépit amoureux* than with the threat posed by Gorgibus, whose blocking function fades after his initial authoritarian outburst against the pernicious effects of novel reading. Even at the end of the play, Gorgibus's renewed threat to impose Valère on Célie quickly evaporates, partly by circumstance, partly by his change of heart: it is enough that Lélie is 'riche en vertus' (last scene). Unlike Don Pèdre, Gorgibus suffers no humiliation; he is reintegrated quickly into the emerging world of the young.

The absence of trickery accounts for the sketchy roles played by the auxiliaries. Gros-René, Lélie's valet, appears only once (7), to complain about his fatigue and hunger; Célie's *suivante* gives a charmingly naïve speech on the virtues of having a husband (even an unwanted one): 'Enfin il n'y a rien tel, Madame, croyez-moi, / Que d'avoir un mari la nuit auprès de soi' (2). Having no continuing functional importance, these two characters merely set off, by their down-to-earth preoccupations, the high-mindedness and exaltation of the lovers.

The fact that *Sganarelle* is built on the systematic use of quid pro quos has other consequences as well, particularly in the different sort of ironic relationship established with the audience. As trickery is absent, there can be no complicity between spectator and character. The game is in a sense being played against all the personages and our pleasure stems from the confusion of the victims in the imbroglio, contrasted with our total understanding of the situation. Instead of the mixture of second- and third-person irony obtained in plays based on *fourberie*, we experience only third-person irony. We know all, the people on stage know little or nothing, and there is no mediator between 'us' and 'them'. At the same time this ironic situation is made more complex by the fact that all four main characters are enmeshed in it and react in different ways to the kaleidoscope of false impressions they behold.

Our superiority in these ironic perspectives helps explain the easy euphoria which suffuses this simple, good-humoured comedy. Also, this sense of well-being is directly related to the preponderant fortuitousness of the action. The more arbitrary the plot the more it denies the temporal causality which is part of our human condition and a prime source of anxiety for us. Freed from all determinisms (even that tenuous one of the trickster planning his stratagems), events can spring up spontaneously at the whim of the comic spirit.

The chief reason, however, for the charm of this play is Sganarelle himself. As with *Le Médecin malgré lui* there is a basic counterpoint between the ideal marriage in the making through the love plot and a 'real' marriage in the lower classes with its wrangling and disputes. The two Sganarelles, one a rustic, the other a 'bon bourgeois,' are cut from the same cloth. Both are suspicious, choleric, coarse in their conjugal life. Both wives are cast as victims, but Martine is clever enough to avenge herself, while Sganarelle's wife, humourless and self-righteous, can do little more than rail.

It would be well, though, not to dwell on the rather superficial similarities of the two plays and the two Sganarelles. The hero of *Le Médecin malgré lui* moves in the course of the play toward the role of helpful auxiliary, the ally of the young. The *cocu imaginaire*, on the other hand, does nothing to bring the lovers together, indeed, his credulity results indirectly in the lovers' quarrel which nearly separates them for good. While the earthy, spontaneous vitality of the would-be doctor's character puts him on the side of life, we find no such functions in his present counterpart. True, Sganarelle's first gestures over Célie while she is in a faint (he puts his hand on her breast and moves his face toward hers, ostensibly to determine whether she is alive or not) are amusingly suggestive, but one must dispute a priapic interpretation of his entire role: if, as Gutwirth contends, 'il s'accommoderait fort bien de Célie sans doute' (p 71), why does he not linger over her rather than go immediately for help, and why is there no hint of desire during their remaining encounters? On the contrary, the logic of a play based on false appearances dictates that Sganarelle's wife should jump to the *wrong* conclusion.

Be that as it may, Sganarelle belongs on the 'other' side of comedy, along with Gorgibus, because they symbolize values that must be exorcised. The father is, for instance, the spokesman for paternal authority in general. His words to Célie in the beginning scene are not forgotten:

> Je n'aurai pas sur vous un pouvoir absolu?
> Et par sottes raisons votre jeune cervelle
> Voudrait régler ici la raison paternelle?

Like Arnolphe he hates the liberalizing influence of sophisticated reading because it is a threat to his authority. In harmony with his joyless vision of human relationships, Gorgibus rather prescribes to his daughter a diet of self-mortifying, austere religious tracts (eg, 'les doctes *Tablettes* / Du conseiller Matthieu' [1]). In this context, the reading of novels like *Clélie* must be seen as part of the cultured play of the wellborn, the analogue in seventeenth-century terms of Frye's pragmatically free society.

What of Sganarelle's values? His stupidity, vanity, braggedocio, and cowardice place him close to the *capitano* type, one of the ridiculous stock figures of the *commedia dell'arte* and seventeenth-century comedy in general. His conceited self-portrait is very much part of the pattern:

> Peut-on trouver en moi quelque chose à redire?
> Cette taille, ce port que tout le monde admire,
> Ce visage si propre à donner de l'amour,
> Pour qui mille beautés soupirent nuit et jour ... (6)

We laugh of course at Sganarelle, but it is derisive laughter directed at his faults and particularly the comic contrast between his heroic pretentions and his pusil-lanimity.[4] His delightfully parodic Cornelian monologue ('Courons donc le chercher, ce pendard qui m'affronte ... ' [17]) and his efforts to flog himself into defending his honour against Lélie (*'se donnant des coups de poings sur l'estomac et des soufflets pour s'exciter'* [21]) validate the comparison with the *miles gloriosus* type.

Sganarelle's funniest trait, however, is his preoccupation with *cocuage*. Like Sganarelle, all of Molière's *cocus* are *imaginaires*. The worried husband-to-be or husband in fact (even Dandin) never has proof positive, nor can *we* be sure that adultery has actually been consummated. As a derisive trait, the obsession of *cocuage* must remain only an obsession; a real victim is far less funny than an imagined one.

Further, this theme belongs to the 'représentation caricaturale du bourgeois' (Bénichou 176) and is part and parcel of the possessive and repressive ethic the middle class is made to project into comedy. Directly linked to domestic tyranny, it is seen as well as a direct result of it. In Bénichou's words, 'la confiance encourage la fidélité ... la contrainte, au contraire, crée la haine et la révolte' (p 193). The point is made time and time again in Molière: if wives are tempted to become unfaithful, the blame must fall, not on them, but on those who try to enslave them.

Misogyny underlies the fear of cuckoldry (Bénichou 179), just as hatred and distrust of women had driven Gorgibus to impose edifying and debasing sermons on his daughter. We have gone deeply into the anti-comic camp with Gorgibus and Sganarelle and the implications are clear and familiar: that wellborn women must be trusted, allowed a social life, be free to make their own decisions, and that men should understand these necessities of civilized living. Whence another reason why *cocuage* is never consummated in Molière: an actual betrayal would betray as well the sense of confidence which animates the 'right' society. We are back in short to the 'fantaisie de triomphe' of comedy, founded on the belief that it is safe to say to the wellborn: 'Fay ce que voudras.' Although imbued with simple Gallic humour, this high-spirited farce points ahead to the most serious implications of such masterpieces as *L'Ecole des femmes*.

L'AMOUR MÉDECIN

Like *Sganarelle*, *L'Amour médecin* introduces us to a characteristic, recurring theme in Molière's theatre. Despite the extent and bitterness of medical satire in this comedy, however, the plot itself is based on the same rudimentary archetypal structure as in the two preceding plays. Once again a young girl (Lucinde) and a young man (Clitandre) wish to marry, but Sganarelle, cast in this comedy as the domineering parent, will have none of it. Not that he has another spouse in mind for his daughter, nor any particular criticism of the one Lucinde has actually chosen; he gives his reasons in a short monologue: 'A-t-on jamais rien vu ... de plus impertinent et de plus ridicule que d'amasser du bien avec de grands travaux, et élever une fille avec beaucoup de soin et de tendresse, pour se dépouiller de l'un et de l'autre entre les mains d'un homme qui ne nous touche de rien? Non, non: Je me moque de cet usage, et je veux garder mon bien et ma fille pour moi' (I, 4).

Sganarelle combines, then, with the authoritarianism of his paternal role the possessiveness of a *barbon* lover as well as the traditional avarice of the blocking figure. In this combination of traits, he is a singular character in Molière. Most fathers are willing to relinquish their offspring provided the latter accept the intended spouse; Sganarelle's naïve egoism urges him to keep his child by his side forever. A kind of arrested father-child relationship is underscored by all of Sganarelle's encounters with his daughter: stubborn, unhearing silences, domineering anger, and above all such baby talk as: 'Allons donc, découvre-moi ton petit cœur. Là, ma pauvre mie, dis, dis; dis tes petites pensées à ton petit papa mignon' (I, 2).

Yet, Sganarelle is hardly a threat. His treatment of Lucinde betrays a basic infantilism in his own character complemented by the stupidity and gullibility of the clown figure he embodies. As a result, the tricks by which he is defeated need not be very ingenious. Lisette functions in her role of *suivante* as the agent of *fourberie*: it is she who sees to it that Clitandre gets into the household disguised as a doctor. Having diagnosed Lucinde's illness as 'un désir dépravé de vouloir être mariée,' Clitandre persuades Sganarelle to agree to a mock marriage ceremony. 'Comme il faut flatter l'imagination des malades, et que j'ai vu en elle de l'aliénation d'esprit ... je l'ai prise par son faible, et lui ai dit que j'étais venu ici pour vous la demander en mariage' (III, 6). The ironic effects built up by these successive stratagems reach their climax when the disguised Clitandre is able to tell Lucinde of his marital intentions in the presence of the father who laughs fatuously at the way his daughter is supposedly taken in (III, 6).

As with Don Pèdre, Sganarelle's subsequent humiliation is twofold: he must endure the knowledge of having been gulled and the taunts of Lisette: 'Ma foi! Monsieur, la bécasse est bridée, et vous avez cru faire en jeu, qui demeure une verité' (last scene). Sganarelle also finds himself in the midst of a festive atmosphere which he will not join. The role of the Sénateur-master of revels is taken here by the final ballet of 'les Jeux, les Ris et les Plaisirs', but Sganarelle is forced to join the dance, the final touch of the scapegoat ritual to which he has been subjected. Yet the impression of exorcism is mitigated by the clownish flatness of Sganarelle's character and his basic infantilism. We are in a world of farce where apparent cruelty hides, in reality, a fundamental indulgence and good humour.

The functional plot of *L'Amour médecin* is extremely slight when one weighs the above elements against the total length of the play. We know, of course, that Molière contrived it very quickly, whence the overall impression of improvisation; the rather gratuitous first scene, for instance, reminds us of an oriental apologue: Sganarelle asks advice of several people as to how to relieve Lucinde's melancholy, and each counsels according to his own self-interest. The chief elaboration on the romantic plot, however, is the portrayal of doctors and medicine. The theme of cuckoldry in *Sganarelle* was linked to the main action by the quid pro quos by which each character thought himself betrayed. Here, Lucinde's sudden 'illness' justifies the appearance on stage of the medical profession, and Sganarelle's fatuous insistence on a 'quantité' of doctors (I, 6) explains why there should be so many. But, as with *Sganarelle*, the theme in counterpoint is important, not because of its tie with the plot, but because it adds an important dimension to the moral statement of the play.

The whole of the second act and the first scene of the third are given over to the five doctors who constitute the primary targets for Molière's satire. The theme is prolonged for the rest of the third act as well by Clitandre's impersonation of a medical practitioner. On the whole, the wrongs ascribed to doctors and their craft are the same as revealed in other plays: ignorance, ineffectualness, and charlatanism. Yet, *L'Amour médecin* has two features that set it apart. The comic element is heightened by the sheer effect of repetition. Four doctors appear for the consulation in II, each strongly individualized and caricatured, and they are joined by a fifth shortly thereafter. In no other play is there such an accumulation. And, more significantly, in no other play do we see the profession *from within*. Among themselves in II, 3, and III, 1, they are free to drop the mask and betray their callousness, contentiousness, and concern with 'formalités.' Seemingly unmindful of their patient, they casually discuss their itineraries through Paris, the relative merits of horse and mule travel, and the case of a doctor who failed to heed the opinion of his *ancien*.

Their disputatious nature, however, causes the mask to fall later when it should be on: Tomès and Fonandrès quarrel before the perplexed Sganarelle over the proper treatment of Lucinde's illness. This incident brings about the second scene mentioned: a fifth and presumably more prestigious doctor, Filerin, scolds the other four for their public controversy and reminds them of the need to hide internal dissension 'sans découvrir encore au peuple ... la forfanterie de notre art' (III, 1). Such is the cynical frankness of remarks attributed to the medical profession in this scene that it resembles astonishingly the bitter denunciation of medicine by Béralde in *Le Malade imaginaire*, even to the wording; in both cases the language of medicine is described as a 'pompeux galimatias.' That the most eloquent and least ridiculous doctor of the lot could be echoed in Molière's last play by an impassioned foe of the profession only heightens the retrospective impact of this scene.

On a satirical level we see, then, in *L'Amour médecin* a particularly biting commentary on doctors and doctoring. In the context of this study, however, we must pass from this rather obvious level to a more general archetypal meaning. To begin with, doctors embody alien values: not only more general ones like crass ignorance and hypocrisy but a peculiarly 'doctoral' trait: solemnity. His utter lack of humour, symbolized by the lugubrious black gown he wears, puts the doctor in the archetypal category of kill-joys, a dour figure who bores us by his jargon and barren logic, who dismays us by his vindictiveness before wit and criticism. Festiveness, joy, laughter are beyond him, so he must take his place beside the heavy father, the tyrannical *barbon* lover, as a figure to be exorcized. And the doctors of *L'Amour médecin* are indeed exorcized – not by the usual means of trickery and humiliation, but by simply being themselves on stage and by lending themselves unwittingly to our derisive laughter.

Unlike his fellow *alazones*, however, the archetypal doctor bears a metaphysical stamp. If comedy is the celebration of life, it is also, explicitly or by implication, the 'carrying out,' or exorcism of death. The stopping of time at the end of the traditional comedy, the projection into the unchanging future of the young lovers, deny the reality of chronological time and our eventual end. But death itself can be more directly devalued, as it is when the point of ritual death passes without catastrophe. Molière's doctor figure can be seen, I think, as fulfilling somewhat the same function. We need not look far for signs of this death-figure role: his ominous garb, his terrifying mien, his ugliness. A suggestion of supernatural power, of black magic puts an aura of dread around him. He utters strange words that arouse basic fears of death and pain in us. Because he can tamper with our bodies he has control over life; and since his art is false, that control becomes the power to kill. Words like 'mort,' 'mourir,' 'tuer' — words so alien to comedy — cluster characteristically around Molière's doctors.

This nightmare image must of course be reduced to comic proportions. Illness is no more real in Molière than cuckoldry: we find only feigned or imaginary disease; such is the tenacity of life that the doctor's worst depredations cannot make an end, for instance, to Argan's vitality. The unreality of death and illness in Molière makes the doctor a much less fearsome personage. His words, moreover, are deflated by their very absurdity and the grotesque way they are proffered by, for example, the ponderous Macroton, and Bahys with his staccato delivery (II, 5). Finally, the allusions to death are fundamentally comic in their context of wit and ridicule. Thus Lisette, who tells the five doctors with mock indignation that 'un insolent ... a eu l'effronterie d'entreprendre sur votre métier, et ... sans votre ordonnance, vient de tuer un homme d'un grand coup d'épée au travers du corps' (III, 2).

By devaluing the doctor's terrifying aspect and powers to do harm, by transmuting dread into laughter, comedy expels death as the ultimate alien element. And the basic archetypal dialectic causes another kind of medicine to come into being, a life-affirming one dedicated to joy and vitality — 'l'amour médecin' in a word. We have already seen Sganarelle embody that function in Le Médecin malgré lui; there the 'real' world of true doctors was present only by implication. In L'Amour médecin, Clitandre makes us forget the grotesque doctors we have actually seen, just as Toinette will prove a joyful foil to the Diafoirus. In each case, the actual doctors are deflated death figures, while the practitioners of love medicine, all impostors in medical terms, are exalted symbols of life. Or, to be more accurate, the real practitioners turn out to be impostors, while the false doctors turn out to be the real ones who affirm the most vital revivifying function.

Clitandre's successful 'cure' both deflates doctors and their dangerous charlatanism and rids comedy of the double threat of tyranny and egoism in the person of Sganarelle. In the last scene the curative power passes from Clitandre to comedy itself and its allied arts of ballet and music:

> Sans nous tous les hommes
> Deviendraient mal sains,
> Et c'est nous qui sommes
> Leurs grands médecins.

Thus life and art blend in a joyous hymn of optimism.

LA COMTESSE D'ESCARBAGNAS AND MONSIEUR DE POURCEAUGNAC

In their satire of provincial nobility, these plays add a geographical dimension to the seventeenth century's moral view of comedy. The relatively timeless concepts of a 'pragmatically free society' and a world 'in ritual bondage' appear in the classical *Weltanschauung* as linked to a social hierarchy: repressiveness and fatuous self-importance are attributes of the bourgeoisie while the ideal of elegant play and high-minded confidence reigns solely in the aristocracy. The pleasure principle can be legitimate only at the top of the hierarchy, for the high-born alone possess the moral excellence to live in harmonious freedom.

The nether world of comedy extends outward into the Provinces as well as downward into the Paris bourgeoisie around and below that tiny island of good taste called 'La Cour et la Ville.' Even people of rank in the provinces are visualized in such grotesque terms that their claim to nobility must be spurious; such characters as the Comtesse d'Escarbagnas and Monsieur de Pourceaugnac appear as pretentious fakes, ridiculous caricatures deserving of the worst kind of mortification. Both plays, then, constitute basically an exorcism of an alien world and its false values – an exorcism so unrelenting and fierce in the case of *Monsieur de Pourceaugnac* that the whole play strikes us as a scapegoat ritual. And while *Monsieur de Pourceaugnac* may be the better play, Hubert's contention that *La Comtesse d'Escarbagnas* 'does not contain anything that cannot be found in other plays of the master' (p xiii) must be disputed. As the playwright's only picture of provincial nobility *in its own setting*, it has its unique place in Molière's canon.

The initial dynamism of each comedy is furnished by the traditional romantic love plot. In *La Comtesse d'Escarbagnas*, Julie and the Vicomte, *honnêtes gens* inexplicably marooned in this farcical world of Angoulême aristocracy, are unable to marry because of disagreements between the two sets of parents. In order to see his beloved as often as possible without arousing suspicion, the Vicomte accepts, like the good courtly hero he is, a double servitude from his lady: he will keep his own affections secret and will, as an added precaution, feign a respectful passion for the Comtesse. In this sketchy plot, the obstacle is not even personified, and the Vicomte's role as the ostensible rival of provincial functionaries like Monsieur Tibaudier and Monsieur Harpin is hardly plausible. We are again in a world of fantasy; the fortuitous nature of these story components is underscored by a particularly abrupt resolution: a letter is delivered to the Vicomte informing him that he may marry his beloved.

Our interest shifts very early in the play to the real dynamic centre of *La Comtesse d'Escarbagnas*, the game of *eiron* against *alazon*. A tone of play is dominant at the outset: 'Cette feinte dont vous parlez,' Julie tells the Vicomte, 'm'est une comédie fort agréable. ... Notre comtesse ... est un aussi bon personnage qu'on en puisse mettre sur le théâtre' (1). As the game involves dissimulation and impersonation, Julie's dramatic metaphors become singularly apt. The whole play was written, of course, to frame another: a lost pastoral at Saint-Germain where it was created, and *Le Mariage forcé* later at the Palais-Royal. It is natural, then, that the play-within-a-play should be anticipated thematically by the numerous theatrical allusions and, indeed, by the transparency of its plot conventions. Julie's word 'comédie,' moreover, leads us in two complementary directions, that of 'feinte' or acting, and that of being an object of derision. Thus, 'donner la comédie' can be the conscious task of a stage director. In this context, the Vicomte has a double role, for he is apparently both the author and director of the play framed by *La Comtesse d'Escarbagnas* (cf. 'ma musique ... ma comédie ... mes entrées de ballet' [5]), and the chief actor in the game played against the Comtesse and her entourage. On the other hand, ridiculous types by their very lack of awareness tend to draw our laughter. This is, for instance, what Philinte tries to make Alceste understand when he tells him 'cette maladie, / Partout où vous allez, donne la comédie' (*Le Misanthrope*, I, 1).

Like the doctors of *L'Amour médecin*, the Comtesse is ridiculous simply by being herself on stage. But the exorcism aspect of the play is underlined by the genteel aggression of which she is a victim. The main weapon by which she unknowingly is castigated is conscious irony. Both Julie and the Vicomte punctuate the proceedings with double-edged comments that flatter her and spur her on to more foolish remarks. Julie leads the good lady into an amusing account of her success among 'les galants de la cour' by the remark: 'Je pense, Madame, que, durant votre séjour à Paris, vous avez fait bien des conquêtes de qualité' (2). The Vicomte's barely hidden sarcasms about Tibaudier's 'poetry' are in the same vein. The lovers function as both observers and participants. Like us, they witness the grotesque and vulgar antics of the Comtesse and her 'court,' and their remarks as actors reinforce our perceptions and heighten our sense of the ridiculous.

The game is about to conclude with the staging of the Vicomte's 'comédie' at the end of 7; but one last intrusion of reality delays our absorption into a world of fantasy. The jealous Harpin bursts in upon the stage of the play-within-a-play and berates the Comtesse for the affection she shows her other suitors. Accused of interrupting the entertainment he picks up the cue and points out to the lady that 'la véritable comédie qui se fait ici, c'est celle que vous jouez' (8). One can imagine the smile of complicity between Julie and the Vicomte at the unintentional pertinence of the remark. With a further stage metaphor, Harpin leaves the stage as abruptly as he had arrived: 'Voilà ma scène faite, voilà mon rôle joué' (8), and a crestfallen Comtesse apologizes for this 'insolence.'

Julie and her lover have had unexpected support in their game. Harpin has humiliated the Countess in a direct way forbidden to the others and has thus participated forcefully in the aggression. Yet, her world, although shaken, still holds together, and Harpin is remembered chiefly as a *trouble-fête*, a discordant element of seriousness in a world dedicated in one form or another to play – the various 'comédies' of Julie and the Vicomte, and refined *badinage* for which this Angoulême 'salon' strives. Even when the Comtesse learns of the Vicomte's dissimulation, the world of theatre quickly absorbs the participants into a painless triumph of convention: announcing to the Countess that he intends to marry Julie, the Vicomte adds: 'si vous m'en croyez, pour rendre la comédie complète de tout point, vous épouserez Monsieur Tibaudier, et donnerez Mademoiselle Andrée à son laquais' (last scene).

This light-hearted dénouement makes us forget that Julie and the Vicomte are really intruders in the unredeemable world of the 'province'; they try to hold aloft the flame of true refinement with their elegant banter, the witty sonnet recited by the Vicomte in 1. The play is really a kind of private joke which they are good enough to let us in on. Totally different is *Monsieur de Pourceaugnac*: here Paris has not sent a detachment of *honnêtes gens* to show up provincial nobility, but a *hobereau de province* has been rash enough to invade the citadel of refinement. Monsieur de Pourceaugnac is now the intruder, but *he* must be driven out. Thus this play too is built upon a systematic aggression – as ferocious and unrelenting as the previous one had been gentle and refined.

Once again a love plot provides the initial momentum of the play. As in *Sganarelle*, the father (Oronte) has promised his daughter to the suitor whom she loves (Julie – once again – and Eraste); but the prospect of a wealthier son-in-law makes him go back on his word. The rival lover is none other than Monsieur de Pourceaugnac, who has just arrived to claim his bride. Besides being a laughable interloper, then, Monsieur de Pourceaugnac places as well an obstacle in the path of true love. His role as a scapegoat is functionally linked to the plot, not a thematic prolongation of it (as with the doctors in *L'Amour médecin*, for example). In this sense the play resembles those which will be studied in the following chapter, where a powerful blocking figure is at the centre of the anticomic world. Having no legal power, however, Pourceaugnac never looms as a serious threat; and the accumulation of tricks played against him, the sheer delight his tormentors take in his discomfiture, make him more of a butt than an adversary, a witless outsider rather than a true blocking character.

'Nous avons préparé un bon nombre de batteries pour renverser ce dessein ridicule' (I, 1). Eraste's military image is apt, for one has the impression of a vast, elaborately contrived campaign about to be launched against the would-be husband. The lovers and their three auxiliaries form the shock troops who operate directly against Pourceaugnac by means of impersonation, and indirectly through their unwitting allies, themselves victims of trickery. Father, doctors, and representatives of justice, all contribute to the bewilderment of the Limousin. Even the traditional *alazones* team with the *eirones* in this world of trickery.

Paris quickly becomes a nightmare world for the Limousin. In an extraordinary speech in II, 4, Pourceaugnac summarizes in telegraphic style his experience of being incarcerated as insane. The fragments of dialogues and singing he has heard, strung together in this droll way, reveal his terror before each component element and his perplexity before the whole series of events. In a sense, we have here a parody of Barthes' 'scène racinienne,' a comic trauma seared into memory: 'Je vous laisse entre les mains de Monsieur. Des médecins habillés de noir. Dans une chaise. Tâter le pouls. Comme ainsi soit. Il est fou ... ' etc.

What is important in the many *fourberies* of which Pourceaugnac is the victim is the breathless pace of the action and the number of people involved. The climax is reached when Pourceaugnac is threatened with hanging for bigamy. As an ultimate humiliation he is forced to disguise himself as a woman – 'nous avons l'impression d'assister à une atroce pitrerie,' comments Adam (p 378) – and listen to two 'suisses' enjoying in advance the grisly spectacle of seeing the bigamist 'gambiller les pieds en haut devant tout le monde' (III, 3). By all evidence the threat of hanging is real; the apparatus of justice pursuing Pourceaugnac does not appear to be an invention of the *fourbes*. The Limousin is recognized and arrested by an *exempt*; only a timely bribe allows him to return home safe and sound, bewildered and angry. His inability to comprehend the situations he has lived through has insulated him, however, against the most crushing come-uppance of all, awareness of his own foolishness. As Hubert rightly notes, 'unlike his fellow dupes in Molière's repertory, the Limousin gentleman never wakes up, no doubt because knowledge and discovery in this play do not matter in the least' (p 199).

To explain the apparent cruelty of the treatment meted out to Pourceaugnac, we must once again proceed from the principle that if there is punishment, there must be crime. The Limousin would inflict himself on a much younger lady whom he has never seen. After betraying his legal formation by an outpouring of lawyer jargon, he refuses to own up to being in the *noblesse de robe*. 'Je suis gentilhomme,' he stoutly maintains (II, 10).[5] This is the original sin of the comic butt: incongruity between reality and appearance, the desire to keep the mask in place even when it has actually fallen.

In the final analysis, however, Pourceaugnac's fault is consubstantial with his characteristic stupidity (repeatedly emphasized in the play) and his role as an outsider. As Nérine, Julie's *suivante*, exclaims early in the play: 'S'il a envie de se marier, que ne prend-il une Limousine et ne laisse-t-il en repos les chrétiens?' (I, 1).

No sooner is the scapegoat expelled than the play ends in reconciliation. Eraste pretends to have rescued Julie from the clutches of Pourceaugnac and is awarded the girl by a repentant father who, cured of his avarice, promises a generous dowry for his daughter. A renewed and reconciled society, rid of the intruder and his alien values, witnesses the apotheosis of the pleasure principle in a song and dance by 'plusieurs masques': 'Ne songeons qu'à nous réjouir: / La grande affaire est le plaisir' (III, 8).

LES FÂCHEUX

The primary characteristic of a *fâcheux* is to be importunate: 'qui dérange,' as the *Dictionnaire Robert* puts it. Thus we are not necessarily dealing in this play with intrinsic faults like miserliness or tyranny, but with annoyances that arise out of a particular situation, events that interefere with the accomplishment of a particular purpose. At first, pure chance seems the power behind the scenes; but as obstacles build up, the impression of a supernatural conspiracy is stronger and stronger, and the sense of harassment and irritation becomes all the more acute since these multiple frustrations are compressed into a three-act format.[6]

All this reminds us of *L'Etourdi*. But in the earlier play, the *contretemps* frustrate carefully elaborated plans of the valet, Mascarille. That is, there is a strong initial energy at work: the driving optimism of the archetypal buffoon undaunted in the face of an apparently malevolent 'sort.' Eraste, the hero-victim of *Les Fâcheux*, is cast in a completely different role. He must muster all his energies merely to hold his position. He desperately wants to keep his mind and eyes on his beloved; the waves of people who accost him are *fâcheux* chiefly because they distract him from this goal.[7] Circumstances force him to seek out the lady in a public place (presumably a fashionable promenade like Cours-la-Reine) and he must prevent the public from forcing him out or absorbing him. He quite literally loses his position during the *intermèdes* when dancing *fâcheux* drive him off the stage. Eraste's valet, moreover, is at the farthest remove from Mascarille. He is more like the second *zanno* of the *commedia*, a bumbler who only adds to his master's sense of frustration. He is in fact one of the prominent *fâcheux* of the play and the only recurring one:

> Au diantre tout valet qui vous est sur les bras,
> Qui fatigue son maître, et ne fait que déplaire
> A force de vouloir trancher du nécessaire!   (I, 1)

The absence, then, of a sense of affirmative energy, of joyous inventiveness leaves this play with a dominant impression of annoyance. This tone of cumulative irritation, of suppressed anger exploding into diatribes and hyperbole reminds one of literary satire where the narrator casts himself as the victim of fate. Boileau's annoyance at 'Les Embarras de Paris' is analogous to the impotent anger which suffuses Eraste's description of his encounter at the theatre with the first *fâcheux* of the play.

Eraste's sense of frustration is heightened in another way. Instinctively polite, Eraste cannot vent his spleen. He even denies himself the luxury of the irritated aside, a device one would expect to find under the circumstances, but which is virtually non-existent in the play. At best he resorts to veiled sarcasm. When the inept dancer says proudly, 'Je me moque, pour moi, des maîtres baladins,' one can imagine the wry tone of Eraste's terse: 'On le voit' (I, 3). Only with the mad inventor, Osmin, does he drop somewhat his native civility. And he does explode repeatedly against his valet with cathartic imprecations like 'Que la fièvre te serre.' Finally, the obsessional nature of Eraste's apprehensions is underlined by the frequent repetition of the word *fâcheux*, usually in a time of irritation.

The functional plot itself confirms our impression that the primary *élan* of comedy – the young man's pursuit of the young lady – is quite subdued in *Les Fâcheux*. The romantic element is tenuous in the extreme; as Molière himself admits, 'je me servis du premier nœud que je pus trouver' (*Avertissement*, vol. I, p 365). Eraste has already won his lady Orphise, but the latter's *tuteur*, Damis, has forbidden his ward to see the young man. We would expect Damis to be one of the more prominent *fâcheux*, not only for Eraste but for the whole comic dynamism; his is the supreme sin of standing in the way of true love. But Damis does not appear until the end of the play and is mentioned only twice before that. And when he does come on stage it is to experience a complete change of heart and allow Orphise to marry Eraste.

Both aspects of the love plot are thus muted. Eraste and Orphise exchange comparatively little dialogue, and their obstacle, Damis, is hardly exploited at all as a blocking figure. The comic myth recedes before the assault of the *fâcheux*.

This succession of annoying characters seems at first glance mechanical, but Molière develops the situation in a surprisingly complex way. Generally speaking, no *fâcheux* appears more than once; but to give some element of continuity, Molière has La Montagne, Eraste's bumbling valet, make three appearances. The theme of importunateness is prolonged in space as well. Orphise is herself set upon by her own lot of *fâcheux*, one of whom causes indirectly a falling out between the lovers. She is unable to rejoin Eraste because she is trapped by 'quelque provinciales, / Aux personnes de cour fâcheuses animales' (II, 3). In two cases, a *fâcheux* labels another character by the same word (Dorante, the hunter, who showers contempt on the *campagnard* [II, 6] and the mad inventor Ormin, who describes Caratidès as a 'vieux importun, qui n'a pas l'esprit sain' (III, 3). This device of the pot calling the kettle black reinforces the self-blindness and fatuousness characteristic of some of the *fâcheux*. Finally, the full range of social types comes out in the *intermèdes* where 'joueurs de mail,' cobblers, and a gardener take their turn in tormenting Eraste. The verbal extravagance of the *fâcheux* in the play proper is paralleled by a physical dynamism in the *intermèdes*. Having been tormented by words, Eraste is now a victim of aggression by dance.

We find a certain moral diversity as well among the speaking *fâcheux*. Some exhibit intrinsic faults while others simply arrive at the wrong time. The 'question galante' which Eraste is asked to arbitrate in II is a proper social game and would probably elicit Eraste's interest at another time. On the other hand, the eccentrics – those whose obsession by one kind of activity throws their whole personality off balance – call forth our derisive laughter. The card fanatic, the hunter, the pedant, all with their specialized jargon, the inventor with his *idée fixe* about turning the seacoasts of France into one huge port – these would be bores in any circumstances.

The depth and complexity of these portrayals explain the second resolution of the comedy, a resolution which quite properly overshadows the union of the lovers. Just as the reconciled Damis speaks in III, 6 what would ordinarily be 'sweetness and light' curtain lines in Quentin Hope's suggestive typology ('Molière's Curtain Lines,' *French Studies* 26 [April 1972] 145-7): 'Célébrons l'heureux sort dont vous allez jouir, / Et que nos violons viennent nous réjouir,' the *fâcheux* make a last assault as a group of '*masques entrent, qui occupent toute la place.*' Eraste, outraged at this final torment, has these 'gredins' run off stage. Thus the final ballet accomplishes the real exorcism. The retreat of the masks signals the definitive defeat of the *fâcheux*, and a pleasant dance of shepherds and shepherdesses concludes the play. The plague of *fâcheux* is over, the real celebration can begin. The thematic unity of the main play and the interludes in this, Molière's first *comédie-ballet*, proves the playwright's success in the task he had assigned himself: 'ne faire qu'une seule chose du ballet et de la comédie' (*Avertissement*, vol. I, p 365).

This chapter began with a short comedy, *Le Sicilien*, which can be considered in fact a schematized prototype of purely functional comedy. The remaining plays studied derive their dramatic interest from thematic extensions of this functional plot. Alien elements usually embodied in a principal blocking character are presented here more diffusely, as part of a humorous society whose role is out of proportion with the actual premises of the comic plot. Our attention is focused in *Sganarelle* upon cuckoldry and the quid pro quos by which the theme is developed; medical charlatanism is at the centre of *L'Amour médecin*, although only loosely tied to the plot; our interest in *La Comtesse d'Escarbagnas* and in *Monsieur de Pourceaugnac* is drawn away from the slender romantic element to the theme of provincial pretentiousness; finally, the comic plot in the play just studied is trampled by the crowd of *fâcheux* that pass before us. In all these cases something standing in the way of love, or opposed to it in some way, is exorcized – either by a satirical portrait sketched by the dramatist or by some humiliation suffered within the play, or both. In the latter three plays we note an additional principle of repetition and accumulation: the dissimulated jibes directed against the Comtesse and her world by Julie and the Vicomte, the succession of humiliations suffered by Pourceaugnac, the series of annoyances plaguing Eraste. But this periodicity must not be confused with the chief characteristic of the comedies analysed in chapter 2. The emphasis is not on vitality and resourcefulness. An intense feeling of frustration pervades *Les Fâcheux*, and the tricks played against the country Comtesse and against Pourceaugnac are intended less to show the resourcefulness of the tricksters than to enable us to laugh at the expense of a fool.

We have been dealing, then, with comedies where exorcism is an important element; that is, where the moral dialectic of comedy is so strong that the anti-comic world – the world of ritual bondage – must be symbolically rejected in order for the new society to take its place. But this process can be carried out much more compellingly in a single blocking character whose wrongdoing stems from his very role in the comic plot. We might speak in this regard of a purely functional aspect, where the action arises from what Barthes calls 'figures' acting in their 'rapports de force.' In the comedies to which we shall now turn, a major part of the play consists in the elaboration of these basic relationships and extensions.

4

Exorcism: The Heavy Fathers

The blocking characters for which Molière is justly famous are far more than the irritating intruders and pretentious and ineffectual fools who are caricatured and baited in the plays just studied. By the authority they enjoy, whether justified or usurped, and by their relentless monomania, they loom as real dangers to the comic order. Here the dialectic of desire and fear reaches its point of highest tension in Molière.

In *L'Ecole des maris* and *L'Ecole des femmes*, where the father figure is himself humiliated and expelled, the exorcism element is strong and, in the case of Arnolphe, it may seem cruelly unjust. In both cases parental authority is depicted as assumed. Sganarelle and Arnolphe are merely guardians of their respective 'daughters' and intend moreover to marry them. The remaining comedies in this category present true parents, however arbitrary their exercise of authority. In two of them, *Tartuffe* and *Les Femmes savantes*, the heavy father is the victim of someone else's hypnotic appeal and cunning. Hence, the guilt for callous parental tyranny falls in part at least upon the real villain of the piece who in this way becomes the scapegoat. The exposure and departure of the true blocking character enable the parental figure to recognize his mistake. In a final group, the true father is himself the principle of opposition: Harpagon, Monsieur Jourdain, and Argan are all enslaved by an obsession which causes them to rule their families with a heavy hand and make selfish and callous decisions regarding the marriages of their children. In each case their tyranny is broken. But only their sin is exorcized; they themselves remain on stage at the end of the play, fundamentally unaware of their defeat.

That they are parents with natural rights explains, perhaps, this impression of ambiguity. Full humiliation and expulsion would shock our notions of family order, while total integration with no chastisement, even external, would seem a glossing over of a serious fault which had almost had catastrophic results.

Harpagon, Jourdain, and Argan lose the battle against their children but are allowed to glide into a fantasy world which protects them against the full knowledge of defeat. Unlike the other four domineering parental figures, there is no painful *anagnorisis*, no gnawing realization of their own foolishness. Yet, there is a strong contrast in tone between *L'Avare* and both *Le Malade imaginaire* and *Le Bourgeois gentilhomme*. Harpagon's fantasy is lifeless, joyless, and solitary; the victorious society leaves him alone on the stage. With the two *comédies-ballets* the father is absorbed into a new society magnanimous enough to protect the *mamamouchi* and the new doctor from any later comic deflation.

L'ECOLE DES MARIS

This comedy is the first to entertain the serious and prolonged discussion of social issues that has become the trademark of Molière's theatre. Neither in his earlier five-act comedies (*L'Etourdi* and *Le Dépit amoureux*) nor in his popular one-act farces (*Les Précieuses ridicules* and *Sganarelle*) do we find much material of this kind. Whatever moral implications are contained in *Les Précieuses*, for instance, are presented in a highly caricatured and negative way. On the other hand, the neat, almost schematic balance between thesis and antithesis as embodied in Sganarelle and Ariste, from which any ambiguity is eliminated by the exemplary reward-and-punishment ending, has led critic after critic to the notion of a thesis.[1]

The wide-ranging *agon* between Ariste and Sganarelle in *L'Ecole des maris* marks a new direction for Molière in another way. The contrast between norm and aberration will henceforth be underlined by contemporaneous terms and ideas. Molière's comedies become, then, doubly 'realistic.' He continues his satirical vocation; but he also elaborates, or at least hints at, an explicit social ideal as a backdrop to what he ridicules. In the plays at hand, he roots his blocking or ridiculous character in the mores of his own culture (as he had done in a more general way with *Les Précieuses* and *Sganarelle*, his first plays in a distinctly French and contemporary setting). More importantly, he relates by the same token the romantic element to the precise social norms recognized and celebrated ritually in his own time: a life of elegant play and self-indulgence in a larger context of aristocratic civility and its sentimental expression.

In this light, Molière can easily pass as a philosopher reacting with native indulgence and generosity on the side of youth against tyrannical egoism, and promoting the cause of kindness and understanding. It may well be, of course, that the dramatist held these views, but whether he did or not is without importance. The play, not Molière, speaks to us and conveys its meaning by form; and from that point of view, the *agon* of *L'Ecole des maris* can be much more pertinently seen as a specific structural analogue of the comic myth. Molière is not baldly 'philosophizing'; he is simply making more explicit, more detailed, the social relevance of the comic structure in his own time.

While the ethical polarization of the play is so great that one could almost speak of a *moralité*, the functional relationships among the characters admit of curious ambiguities. The initial parallelism suggests the standard double plot: both Ariste and Sganarelle intend to marry their respective wards, Léonor and Isabelle. Having taken care of the two girls from childhood, they each have a double function as 'père' and 'époux'; as their moral fatherhood is confirmed legally by a contract, they are both free to use that authority to impose themselves as husbands or make other dispositions as they wish (I, 1). Thus the action takes place, as Gutwirth puts it, in 'un intervalle hybride, où le mari qui ne l'est pas encore peut être trompé sans dommage et le mariage s'abolir avant d'avoir jamais été' (p 103). Two contrasts deepen the situation: the difference in age between the two brothers – Ariste is a *senex*, Sganarelle a *barbon*[2] – and, naturally, their incompatible views on the education of women.

The intrusion of Valère creates the functional plot as such. The affection between Ariste and Léonor, assured because Ariste subscribes already to the ideals of freedom and confidence implicit in the play, will recede into the background and serve as a foil for the 'blondin-berne-barbon' action.

In the typical comedy the initiative and energy for contriving the defeat of the obstacle figure comes from the young man or, more specifically, from his auxiliary, aided often by a *suivante*. This play, like its successor, *L'Ecole des femmes*, is quite anomalous in this respect. Here it is Isabelle who invents and carries off the stratagems by which she can be free of her 'Argus.' Taking advantage of Sganarelle's gullibility, she makes him an unsuspecting go-between: through him, she declares her love for Valère and has a love letter delivered to the young man. In addition to these premeditated schemes she adds an equally clever one, invented on the spur of the moment at the beginning of III, which precipitates the comic reversal. Valère joins the game of deceit belatedly, when the play is half over. The two auxiliaries, Léonor's *suivante*, Lisette, and Ergaste, Valère's valet, have very small roles as commentators on the action, not as participants.

As in other Molière comedies, the *eiron-alazon* conflict gives rise to strong effects of dramatic irony. The playwright exploits especially the systematic double-entendre used by the lovers in their messages and in their face-to-face meeting in II, 9. Feigning indignation at Valère and his designs to marry her, Isabelle gives him his cue under Sganarelle's very nose:

Il faut que ce que j'aime, usant de diligence,
Fasse à ce que je hais perdre toute espérance,
Et qu'un heureux hymen affranchisse mon sort
D'un supplice pour moi plus affreux que la mort.

Characteristically, this second-person irony has a third-person echo from Sganarelle, against whom the game is played: 'Oui, mignonne, je songe à remplir ton attente.'

Sganarelle is made ridiculous in this way throughout the play, but, as with Don Pèdre in *Le Sicilien*, the harshest punishment is reserved for the end: the awareness of being duped and of having contrived unwittingly the marriage of his future wife with his rival. The world formed at the end of the play has no room for him and he leaves the stage after a bitter outburst against womenkind.

What is the corruption that he carries off to leave a purified society behind him? Actually, the *faute comique* is not difficult to assign: Sganarelle propounds the wrong theories of education and ridicules the right ones. There are in fact three schools in this play: the 'école du monde' in which the enlightened Ariste has formed his ward, the kind of preventive custody of which Isabelle has been victim, and, on a different level, the *école* of the title: the school of ridicule for which Lisette becomes the recruiting officer in the curtain lines addressed to the audience: 'Vous, si vous connaissez des maris loups-garous, / Envoyez-les au moins à l'école chez nous' (III, 9). Having professed the wrong precepts in the school for wives, Sganarelle becomes an unwilling pupil in the school for husbands.[3]

While he functions both as future husband and as father, Sganarelle's *alazoneia* involves chiefly his role as *précepteur*. Significantly, he spends more time ridiculing Ariste's beliefs than in defending his own. The smug and mean side of his temperament comes out to give a strong moral colour to his already objectionable philosophy:

> Vous souffrez que la vôtre aille leste et pimpante:
> Je le veux bien; qu'elle ait et laquais et suivante:
> J'y consens; qu'elle coure, aime l'oisiveté,
> Et soit des damoiseaux fleurée [flairée] en liberté:
> J'en suis fort satisfait. (I, 2)

To the sneering irony of feigned agreement Sganarelle adds an injurious and degrading suggestion of animals smelling out a female for coupling. His own ideas, expressed immediately after the above lines, are thus situated in a context of arrogance and coarseness:

J'entends que la mienne
Vive à ma fantaisie, et non pas à la sienne;
Que d'une serge honnête elle ait son vêtement,
Et ne porte le noir qu'aux bons jours seulement,
Qu'enfermée au logis, en personne bien sage,
Elle s'applique toute aux choses du ménage,
...
Qu'aux discours des muguets elle ferme l'oreille,
Et ne sorte jamais sans avoir qui la veille. (I, 2)

Sganarelle's pervasive egoism is only enhanced by the peremptory tone of these 'maximes sévères' which he himself devalues by making them a function of his 'fantaisie.' The underlying idea is the rejection of all fashionable social norms: clothing, civility, intelligent conversation, and *galanterie*. He has already ridiculed the costume worn by the 'muguets' banished from Isabelle's presence (I, 1), and Ariste's own attempts to conform to the edicts of fashion: 'je vous vois porter les sottises qu'on porte' (I, 1). His own vestimentary ideal is the outmoded clothing worn by his 'aieux,' the male equivalent of the colourless 'serge honnête' by which Isabelle must dull her beauty. To be sure Molière pokes fun at exaggeration and ostentation in fashionable circles too; but what Sganarelle advocates here is on the level of the wing collar and the pince-nez today.

By imprisoning his ward and imposing boring domestic tasks on her, Sganarelle denies the highest aspirations of the French seventeenth century: witty conversation among cultivated people, men and women alike, in a relaxed atmosphere of spontaneous play. Small wonder that Lisette, Léonor's *suivante*, exclaims indignantly: 'En effet, tous ces soins sont des choses infâmes. / Sommes-nous chez les Turcs pour renfermer les femmes? ' (I, 2) As in *Le Sicilien*, this near-incarceration of women is seen as a barbarian intrusion. Lisette's vigorous protest introduces the tone of indignation and pathos by which Isabelle gives expression to her predicament and which will serve as a justification not only for her deceit, but for her boldness, which runs counter to normal feminine decorum:

Je fais, pour une fille, un projet bien hardi;
Mais l'injuste rigueur dont envers moi l'on use,
Dans tout esprit bien fait me servira d'excuse. (II, 1)

Sganarelle's whole programme of studies has been offered as a self-righteous antithesis to a caricatured version of Ariste's own ideal. But Molière does give Ariste an opportunity to speak his own mind and in no other play do we find the comic ideal of indulgence, freedom, good fellowship, and social solidarity so explicitly stated as in his words concerning Léonor's education:

> J'ai souffert qu'elle ait vu les belles compagnies,
> Les divertissements, les bals, les comédies;
> Ce sont choses, pour moi, que je tiens de tout temps
> Fort propres à former l'esprit des jeunes gens;
> Et l'école du monde, en l'air dont il faut vivre
> Instruit mieux, à mon gré, que ne fait aucun livre.
> Elle aime à dépenser en habits, linge et nœuds:
> Que voulez-vous? Je tâche à contenter ses vœux.   (I, 2)[4]

Ariste, the first of a line of 'good fathers' that will include the Enrique of *L'Ecole des femmes* and the Anselme of *L'Avare*, is a veritable spokesman for the pleasure principle and his role will be the same when he becomes husband instead of foster-father. Sganarelle, shocked already at Ariste's easygoing guardianship, is astounded:

> Quoi? si vous l'épousez, elle pourra prétendre
> Les mêmes libertés que fille ou lui voit prendre?
>
> ARISTE
> Pourquoi non?   (I, 2)

A wayward child can at worst embarrass the father; a wayward wife can do much more harm to her husband. We encounter once again, then, the theme of cuckoldry, the dominant fear of the domineering spouse, and the exemplary punishment which awaits him. All tyrants in marriage bring about their own downfall, a point which Ergaste makes explicit at the end of the play as he turns the knife in Sganarelle's wound: 'Au sort d'être cocu son ascendant l'expose, / Et ne l'être qu'en herbe est pour lui douce chose' (III, 9). Tyranny, misogyny, and fear of the proverbial horns are thus thematically related as part of the alien world which Sganarelle and his counterparts represent.

But Sganarelle is much more than a spokesman for his world, a mere purveyor of ideals, false or not. Molière fleshes him out quickly but effectively. His rejection of society is not a reasoned, deliberate course of action; as with Alceste, it is an involuntary result of his own predisposition. Such epithets as 'farouche humeur' (I, 1), 'bizarre fou' (II, 4), 'loup-garou' (II, 4 and III, 9) make his temperament clear. His own actions – his rudeness to Ariste whom he taunts about his age, his humourless and censorious attitude generally – put the finishing touches on this picture. In another anticipation of Alceste, he is revolted by the *laisser-aller* he sees around him in Paris:

> Au lieu de voir régner cette sévérité
> Qui composait si bien l'ancienne honnêteté

he yearns to settle in the country where, 'grâces aux Cieux, / Les sottises du temps ne blessent point mes yeux' (I, 3).

In short, Sganarelle does not simply speak his mind, but his whole personality. This kill-joy has no place in the reasonable and harmonious society constituted by his own defeat; he and the world he represents must depart.

In this rare case trickery alone suffices to bring about the comic triumph. No miraculous intervention from the world of fantasy, no striking example of 'la pensée magique' turn the tables – unlike the other *Ecole, Tartuffe*, and *L'Avare.* Sganarelle's stupidity, passivity, and gullible nature make him an easy victim and a small threat, a minor intrusion into the healthy world which Ariste seems to protect and guarantee by his very presence.

'To a seventeenth-century audience,' Hubert rightly observes, 'neither Ariste's extreme permissiveness, nor Sganarelle's workhouse techniques would have seemed realistic or even theoretically tenable positions' (pp 48-9). Both ideals are transfigured; Sganarelle's by caricature, Ariste's by idealization. By the same token it is absurd to condemn Ariste's marriage to Léonor as 'contre nature' and foresee for the latter a destiny like that of Madame de Clèves.[5] We simply have in this dénouement two forms of an ideal of marriage: the familiar fantasy of comedy where young man and girl join hands in an eternal present of happiness, and another which is an idealized form of the typical seventeenth-century marriage where the bride was much younger than the husband. Molière usually shows this type of union as tyranny by devaluing the husband or future husband into a *barbon* like Sganarelle. The conventions of the genre in which he worked would naturally cause him to make this transformation. But once – and only once – in his career he turned the good father into the kind spouse.

L'ECOLE DES FEMMES

That *L'Ecole des femmes* is an elaboration of *L'Ecole des maris* can be seen not only in the thematic material – the education of women and their social role – but in the structure itself. We recognize Arnolphe as a prolongation of Sganarelle, while the lovers Horace-Agnès become the counterparts of Valère-

Isabelle. The role of trickster devolves once again upon the young lady, while the auxiliaries Alain and Georgette, like Lisette and Ergaste, are episodic characters who merely widen the comic perspective.

These obvious resemblances should not deceive us, however. A close reading of both plays leaves no doubt that Molière's comic art matured immeasurably in the two years which separate these two *Ecoles*. To begin with, there is the unforgettable Arnolphe, 'la figure,' in Bénichou's words, 'la plus achevée que Molière ait donné du bourgeois amoureux. ... tour à tour croquemitaine solennel, barbon grivois, et surtout propriétaire jaloux' (p 178). Indeed, the playwright gave Arnolphe such depth and complexity as the comic butt that the seventeenth-century audience, accustomed as it was to rather one-dimensional buffoon types like Sganarelle, was thrown off balance. That a character in this function could willingly and generously give money to Horace broke with the narrow habits that Lysidas is meant to caricature in *La Critique*: 'Puisque c'est le personnage ridicule de la pièce, fallait-il lui faire faire l'action d'un honnête homme? ' (6).

While in his function as blocking character Arnolphe has the same three roles as Sganarelle in *L'Ecole des maris* – father figure, future husband, and tutor – it is worth noting right away that his rights as guardian are spurious compared with the contractual arrangement in the first *Ecole*. That he has in effect bought Agnès as a child makes his legal hold shaky and his determination to marry her questionable in the extreme. And, most significantly of all, we see in this play the teacher *at work*. Principles formerly argued in the abstract are now applied on stage; enactment replaces narration.

Thus, in the best professorial tradition, Arnolphe first gives a formal, *ex cathedra* lecture, then has his pupil participate actively in the lesson. His ponderous 'discours sur le mariage' with its laboured periodic style and heavy use of *exempla* is one of the high points of the play:

> Le mariage, Agnès, n'est pas un badinage:
> A d'austères devoirs le rang de femme engage,
> Et vous n'y montez pas, à ce que je prétends,
> Pour être libertine et prendre du bon temps.
> Votre sexe n'est là que pour la dépendance:
> Du côté de la barbe est la toute-puissance.
>
> ...
>
> Et ce que le soldat, dans son devoir instruit,
> Montre d'obéissance au chef qui le conduit,
> Le valet à son maître, un enfant à son père,
> A son supérieur le moindre petit Frère,

N'approche point encor de la docilité,
Et de l'obéissance, et de l'humilité
Et du profond respect où la femme doit être
⌐Pour son mari, son chef, son seigneur et son maître.⌐   (III, 2)

Here, concentrated in a few verses, is the entire 'programme of studies' so diffusely presented in the earlier play. Arnolphe's dour view of marriage is underlined by a whole series of analogies with other hierarchical entities: military, family, social, and – most significantly – religious.

The comparison of marriage with the monastic vocation makes Arnolphe's role merge into that of 'directeur de conscience,' a role he himself is aware of playing (III, 1). True to type, he threatens his ward with hell-fire which will make her soul 'noire comme un charbon' and sermonizes generally on the after-life perils of 'femmes mal vivantes' (III, 2). These naïve attempts to terrorize Agnès lead Arnolphe to the second part of the lesson: 'Les Maximes du Mariage' (III, 2). These precepts which provide the wife with a convent-like 'exercice journalier' make of marriage once again a kind of religious mortification, a preparation for total self-abnegation:

Ainsi qu'une novice
Par cœur dans le couvent doit savoir son office,
Entrant au mariage il en faut faire autant.

When we go below the obvious comic value of Agnès' uncomprehending and mechanical reading, we find a lesson in austere solitude. The burden of these 'maximes' is that the virtuous spouse must eschew all normal social life. She must receive only her husband's guests, avoid 'belles assemblées' and such fashionable entertainments as 'promenades' and 'repas champêtres.' Once again, the blocking character rejects the whole social ideal of the seventeenth century; Ariste's 'école du monde' is implied even more forcefully in this negative picture. More generally, the reign of pleasure which the dénouement of comedy is supposed to institute falls under the shadow of Arnolphe's repressiveness. Agnès herself makes this contrast explicit in standing up to Arnolphe and in justifying her love for Horace:

Chez vous le mariage est fâcheux et pénible,
Et vos discours en font une image terrible;
Mais, las! il le fait, lui, si rempli de plaisirs,
Que de se marier il donne des désirs.   (V, 4)

As with Sganarelle, Arnolphe's reason for imposing slavery on his wife is a mean and foolish one: fear of cuckoldry. But what is largely a point of honour for Sganarelle becomes a mania for Arnolphe. He is both fascinated and horrified by his obsession. He shows a morbid curiosity about others and a sniggering delectation in their conjugal misfortunes: 'des tours que je vois / Je me donne souvent la comédie à moi' (I, 4). He even keeps a notebook ('tablettes') of such 'contes gaillards.' In short, there is much of the *voyeur* in this man so ready to chortle at cuckolds and so avid for graphic evidence of their plight.

His readiness to mock Parisian *cocus* stems of course from his absolute confidence that he can never be of their number. The most distinctive form of egoism and conceit in Arnolphe is this sense of invulnerability:

> Héroines du temps, Mesdames les savantes,
> Pousseuses de tendresse et de beaux sentiments,
> Je défie à la fois tous vos vers, vos romans,
> Vos lettres, billets doux, toute votre science
> De valoir cette honnête et pudique ignorance. (I, 3)

He throws down the gauntlet before what he scorns elsewhere as 'une femme d'esprit,' the cultivated, well-bred *salon* lady at ease in the social game of *galanterie*. What he caricatures throughout the play is the norm of which his whole pedagogical programme is a gross violation. In his narrow view of womankind, freedom can lead only to infidelity, while sequestration is the sole guarantee against woman's perverse nature. Cuckoldry is once again linked to a fundamental misogyny, and the precautions taken to avoid this 'disgrâce' serve only to hasten it.

Such is the lesson that Chrysalde tries to convey. As the burden of his argument is simply that chance alone determines whether one is or is not to be *cocu*, critics like Adam (p 284) have seen him as symbolizing an extreme of dubious *complaisance* expressed in mediocre platitudes. There is, of course, a tone of teasing irony, of quiet jocularity in Chrysalde's speeches which a too literal interpretation of *what* he says makes us forget. But he is not just winking in our direction with his easy-going *maximes*. As an 'honnête homme,' Chrysalde would subscribe to the aristocratic notion that a trusted woman will live up to expectations because of her wellborn nature, while the same woman will punish tyranny in the way most humiliating for her tyrant. Chrysalde seems to be hoping that if Arnolphe accepted cuckoldry as a matter of fate he would relax his vigilance and lessen the danger of wifely infidelity. Chrysalde is not merely an ironic antithesis for Arnolphe's ideas, as was Ariste for Sganarelle's; he is coping with the immediate and personal problem of how to save a friend from a fate which he dreads, but which he is at the same time inviting.

Were Arnolphe's conceit expressed only in this trivial context, the punishment he suffers might go beyond his crime. But he is guilty of a far more serious form of egoism. Not only does he wish to dominate, but to mould. Thus he encroaches 'upon the functions of God as creator' (Hubert 81). Nowhere does this trait come out more strongly than in his jubilation after the marriage lesson:

> Je ne puis faire mieux que d'en faire ma femme.
> Ainsi que je voudrai, je tournerai cette âme;
> Comme un morceau de cire entre mes mains elle est,
> Et je lui puis donner la forme qui me plaît. (III, 3)

There is no need to underline the profusion of forms relating to the first person or the self-revealing aptness of the shaper-of-wax image. In *L'Ecole des maris* Isabelle is like any other young heroine – normally mature, articulate, pathetic, and already in love. Sganarelle's tyranny has not prevented his ward from becoming a woman. As a result, when he uses affectionate diminutives like 'mon petit cœur,' 'ma pouponne,' he emphasizes his own infantilism more than Isabelle's. Agnès, on the other hand, is extraordinarily unique: Arnolphe has succeeded in keeping her a child, and only through the other schoolmaster of the play, love, does she become herself. This sense of self-fulfilment, of self-realization in the very course of the action, so exceptional in a dramatic tradition centred on fixed types, is one of the main reasons for this comedy's compelling appeal.

The general comic fault of *alazoneia* is tellingly particularized, then, in the person of Arnolphe. Three forms of tyrannical authority – father, husband, and teacher-religious educator – are extended almost to cosmic dimensions in Arnolphe's determination to have a life-long child bride. The reason for such single-minded and unfeeling conduct: 'sauver mon front de maligne influence' (I, 1). His unconscionable mirth in seeing the same influence mark others is additional evidence, if any is needed, that Arnolphe deserves his fate. Comic justice must then prevail. The play is but one long aggression practised on him. He is constantly reminded of the excruciating distance between purpose and result, intention and outcome. Even in his love for Agnès he is driven to declare to her: 'Tout comme tu voudras, tu pourras te conduire' (V, 4). He himself is stunned by this *carte blanche* he gives Agnès to cuckold him.

This kind of perception in the comic butt occurs usually at the dénouement where it becomes part of the exorcism. Until then the scapegoat figure may have been insulated against the painful knowledge of his limitations, of the deceptions perpetrated against him. In *L'Ecole des maris*, Sganarelle, by unknowingly serving as a go-between for his intended wife and her beloved, naturally arouses our derision. But only at the end, when he is aware of having been gulled, is his punishment real for him. Arnolphe, too, perceives at the dénouement that both Agnès and fate have carried the day. Unlike Sganarelle, he does not even have the privilege of exploding into misogynistic invective; only a stifled 'Ouf!' signals the end of the exorcism, the moment of agonising enlightenment. The *Ecole des femmes* has become a School for Husbands.

The profound originality of *L'Ecole des femmes*, however, is that this pattern of ignorance-to-awareness becomes a function of the whole plot, not just the resolution. Each act save the second begins with an upward movement in Arnolphe of confidence and self-assurance reaching a high point in a dialogue with Horace. Horace in turn reverses the movement by revealing unexpected and painful news to Arnolphe who then pours out his frustrations in a monologue. Act III illustrates this mechanism admirably. Arnolphe is delighted at the beginning of the act because Agnès, as he had directed, has dutifully thrown the 'grès' at Horace. The girl's docility during her lesson, both in listening so carefully to his lecture on marriage and in reading the 'maximes' so earnestly brings Arnolphe to a pinnacle of self-satisfied delight in his master-potter monologue. Horace arrives to recount the humiliation of having had a stone hurled at him. Arnolphe is hardly able to contain his delight, only to have it transformed into stifled rage when the young man reveals that a love letter was thrown as well. To maintain his advantage over Horace (who does not know of course his interlocutor's double identity) he must contain his frustration as he had his exultation. His pent-up anger is perhaps punishment enough, but he must also hear the tender words contained in the letter and the injurious epithets applied to him: 'Ce franc animal, / Ce traître, ce bourreau, ce faquin, ce brutal' (III, 4). Only with Horace's departure can he enjoy the dubious relief of a bitter monologue.

The very fact that this pattern recurs four times accentuates the impression of a perverse fate:

> Quoi! l'astre qui s'obstine à me désespérer
> Ne me donnera pas le temps de respirer?
> ...
> Et je serai la dupe, en ma maturité,
> D'une jeune innocente et d'un jeune éventé? (IV, 7)

And Arnolphe's plight is all the more frustrating as he thinks of his enormous head start in the game: his life experience and his trump card of foreknowledge.

From scattered suggestions in *L'Ecole des maris* – especially in II where Isabelle's *récit* to Sganarelle of her encounter with Valère is followed by a fatuous self-congratulatory monologue by the *barbon* – Molière has created this unique ironic structure which both reveals and punishes the fault of the protagonist. The absurdity of the charge levelled by seventeenth-century French critics that *L'Ecole des femmes* consisted entirely in 'récits' becomes all the more manifest. Molière's spokesman in *La Critique* is quite right in insisting that 'les récits eux-mêmes y sont des actions, suivant la constitution du sujet; d'autant qu'ils sont tous faits innocemment, ces récits, à la personne intéressée, qui par là entre, à tous coups, dans une confusion à réjouir les spectateurs' (6). And another friend of Molière, Uranie, chimes in with: 'Pour moi, je trouve que la beauté du sujet de *L'Ecole des femmes* consiste dans cette confidence perpétuelle; et ce qui me paraît assez plaisant, c'est qu'un homme qui a de l'esprit, et qui est averti de tout par une innocente qui est sa maîtresse, et par un étourdi qui est son rival, ne puisse avec cela éviter ce qui lui arrive' (6). Implicit in these judicious remarks are the modern notions of dramatic irony arising from the play of knowledge and ignorance and of the irony of fate with its outcome contrary to all expectations.

As with *L'Ecole des maris*, the auxiliaries are episodic and non-functional. The role of trickster is carried by the young lady herself. As love matures Agnès it develops in her the means for realizing her inclinations, or at least for putting up a fight against those who wish otherwise. Yet, in the final analysis love and the stratagems it inspires are not enough to bring about the comic resolution. We are dealing with a far more dangerous obstacle force here than the simple and buffoonish Sganarelle. Arnolphe 'a de l'esprit'; he struggles against his 'astre' because he knows what is happening to him. If this knowledge is painful, it also gives him an active and therefore menacing role in the plot. The trump card obtained from his double name is, in short, an enormous advantage; by all criteria of verisimilitude he should win. The real world, the world of authority and power, intrudes here with disquieting force. Indeed, that final downturn in the lovers' fortune, that impression of imminent defeat (Frye's 'point of ritual death') is strongly marked in this play. First, Horace is believed dead at the beginning of V, having fallen from the ladder he was using to abduct Agnès. He is 'ressuscitated' immediately, but Arnolphe promises another form of symbolic capital punishment to Agnès should she refuse him: 'un cul de couvent me vengera de tout' (V, 4). The forceful coupling of two forms of incarceration – convent life and the 'cul de basse fosse' with all its horrible overtones – drives home a powerful impression of death-in-life in store for the young girl.

The more dangerous the obstacle figure, the more striking the operation of 'la pensée magique.' It is no surprise that Arnolphe is undone only by a miraculous intervention from the outside. He is so powerful and the values he represents so 'real' that he must be defeated by fantasy. The world of youth, indulgence, trust, and pleasure returns to L'Ecole des femmes with the arrival of Enrique, the good genius of comedy.

The play ends with the constitution of a new society, or, to be exact, the reuniting of an old family. Agnès finds her true father and is reintegrated into a relationship which fate had disrupted so many years before. Compounding this chance separation was the threat of usurped authority by Arnolphe. His claim on Agnès has been shown to be spurious and the bondage he has imposed morally reprehensible. No other play, except perhaps L'Avare, illustrates so well the ternary rhythm of comedy as described by Frye. The middle phase of ritual bondage is clearly Arnolphe's; freed from the threat of slavery, corruption, and unhappiness which has interrupted its destiny, Enrique's family can be reunited as the pragmatically free society which embodies the comic ideal. In this context, there can be no other issue for Arnolphe than expulsion. Everything has already happened for the best. The fate which had frustrated Arnolphe's designs had already arranged the marriage that crowns the play. The good fathers who have been the agents of this fate, Enrique and Oronte, join Chrysalde in enveloping the lovers in their benignity.

TARTUFFE

Among the 'heavy father' plays none comes closer than Tartuffe to what Frye calls the ironic phase of comedy where 'the demonic world is never far away' (p 178). Whatever the comic force of many scenes, the ominous mood that hangs over the play remains with us long after the dénouement.[6] A cancer of bondage and corruption has set into the play's society and, even after it is extirpated at the comic reversal, the concluding verses speak more of relief and gratitude than of exultation and victory.

While Guicharnaud studies Tartuffe in the context of two other supremely problematical plays of Molière, Le Misanthrope and Don Juan, the play belongs here in our analysis because, unlike the other two, it does embody the comic myth. However much Tartuffe and his dupes dominate the action, the romantic formula comes out as Valère and Mariane seek to realize their happiness in the face of Orgon's obstinacy and Tartuffe's malevolent influence. Once again, however, Molière has forged out of these familiar conventions a truly individual creation. Just as the repeated pattern of humiliations gives a particular flavour to L'Ecole des femmes, here the shift towards the demonic accounts for the special mood of Tartuffe. Both poles in the dialectic move toward an ironic vision: the love plot is muted and suffused with pathos, while the blocking character, probably the most sinister in Molière, very nearly imposes his nightmare vision on the play's society.

The boy-meets-girl theme is announced almost as an afterthought, in an anti-climactic moment after the compelling first scene. Damis entreats Cléante to remind Orgon that Mariane has been promised to Valère: 'Si même ardeur enflamme et ma sœur et Valère, / La sœur de cet ami, vous le savez, m'est chère' (I, 3). This double pairing of brothers and sisters points toward a dual marriage at the end; but in actual fact we never hear of Damis's love interest again. Even the first relationship is clouded immediately by the *dépit amoureux* of II and by the threat of a forced marriage between Mariane and Tartuffe which hangs over the whole action. Valère appears again only at the very end of the play; his purpose is not to court Mariane but to warn Orgon that he must flee. Only during the *dépit* scene do the lovers meet on stage; even then they have little time, after their mutual recriminations, to exchange words of love. By way of comparison, the two sets of lovers in *L'Avare* meet often enough to keep up the romantic continuity of the action and sustain a refined tone in their exchanges.

Another characteristic of *Tartuffe* is that the impression of imminent defeat usually contained in the moment of ritual death is diffused through the play; at more than one point, the energy of the young appears to be spent, the nightmare seems on the verge of becoming reality. In II, 3, Mariane, stunned into horrified passivity at the prospect of marriage with Tartuffe, can think of only one way out: 'De me donner la mort si l'on me violente.' The resistance of youth is at a dangerous ebb and Dorine must take up the cause of life and hope. Her affectionate sarcasm: 'Fort bien: c'est un recours où je ne songeais pas' begins to restore Mariane's sense of resolve. Near the end of III, the threat of death takes another form as Orgon screams at his son: 'Je te prive, pendard, de ma succession, / Et te donne de plus ma malédiction' (III, 6). Each of these acts, in its way, is a symbolic form of murder. Damis no longer exists, Tartuffe has replaced him as legal heir.

Mariane's tearful entreaty to her father in IV, 3: 'souffrez qu'un couvent dans les austérités / Use les tristes jours que le Ciel m'a comptés' renews, in a different form, her despair of II. The threat of convent life is usually preferred by a blocking character to a recalcitrant girl (Arnolphe's intention to lock up Agnès in 'un cul de couvent' is a case in point), but here claustration is a form of symbolic suicide, morally defensible of course, but still an admission of defeat, a renunciation of the comic dream. The elevated, almost tragic diction of Mariane's speech (eg, 'tristes jours') confers on the scene a degree of pathos rare in Molière[7] Her pleading words are underscored by her gesture as she sinks to her knees to implore her father. There is more in this than mere comment on Orgon's inhumanity. Molière blurs the whole comic fantasy. Gone is the bright, cheeky young girl like Elise in *L'Avare*, standing up to her father and confident of ultimate victory; Mariane is placed before an intolerable vision of ruined expectations and life-long misery.

These somber anticipations culminate in the customary point of ritual death of the play, placed appropriately just at the end of IV: Tartuffe's snarling turnabout as Orgon attempts to expel him from the house: 'C'est à vous d'en sortir, vous qui parlez en maître' (IV, 7). Coming as a startling dramatic contrast after Elmire's success in unmasking the hypocrite, this reversal provokes the sudden alarm at the end of the act and the black mood that haunts most of V. For the impact of Tartuffe's victory goes far beyond the range of the normal counterturn. In *L'Ecole des femmes*, for instance, only the fortune of the lovers is affected by Arnolphe's near triumph in V; here, on the contrary, the whole family trembles under the threat of expulsion and confiscation. What would constitute the pragmatically free society at the dénouement finds itself in danger of being thrust off the stage into a nightmare of poverty and homelessness.

This sustained mood of despair and betrayal is reinforced by repeated allusions to Orgon's perfidy. Cléante reminds him that Valère 'a parole de vous' and appeals to his self-respect: 'Vous voulez manquer à votre foi? ' (I, 5). Orgon's intention to marry Mariane off to Tartuffe is thus more than mere obstinacy; it is an act of treachery quite in keeping with the atmosphere of moral opprobrium that dominates the play.

There is much, then, in the very structure of *Tartuffe* that dampens the normal energy of comedy. The *élan* of the young, their confidence in the future, is seriously undermined. The blocking character in turn acquires a dimension of demonic power that takes us often beyond the range of derisive laughter.

The obstacle function has been displaced from its normal locus, the heavy father, to the knave. Tartuffe's energy and guile make him a sorcerer; he has literally bewitched Orgon, who seems to turn helplessly around a larger and more ominous body. This too marks the play as exceptional. In normal comedy, the young can count on the blocking character's credulity and egoism in their contest with him — witness Sganarelle and Arnolphe who serve unwittingly as a go-between for rival and ward. In *Tartuffe*, however, the impostor has turned faults to advantage. That Tartuffe gives Orgon's native egoism all the nourishment it needs constitutes the secret of his hold over him. Heavy fathers are usually choleric and selfish; Tartuffe legitimizes these traits by transforming petulance into the anger of the righteous against sin, selfishness into religious duty.[8] Who else could present innate narcissism as lofty detachment from the things of this world: 'Je verrais mourir frère, enfants, mère et femme, / Que je m'en soucierais autant que de cela' (I, 5)?

The normal comic stratagem can play only a minor role in this work. As

Orgon's be-all and end-all, Tartuffe can insure that Orgon's stupidity will not be turned against him. Trickery, if it is used, must contend with a clever, perceptive man who has usurped the authority of the head of the house; tyranny and guile together constitute a formidable obstacle. It is Elmire, the archetypal good mother on the side of the young, who must in desperation take up the function of *fourberie*. The learning experience of the first seduction scene (III, 3) provides her with the role that will prove Tartuffe's undoing. In IV, 5 she becomes an actress in 'a sovereign exercise of dramatic irony' (Moore, *Molière* 60). The perspectives of dissembler, victim, and 'spectator' (Orgon hidden under the table) shift and interact with ever-increasing comic impact. In a kind of poetic justice, Elmire captures Tartuffe through his sole weakness, lust, just as he had played on Orgon's credulity and egoism.[9]

As with *L'Ecole des femmes*, however, trickery is in itself not enough to bring about the comic reversal. Elmire exposes Tartuffe and breaks his spell over Orgon. But in the meantime psychological domination has been replaced by a quasi-legal hold. Because of Orgon's misguided generosity and trust, Tartuffe now possesses the household and has in addition the power of blackmail over his benefactor. The penniless adventurer has attained the wealth and position that had been his goal all along. He no longer has even to marry Mariane; prosperity has been dropped into his lap. By all canons of reality he has won and should stand triumphantly in centre stage as the family goes forth into destitution.

The final resolution must come from beyond the realm of probability; only a miracle can break up this demonic world. As in *L'Ecole des femmes*, the greater the force of reality the stronger and more effective must be the wish-fulfilment function which exorcizes it. As absolute evil is about to triumph in *Tartuffe*, only divine intervention can save the situation. Thus the *deus ex machina* of the Exempt, gratuitous and miraculous as it is, is a direct and logical response to the archetypal premises of the play. Only the anointed King, or his surrogate, can exorcize the demon. This is the real reason for Tartuffe's return on stage in V: an exorcism in *absentia* would have little dramatic force. To sharpen the effect Molière is careful to localize and emphasize the exact moment of the reversal. As Tartuffe spitefully tells the Exempt: 'daignez accomplir votre ordre, je vous prie' (V, last scene), he finds the hand of justice upon his own shoulder. The corrupted law which has made Orgon a victim is purified by royal benevolence. As a matter of fact, an outside providence, as in *L'Ecole des femmes*, has already done things right. Enrique had intended all along to give Agnès to Horace: the King had already decided to right the situation, while allowing Tartuffe the illusion of triumph to see how far he would go.

Tartuffe plummets, then, from victor to scapegoat. He is removed from the stage, and with him go the evils with which he had infected the house: cupidity, lust, inhumanity, hypocrisy, double-dealing. Orgon, awakened as from a night-mare, gathers his reconciled family about him and blesses the union of Valère and Mariane. The guilt for Orgon's derogation of the norm has been effectively discharged upon the knave, who bears a twofold culpability.[10] It is just, then, that we should imagine Tartuffe suffering some unnamed legal punishment, befitting the monstrous threat he had held over the family. The play transcends the normal exorcism of humiliation and exclusion, where the realization of folly is its own punishment. Tartuffe is the only scapegoat in Molière whose chastise-ment takes legal form – another reason why the King, as the ultimate dispenser of justice, must be the providential force here.

But the question remains: is Tartuffe really humiliated? Is there the same painful comic *anagnorisis* that drives Arnolphe off the stage at the end of *L'Ecole des femmes*? Because the impostor seems defiant, stoic, and unrepen-tant as he leaves us, we cannot laugh and we cannot forgive. Evil has gone too far, and is too unregenerate, to elicit derisive mirth; good has been too severely tried for immediate, unalloyed euphoria.

In *Tartuffe*, the dialectic of the comic myth shifts away from the normal re-sponses of happy complicity and derision. The romantic plot is coloured by pathos, while the blocking figure transcends the normal, laughable *alazoneia* of comedy. But there is more to this play than a generic plot; the social meaning of the *mythos* as exemplified in *Tartuffe* raises difficult questions of comic norms which will no doubt always be debated.

It is significant that the issue over which the first battle is fought (I, 1) is that of social entertainment. Madame Pernelle fulminates against the frequent visitors who turn the house into what she condemns as 'la cour du roi Pétaut.' All through her skirmishes with the other members of the family she complains about the 'propos oisifs,' the 'mille caquets divers' which dominate in this 'tour de Babylone, / Car chacun y babille, et tout du long de l'aune.' She turns her wrath especially on her daughter-in-law, Elmire: 'Vous êtes dépensière; et cet état me blesse, / Que vous alliez vêtue ainsi qu'une princesse.' Elmire's crime is wanting to appear fashionable, to look the part of a charming, still attractive lady. Indeed, the text points clearly to a kind of drawing room circle with Elmire as its *dame*. In his first meeting with Elmire, Tartuffe himself alludes to the 'visites qu'ici reçoivent vos attraits' (III, 3). His jealousy arises from the fact that Elmire is naturally subjected to the inevitable play courtships essential to 'la belle galanterie.' This life is viewed by Madame Pernelle's adversaries as a moral norm for which they do not have to apologize: 'En quoi blesse le Ciel une visite honnête? ' (I, 1) asks Dorine.

Tartuffe is then cast from the outset in the role of kill-joy, the self-righteous

adversary of this world of innocent pleasure. The very first derogatory statements made about him – Damis's protest to Madame Pernelle – hammer this
point:

> Quoi? je souffrirai, moi, qu'un cagot de critique
> Vienne usurper céans un pouvoir tyrannique,
> Et que nous ne puissions à rien nous divertir,
> Si ce beau Monsieur-là n'y daigne consentir?   (I, 1)

Damis passes over the issue of hypocrisy – the central one of the play in the
traditional view – to emphasize Tartuffe's sour, censorious attitude toward social
entertainment and his despotism over the family, Madame Pernelle goes one
better in defending her desire to banish society from the house: 'Ces visites, ces
bals, ces conversations / Sont du malin esprit toutes inventions' (I, 1). Social
intercourse is equated with absolute evil; the pleasing chatter of people enjoying
themselves must be replaced by the austere silence of a monastery.

The moral issue here is knotty. The seventeenth-century élite felt keenly no
doubt the contradiction between its ideal of innocent, self-indulgent merriment
in the here and now and the reigning Christian orthodoxy stressing original sin,
abnegation, and the after-life. Hence, a sincere adversary of the pleasure principle would force a disturbing *prise de conscience* in the spectator. That is why
Christian moralizing and other-worldliness must be presented as hypocritical
posturing to attain base ends. If Tartuffe were not a *scélérat*, the comic vision
might be shattered.

Tartuffe's censoriousness is presented, then, as not only extravagant on face
value (cf. Cléante's insistence on a 'dévotion ... humaine [et] traitable' [1, 5] but
profoundly corrupt underneath. If he wishes to protect the family from a supposedly debased society it is in order to have more power over them, to realize
his plan of possessing them utterly. Damis's reference to the 'cagot de critique'
and his 'pouvoir tyrannique' contains the operative words of the play, relating as
they do Tartuffe's chief traits to his central design: dissembling and self-
righteousness at the service of the will to power.

This tyranny is morally perverse as well, for to protest against it is to incur
the dangerous charge of free-thinking. Orgon's veiled threat against his brother-
in-law is a case in point: 'Mon frère, ce discours sent le libertinage' (I, 5). The
atmosphere of gloom and impotence is reinforced, then, by the futility of argument. The moral system of Tartuffe and his dupes is a closed circle. Logic
cannot intrude (as Cléante finds out to his dismay), and the ultimate threat is
always there: the pyre reserved for heretics.

Another principle of corruption in this false world of religious zeal, the one that proves in part his undoing, is naturally his lust for Elmire. Under his solici-tude on her behalf lies his jealousy towards her admirers and his determination to thrust them aside. Elmire will thus be at once more available and more vulnerable to his designs. Even if Tartuffe's courtship were in proper form, even if he were truly the 'honnête homme amoureux' whose mask he wears (Guichar-naud *Aventure* 90), his desire to be Elmire's total society, to have her to himself would sin against the norm of confidence in women to assume their social role. But the hypocrite's *galanterie* is in fact a grotesque caricature of the socialized and civilized love-making that is one of the main articles of the courtly ethic. His sinister declaration of love – 'tout à fait galante' in Elmire's sarcastic words – perverts the language of sainthood and invites wallowing in sexual licence:

> De vous dépend ma peine ou ma béatitude,
>
> ...
>
> De l'amour sans scandale et du plaisir sans peur.   (III, 3)

'Plaisir' here has nothing to do with the comic pleasure principle, nor is Tartuffe's eroticism to be equated with Horace's passion for Agnès. The young love realized with the comic reversal is civilized. Courtship is honourable and takes its time as it passes through well-defined and codified phases; the young man does not force himself upon the young lady, nor does she forget the decorum of her sex. They strive in marriage not for selfish pleasure-taking but for reciprocal giving in a ceremony freely consented to. Physical attraction be-tween lovers in comedy should not be opposed, then, to courtly love, nor should pure sexual *élan* be taken as Molière's norm of comic ardour. On the contrary: by the very personage of Tartuffe raw desire, the libido that can fly in the face of convention and law, is set in contrast to civilized *galanterie*. Pleasure for him is but the violent coupling of animals. When he wrestles with Elmire we see true libido, egotistical, imperious, crude. In both seduction scenes he has the mechan-ical reflexes of a rutting bull as he bypasses the usual ritual of hand-holding, exclamations of love, and rapt looks for more direct measures: a hand on the knee, a stolen caress around the neck and bosom as he admires Elmire's lace: 'Mon Dieu! que de ce point l'ouvrage est merveilleux!, (III, 3). Elmire is forced to point out in IV, 5 that true love is more temperate: 'Quoi? vous voulez aller avec cette vitesse, / Et d'un cœur tout d'abord épuiser la tendresse? ' But this lesson in *galanterie* is lost. Tartuffe's literal brutality excludes him from the company of deferential suitors. Even when he must hide his nature, he is incap-able of conforming to the middle position of respectful civility. He passes rather to the extreme of grotesque prudishness. Molière never portrayed a stronger contrast than that between the chaste monk, eyes averted, who holds a handkerchief before Dorine's *décolleté*, and the lustful knave slavering a moment later over Elmire.

Tartuffe's gross hypocrisy, his unscrupulous quest for material gain, his designs on Elmire ruin whatever validity his moral precepts might have had. His corruption attacks the fabric of society, just as his censoriousness, now completely devalued, threatened its pleasures. No scapegoat stands in more stark contrast to the comic vision or has come closer to destroying it. Thus, for the only time in Molière, we feel that the punishment, no matter how severe we imagine it, cannot be commensurate with the crime.

LES FEMMES SAVANTES

In *Les Femmes savantes* the blocking character for the only time in Molière takes on feminine attributes; Orgon becomes Philaminte. For the archetypal critic this change of sex does not alter function. Barthes' definition of the Racinian 'figures' can be applied as well to the basic types of comedy: '[ils] reçoivent leurs différences, non de leur état civil, mais de leur place dans la configuration générale qui les tient enfermés' (p 21). Philaminte is as much a 'Père' as Agrippine.

Approaching the matter from another angle, Mauron places Philaminte in the 'mère terrible' category along with Madame Jourdain and Béline, the conniving second wife of Argan in *Le Malade imaginaire*. 'Leur apparition,' he goes on to say, 'marque une régression comique vers le régime matrimonial: le père tombe alors dans un état d'extrême infantilisme et de dépendance' (*Psychocritique* 67). To be sure, in all three cases the husband is subjugated by the domineering wife; but it does not follow, as Mauron appears to infer, that the wife acts on the side of the son and helps him obtain the victory over the father (*loc. cit.*). Only Madame Jourdain openly espouses the cause of the lovers, and in that sense she is much closer to Elmire than to the other two. Philaminte and Béline stand in opposition to the love plot, each for her own reasons. But only Philaminte can be labelled a heavy father type, for she has usurped her husband's authority and aims to use it to impose a marriage of her choosing. Béline remains officially subordinate to Argan; she rules only by deceit.

In short, Mauron seems to be following Jung's distinction between the two forms of the anima archetype: the gentle, protective, generous mother, symbolic of the life force, and the terrifying, domineering harridan. But this essentially emotional antithesis does not always work in comedy; a strong-willed mother on the right side of the comic plot is a good mother.

The 'heavy mother' role of Philaminte parallels to a surprising degree Orgon's part as a tyrannical father. The chief victim of her despotism, too, is a daughter. Henriette, the counterpart of Mariane, is in love with someone of fitting age and station, Clitandre, but must accept another husband if the mother has her way. And the rival suitor (Trissotin) is just as repugnant to Henriette as Tartuffe is to Mariane.

As with Tartuffe, Trissotin accepts this offer of marriage out of greed. Both are motivated by desire for material gain, but both endeavour to mask their motives by a pretense of respectability. Such is their skill at dissimulation that they literally mesmerize the dominant figure in the family. Just as Tartuffe was the epitome of selflessness and piety for Orgon, so is Trissotin the *nec plus ultra* of wit and knowledge for Philaminte. To maintain his hold over the family, Trissotin caters to the same sort of native egoism we found in Orgon. Philaminte is selfish and tyrannical by nature, and the pedant gives her a clever excuse for indulging these penchants. Thanks to the learning he has inspired in her, she can vaunt her 'droits de la raison' (IV, 1) in place of the 'droits de la nature' to which she, as wife to her husband, is not entitled. Thus, when Chrysale tries to challenge her, she can justify her resistance on intellectual grounds. Who should govern, she asks rhetorically, 'l'esprit ou le corps, la forme ou la matière'? (IV, 1). In a word, Trissotin has encouraged her to twist half-baked Platonism into a rationale for her will to power. And, like Orgon, Philaminte is more unwilling than unable to see through the hollow sham projected by her hero. Trissotin nurtures in her a *mauvaise foi* by which she can advance or accept good motives for actions whose true mainsprings she refuses to consider. Both characters are more vain than foolish.

In each play the moral issues raised by the intruder split the family into two camps. The ludicrous extreme of credulity and empty-headedness embodied in Madame Pernelle finds its counterpart in Bélise, whose grotesque antics and delusions put her too on the level of farce. Armande, Philaminte's other daughter, must be seen on a higher level of decorum. She is guilty, like the other ladies, of bad faith in her desire to cover innate spite and arrogance with an overlay of superior wisdom and philosophical serenity; when raw anger causes this pretense to collapse and leave her open to her sister's taunt: 'où donc est la morale / Qui sait si bien régir la partie animale [?]' (I, 2), she is as comically naked as Orgon before Dorine's triumphant: 'Ah! vous êtes dévot, et vous vous emportez? ' (II, 2). Yet, it is she who has the task of defending the group's cause in her debates with Clitandre; while her arguments are specious, her eloquence and diction place her on a par with her adversaries. Finally, were she on the level of Bélise's crudeness and naïveté, she would obviously not have been Clitandre's first choice.

In most of the plays studied in this chapter the father figure stands alone against the rest of the household. In *Tartuffe* and *Les Femmes savantes*, however, the alien values promoted by the blocking character are represented by a group. The 'savantes' have a programme to which they would like to convert the members of their family and which they long to impose on society at large; in like manner, the 'tartuffiés' attempt to foist their repressive and joyless ethic on those under their power or influence.

Both works, then, present a claque of generally ridiculous admirers surrounding a gross knave who has learned the trick of turning native despotism to his advantage and who is willing to marry a girl against her wishes to realize his own crass objectives. But Trissotin looms of course as far less a threat than Tartuffe. At no time is he in a position to dispossess the family – his knavery is far less thorough than Tartuffe's. Nor does he have the same amount of time to observe, connive, and control. Tartuffe is a resident 'directeur de conscience,' privy to the deepest and most compromising secrets of the household. Trissotin is more of a passing entertainer, purveying wit and learning for the amusement and edification of the ladies. And while *his* enemies can at worst be charged with bias and anti-intellectualism, the ominous accusation of 'libertinage' hangs heavy over those who would criticize the impostor.

Tartuffe, then, stands far beyond Trissotin. The hypocrite's strength comes from his self-possession, his careful control over his part. He is a skilled actor observing and calculating his effects on others. Only lust cramps this remarkable self-mastery. Trissotin's weakness consists in his being himself most of the time. He believes himself witty and wise, an opinion which the ladies are only too glad to reflect; they all live in a symbiotic relationship, each needing the blandishments of the other. But for us, Trissotin is self-important, mediocre, pedantic, boring, and vindictive. Not only are we told so by Clitandre and others, but, more importantly, he reveals himself this way to us. He is more the fool than the knave, while Tartuffe is only one step short of perfect knavery.[11]

Even when Trissotin plays a conscious role he is flat and unconvincing. Protesting that he is not interested in Henriette's dowry, he flatters her:

> Vos brillants attraits, vos yeux perçants et doux,
> Votre grâce, et votre air, sont les biens, les richesses,
> Qui vous ont attiré mes vœux et mes tendresses:

clichés so lame and threadbare that Henriette can only reply sarcastically: 'Cet obligeant amour a de quoi me confondre' (V, 1).

As in *Tartuffe*, the love plot of *Les Femmes savantes* soon recedes into the background. Mariane and Valère appear together only once before their final reconciliation, and their predicament takes on a tone of pathos, in contrast to the usual robust *élan* of Molière lovers. In the case of Clitandre and Henriette, on whom the love interest of *Les Femmes savantes* centres, there are four meetings. In three of them they share the stage with someone else, and the one moment when they are alone together (I, 3) can scarcely be labelled a love scene. After the rather formal and tense conversation with Armande directly before, one would expect the lovers to exchange exclamations and looks of affection. But we are far from the ardour and spontaneity of the typical *jeunes amoureux* of comedy. It must be said that Henriette, like Philinte in *Le Misanthrope*, is second best; Eliante's first love was Alceste, and Clitandre first courted Armande, a fact that, perhaps, explains the subdued image of passion in both instances. Whatever the explanation, Clitandre, in his scene with Henriette, is more interested in speaking his mind about 'femmes docteurs' and in delivering an eloquent diatribe against Monsieur Trissotin than in verbalizing his passion. Their only genuine talk of love occurs in the presence of two others and near the end of the play:

> CLITANDRE
> Quelque secours puissant qu'on promette à ma flamme,
> Mon plus solide espoir, c'est votre cœur, Madame.

> HENRIETTE
> Pour mon cœur, vous pouvez vous assurer de lui.

> CLITANDRE
> Je ne puis qu'être heureux, quand j'aurai son appui.

> HENRIETTE
> Vous voyez à quels nœuds on prétend le contraindre.

> CLITANDRE
> Tant qu'il sera pour moi, je ne vois rien à craindre. (IV, 5)

This stylized stichomythia reinforced by lofty diction marks an attitude of respectful reserve where spontaneity, giddiness, irrepressible passion have no part. Nor can we speak of pathos, either, as Clitandre and Henriette struggle with the forces in opposition to them. They stand up proudly and firmly against their enemies and marshal all the resources of their intelligence and eloquence to plead their case. Intellect dominates emotion, and the rhetoric of logic takes precedence over the language of passion.

It is no surprise that Clitandre and Henriette are in fact the *raisonneurs* of this play. As spokesmen for the comic norm, they participate in all of the key ideological confrontations: the opening debate over love and marriage between Armande and her sister (I, 1) and the climactic arguments which oppose Clitandre first to Armande and then to Trissotin (IV, 2 and 3). Consequently, the character whom we would expect to be the counterpart of the Cléante of *Tartuffe*, Orgon's brother and detached purveyor of wisdom, is only marginally involved in the moral issues of *Les Femmes savantes*. Ariste, Chrysale's brother, functions as little more than a valet. Like a wise servant he urges resolve and courage upon Chrysale for the coming show-down with Philaminte, and his false-letter stratagem at the end of the play is every bit in the tradition of the resourceful auxiliary.

The tone of refined diction and eloquent argument which pervades much of *Les Femmes savantes* explains the short shrift given the usual means of developing the comic plot: trickery and irony. The auxiliaries, on whom this task usually devolves, are non-existent. Martine is a kitchen maid full of earthy wisdom but a far cry from the great Molière *soubrettes*. The valet figure has no role, although his function is discreetly assumed by Ariste. The dramatic reason for their absence is evident: Clitandre and Henriette are intelligent, self-possessed, and articulate; they can make their own case. The two main activities of auxiliaries, ruse and comment, are out of place in this heroic world. In fact, the lovers of *Les Femmes savantes* are above deception and dissimulation. Henriette encourages her beloved to be more 'complaisant' toward the 'savantes' whims – advice that the high-minded youth firmly rejects: 'Mon coeur n'a jamais pu, tant il est né sincère, / Même dans votre sœur flatter leur caractère' (I, 3). One of the main reasons he is in Philaminte's disfavour is his refusal to cater to her literary pretentions: 'Il sait que, Dieu merci, je me mêle d'écrire,' complains the mother, 'Et jamais il ne m'a prié de lui rien lire' (IV, 1).

Ariste's spontaneous invention to unmask Trissotin is the only ruse in the play. Trickery is replaced by head-on confrontation, dissembling by eloquent verbal contest. The dynamic principle of *Les Femmes savantes* is the *agon* with its full range of tones: passionate sincerity, heavy sarcasm, taunting, persiflage, invective. That is why it is a comedy of set pieces, often lengthy, always carefully ordered, with, as counterpoint, short exchanges of dialogue in the form of stichomythia. This type of scene construction brings us close to tragic diction and explains the persistent impression of heroic comedy in the love plot. Clitandre is the proud plaindealer in the tradition of Nicomède, while Henriette and Armande carry on the one-line taunts so reminiscent of tragi-comedy (cf. I, 2 and III, 5).

However much the *agon* may dominate, the levels of diction vary. The heroic tone of Clitandre, Henriette and, to a degree, Armande, is almost parodied in the confrontation between the two pedants, Trissotin and Vadius, in III, 3. Here stichomythia conveys vacuous praise in a fatuous exchange of compliments:

TRISSOTIN
Vos vers ont des beautés que n'ont point tous les autres.

VADIUS
Les Grâces et Vénus règnent dans tous les vôtres.

TRISSOTIN
Vous avez le tour libre, et le beau choix des mots.

VADIUS
On voit partout chez vous l'*ithos* et le *pathos*.

and, after their quarrel, fish-wife invective:

Allez, petit grimaud, barbouilleur de papier.
Allez, rimeur de balle, opprobre du métier.

The scene ends in fact with a parody of the heroic challenge: 'Hé bien, nous vous verrons seul à seul chez Barbin' – the field of honour being a well-known Paris publishing house.

The key contest on whose outcome the fate of the lovers depends takes place in a middle range of diction. The struggle between the cowed husband, Chrysale, and his virago wife lends itself to a richness of tones. Philaminte seems a kind of female bogeyman, fearsome only in appearance, while Chrysale's heroic self-affirmations come out with a tremor. Good father he is, though, and well intentioned. His natural 'bonté d'âme' (I, 3) as well as his youthful memories incline him to indulgence toward young love:

Tenez, mon cœur s'émeut à toutes ces tendresses,
Cela ragaillardit tout à fait mes vieux jours,
Et je me ressouviens de mes jeunes amours. (III, 6)

The same gentleness, unhappily, makes him shrink before his wife's tantrums.

This struggle takes place in different stages, in a series of skirmishes leading up to the decisive battle in V. Molière exploits Chrysale's vacillations skilfully. Acts II, III, and IV all end with firm resolutions by Chrysale to stand up for his rights and those of the lovers. Whether or not he will live up to his own expectations gives us matter for thought during the intermission and most of the next act. Battle is finally joined when Philaminte advances the marriage date lest her authority be further eroded: 'Dès ce soir à Monsieur [Trissotin] je marierai ma fille' (IV, 4). This now immediate threat brings us as close as we ever get in this heroic play to that moment of pessimism and despair which is the point of ritual death: rather than bow to Philaminte's will, Henriette vows to enter a convent ('Il est une retraite où notre âme se donne' [IV, 5], a discreet and elegant reference to the religious vocation in keeping with the refined tone of the love plot).

The final struggle (V, 3) takes the form, expectedly, of stichomythia: Philaminte and Chrysale give contradictory instructions to the Notaire:

> Mettez, mettez, Monsieur, Trissotin pour mon gendre.
> Pour mon gendre, mettez, mettez, Monsieur, Clitandre.

But even with the unexpected support from Martine, eager to avenge her dismissal, Chrysale fails to carry the day. He falters in his resolve and jumps at an opportunity for accommodation: Trissotin may marry Henriette, and Clitandre may have Armande. Only Ariste's timely ruse allows the father to save face and the lovers to be united. His false news of bankruptcy causes Trissotin to have second thoughts about the opposition against him. Like Tartuffe, Trissotin plays his hypocritical role to the last, but Ariste's simple trick proves him a greater fool than ever. No need here for a *deus ex machina*, an agent of providence from beyond, to take charge. What little evil has been caused by Trissotin can be readily exorcized. *Les Femmes savantes* is the only one of the *grandes comédies* in this chapter where the reversal comes wholly from within the action.

In their triumph, Clitandre and Henriette form a new society. But the degree to which the other members will be a part of it hangs in doubt. In *Tartuffe*, the whole family – former dupes and former victims – is united around a social ideal embodied by the lovers. Orgon undergoes a full and painful *anagnorisis*, a kind of redemption that makes him fit again – temporarily at least – for a just society. Whether Philaminte's realization of Trissotin's avarice and cowardice turns her into a good mother is another matter. She seems unready to renounce her 'philosophie' which she recommends to Armande as a consolation. Her very equanimity in the face of deceit and misfortune: 'Et perdant toute chose, à soi-même il se reste' (V, last scene), suggests an unregenerate egoism. Indeed, she approves the marriage of Henriette to Clitandre not to guarantee the happiness of the lovers but to punish Trissotin: 'J'en ai la joie au cœur, / Par le chagrin qu'aura ce lâche déserteur.' This spite of a wounded ego does not augur well.

While there could possibly be no more Tartuffes in Orgon's life, another Tris-sotin, this time cleverer and more knavish, might easily insinuate himself into Philaminte's.

Similarly, the last words of the play, spoken by Chrysale, are shrouded in uncertainty: 'Allons, Monsieur, suivez l'ordre que j'ai prescrit, / Et faites le contrat ainsi que je l'ai dit.' A newly discovered manhood likely to prevail? The fact that Chrysale was unable to win on his own puts this possibility in doubt. This confidence may well be, as Hope suggests, a delusion comparable to others expressed at the end of the play: Bélise's conviction that Clitandre still loves her, for instance ('Molière's Curtain Lines' 151). Whatever the case, the final atmosphere of *Les Femmes savantes* is one of intriguing ambiguity.

The dominant impression of refinement, reserve, and self-control in the love plot is not the only reason, of course, for the all-pervading intellectuality of *Les Femmes savantes*. The play deals in an intellectual way with intellectual issues. Love, marriage, learning, literary taste, propriety in language – such themes are treated in the way they deserve, with the full arsenal of rhetorical elaboration and ornamentation, and with the most thought-provoking devices of ironic contrast. These subjects are all interrelated; the ideas propounded by the 'savantes' on love and marriage are products of their efforts at self-education, while their need for purity in affairs of the heart leads to a keen sense of linguistic decorum. Thirst for knowledge and efforts at literary creativity are but two forms of a single striving toward enlightenment. Their battle against ignorance and vulgarity finds expression as well in the manifesto of their embryonic 'académie'; the advancement of learning and the fostering of literary and linguistic distinction are only facets of a unified programme.

The way in which these points are debated respects the orderly and analytical development of the play. The subjects of love and knowledge are discussed separately, each in two scenes, one at the beginning and one near the end. The opening *agon* between Henriette and Armande (I, 1) introduces the theme of love which is picked up in IV, 2 in an even lengthier and more closely reasoned debate between Armande and Clitandre. Similarly, the issue of knowledge and its relevance to social life finds expression in Clitandre's biting criticism of 'femmes docteurs' in I and his sharp clash with Trissotin in IV, 3 just after his discussion with Armande.

It would be simplistic, however, to reduce *Les Femmes savantes* to a general debate over precepts where the common sense of Clitandre is pitted against the others' absurdities. These ideas are examined in other perspectives and, with respect to comic impact, the credo of the 'savantes' is devaluated by a fundamental device in Molière: incongruity between practice and precept, intention and result. We have seen what powerful results Molière obtained from this technique in *Tartuffe*; they are no less memorable in *Les Femmes savantes*.

Philaminte and her côterie see love in Platonic terms; its vulgar form debases it to the level of enslavement to the senses, completed in marriage by enslavement to men. Having presented Tartuffe's animal-like instinctuality with such impact, Molière now shows us the opposite comic extreme: disembodied, ethereal feeling devoid of physical drives. But even if the ladies' half-digested Platonism were propounded with understanding, their conduct would present disquieting traits. For they, like all Molière's prudes, suffer from repressed and frustrated sexual desire. Armande's spiteful envy of her sister's happiness is all too evident, while Bélise's 'visions' of being loved by all constitute transparently ludicrous wish-fulfilments. Terms denoting physical delectation and emotional pleasure appear where one would expect reasoned intellectual judgements:

> Epicure me plaît, et ses dogmes sont forts. (v. 879)
>
> ...
>
> J'aime ses tourbillons ... (III, 2)[12]

The most obvious example of displaced sexuality occurs during the reading and commentary of Trissotin's sonnet. The climactic verse calls forth what Jouanny aptly labels a 'spasme' (note 1840):

PHILAMINTE
On n'en peut plus.

BÉLISE
On pâme.

ARMANDE
On se meurt de plaisir. (III, 2)

Finally, the ideal of equanimity implied in such a lofty 'philosophie' is betrayed by still another emotional enslavement, overt this time. As with so many other creations of Molière, Philaminte's chief drive is anger. Heavy fathers are choleric, because wrath is a form of bullying and therefore of domination, and because from the audience's viewpoint it devalues the character at the same time. The temper tantrum, the main form of infantile behaviour in this category of personages, prevents us from taking the blocking character too seriously. Thus the incongruity between the serene philosopher and the 'vrai dragon' whom Chrysale is seeking to tame brings one more comic element into the play.

In a word, the ladies fall far short of the equanimity and spirituality to which they aspire. As if to redeem themselves they try to banish words where they cannot extirpate things. In their ironic naïveté, elaborate taboos around words actually conjure the impurities they supposedly signify. Molière obviously attached great importance to this ludicrous extreme. Henriette's casual mention of 'mariage' in the first lines of the play elicits the same reaction of revulsion in Armande as if she had witnessed married love in action. In like manner, Philaminte first appears in a paroxysm of rage against the kitchen maid, Martine. Along with Chrysale we are prepared to accept the worst hypotheses for the girl's dismissal, but in a carefully orchestrated comic letdown, we learn that she has sinned only against linguistic purity – a wrong comparable in the 'savantes" eyes to the most wretched perversion.

Molière brings one more point of view to bear on this general problem of love and marriage. Chrysale protests against Martine's dismissal, arguing quite sensibly:

> Qu'importe qu'elle manque aux lois de Vaugelas,
> Pourvu qu'à la cuisine elle ne manque pas?
> ...
> Je vis de bonne soupe, et non de beau langage. (II, 7)

Here is the voice of creatural comfort, for whom the only important food is that offered to the stomach. In most comedies this statement is advanced by the valet, more attentive to hunger and thirst than to his master's amorous pursuits. Chrysale's concern with 'bonne soupe' is no more to be taken as a norm than his pronouncements on marriage. The perfect wife is the totally domesticated and ignorant one of former times whom Chrysale evokes with nostalgia:

> Nos pères sur ce point étaient gens bien sensés,
> Qui disaient qu'une femme en sait toujours assez
> Quand la capacité de son esprit se hausse
> A connaître un pourpoint d'avec un haut de chausse. (II, 7)

This appeal to the 'good old days' – always a sign in Molière of ridiculous anachronism[13] – hides a basic narcissism in Chrysale. His wife, like his servants, is there to satisfy his physical needs and to make his life easy. 'Faire aller son ménage' – such is wifely duty and subjection. Chrysale also condemns the quest for knowledge among servants: 'L'un me brûle mon rôt en lisant quelque histoire; / L'autre rêve à des vers quand je demande à boire' (II, 7). Chrysale's perfect household is dedicated to pampering *him*. While his egoism is much less callous and his domination only a wish, his view of marriage strays uncomfortably close to Arnolphe's.

The presentation of love and marriage in *Les Femmes savantes* emphasizes two extremes: constraint and subjection on the one hand, and vengeful self-affirmation on the other, slavery to the senses and rejection of the body. If Molière ridicules the ladies' pretentions to emancipation, it is not to satirize women nor to preach their subservience. For Chrysale's nostalgia is an equally ludicrous extreme. The truth in this ironic polarity lies elsewhere: a marriage between equals, with neither pre-eminent, in a relationship of mutual confidence where body, mind, and soul meet: 'J'aime avec tout moi-même, et l'amour qu'on me donne / En veut, je le confesse, à toute la personne' (IV, 2).[14] Henriette integrates this view of total love into a vision of marriage which is the most explicitly romantic in all of Molière:

> D'attacher à soi, par le titre d'époux,
> Un homme qui vous aime et soit aimé de vous,
> Et de cette union, de tendresse suivie,
> Se faire les douceurs d'une innocente vie. (I, 1)

The other point at issue in *Les Femmes savantes* is the more general one of knowledge. On the level of precept, Philaminte and her circle prefer a 'tête bien pleine' to a 'tête bien faite.' If as a theoretician of *honnêteté* Pascal recommended knowing a little about everything rather than everything about one thing, the 'savantes' want to learn everything about everything: 'Physique, / Grammaire, histoire, vers, morale et politique' comprise their hodge-podge programme (III, 2). They also wish to write, to legislate on language, and to found an 'académie'. Molière further devalues their efforts by showing how ill-equipped they are to carry out their programme. Their muddle-headed view of learning, more a pretext for name-dropping than an impulse toward enlightenment, their counterfeit and derivative literary tastes (brought out so forcefully in the *salon* scene [III, 2]), their capricious vendetta against language – all underline how woefully short in intelligence and judgement these ladies are.

When the pretentions are peeled away, what remains in this embryonic Academy is a crass wish to dominate. The ladies want their linguistic 'proscriptions' to have force of law everywhere; 'Nous serons par nos lois les juges des ouvrages' (III, 2). Learning is a stepping stone to power.[15] Their revulsion at man's dominion over woman is but a transparent desire to reverse the relationship.

It is wrong, however, to interpret this play as an anti-feminist tract. If 'pédantes' are Molière's target, so are 'pédants.' The dogfight in III, 3 between Trissotin and Vadius makes the ladies appear civil and high-minded by comparison. Nor should Chrysale's condemnation of learning be taken as a norm either:

> Vos livres éternels ne me contentent pas,
> Et hors un gros Plutarque à mettre mes rabats,
> Vous devriez brûler tout ce meuble inutile,
> Et laisser la science aux docteurs de la ville. (II, 7)

This is crude egoism; books do not please *him*. If the sole use for Plutarch is to press his shirtfront, he surely deserves the ladies' scorn. But the real reason for his hatred of knowledge is that it draws away attention that should be directed at him: 'Dans ce vain savoir, qu'on va chercher si loin, / On ne sait comme va mon pot, dont j'ai besoin' (II, 7).

Two extremes once again: encyclopaedic knowledge versus total ignorance, both in violation of the *honnête* ideal of learning blended in a balanced life. The quarrel is less between two views of knowledge in the abstract than around the position of learning in one's social image. What Clitandre says of enlightened women applies to men as well:

> Je consens qu'une femme ait des clartés de tout;
> ...
> [Mais] j'aime que souvent, aux questions qu'on fait,
> Elle sache ignorer les choses qu'elle sait;
> De son étude enfin je veux qu'elle se cache,
> Et qu'elle ait du savoir sans vouloir qu'on le sache. (I, 3)

We are back to the seventeenth-century ideal of civility, so well defined by Pascal among others: 'Quand en voyant un homme on se souvient de son livre, c'est mauvais signe; je voudrais qu'on ne s'aperçût d'aucune qualité que par la rencontre et l'occasion d'en user' (*Pensée* 35, Brunschwicg edition). Or in Clitandre's paradoxes: 'La science est sujette à faire de grands sots'; 'Un sot savant est sot plus qu'un sot ignorant' (IV, 3). 'Sottise' is a social sin that is compounded by excessive display of knowledge.

The three societies pictured in *Les Femmes savantes* all contravene the laws of civility: the family with its extremes of erudite ostentation and self-satisfied ignorance; Philaminte's 'salon' with its stupidity and pretentiousness; the hypothetical 'académie' of so little promise. As Clitandre explains, only one society embodies the virtues of which the lesser groups are devoid, the Court:

> Permettez-moi, Monsieur Trissotin, de vous dire
> ...
> Qu'elle a du sens commun pour se connaître à tout;

Que chez elle on se peut former quelque bon goût;
Et que l'esprit du monde y vaut, sans flatterie,
Tout le savoir obscur de la pédanterie. (IV, 3)

Although admired by Molière's immediate posterity, *Les Femmes savantes* has been disdained by some recent critics: 'sa plus mauvaise pièce' as Adam concludes in his angry study of the work (p 392). The play deserves better. It presents in an intellectually challenging and stage-worthy way the widest social vision of any of Molière's comedies. Earlier ideals of married love, tolerance, understanding, liberty, confidence are broadened and blended here into a comprehensive view of life in society, where love, instinct, knowledge, taste, and refinement fuse into a harmonious whole.

L'AVARE

The arrangement of functions in *L'Avare* brings us back from the singularities of *Les Femmes savantes* to the more typical version of the comic myth that we saw in *Tartuffe*. A traditional romantic plot is impeded by the usual paternal blocking character. The love interest again is double: two couples are involved, Valère-Elise and Cléante-Mariane, with the same brother-sister pairing as in *Tartuffe* (although Valère and Mariane do not learn of their blood relationship until the dénouement). Once more, as in *Tartuffe*, two son figures are set in moral opposition: Cléante, like Damis, so explodes in hostility and rebellion against his father that he too earns a curse for his pains; as the antithesis to this 'bad son,' Valère wins the confidence and affection of the paternal figure, as does his homonym in *Tartuffe*. Finally, there is the heavy father himself, egotistical, authoritarian, and inhuman.

The phases of the action recall as well the conventional development of the comic plot with, in the case of *L'Avare*, strong effects of dramatic contrast. The blocking character appears to have been undone by La Flèche's theft of the *cassette*, a feat comparable to Elmire's unmasking of Tartuffe, and Horace's spiriting away of Agnès. But we are catapulted from this sense of triumph to a point of ritual death, just as baleful and terrifying in its implications as Tartuffe's apparent victory and Arnolphe's recapture of Agnès. Elise, like Agnès, is threatened with claustration: 'Quatre bonnes murailles me répondront de ta conduite' (II, 4), the living death, in comic terms, of convent life. Valère, accused of stealing Harpagon's treasure, inadvertently confesses to having won the heart of Elise. He finds himself charged with both theft and seduction and threatened with a hanging. Indeed, the spectre of one of the most grisly forms of capital punishment in the seventeenth century looms on the horizon as Harpagon screams at Valère: 'Tu seras roué tout vif' (V, 4).

But 'la pensée magique' intervenes once more. A situation evolving towards bondage and horror, like that of *Tartuffe* and *L'Ecole des femmes*, is saved only by a miraculous event outside the canons of probability. The spell of the evil father is broken by a force representing paternal benevolence: Anselme, the true father, who restores health and sanity to Harpagon's vitiated family.[16]

Once again, however, Molière has fused these conventions together in a highly individual way. Its surface similarities with other plays should not obscure the qualities *sui generis* of *L'Avare*. The romantic element, for instance, is far more compelling. Both threads of the plot are developed with equal emphasis (unlike *Tartuffe*, where the second thread quickly disappears). In I, 1 and 2 we learn about the reciprocal affection of Valère and Elise and of Cléante's passion for Mariane. The romantic premises are enacted before us, moreover, not casually mentioned as with Damis. These scenes reinforce a romantic atmosphere both by theme and by tone: the heroic rescue from drowning for example, through which Valère has won Elise's love, and the affectionate bantering that suffuses each scene.[17]

Molière is careful to maintain the continuity of this atmosphere. Three important scenes in III (7, 8, and 9) bring three of the four lovers on stage (Elise, Mariane, and Cléante). The civility, refinement, and elegance of their conduct are all the more highlighted by Harpagon's ridiculous attempts to emulate the sophistication of 'la belle galanterie' as he courts Mariane. Molière further reinforces the love interest as Mariane and Cléante convey their true feelings to each other before an unsuspecting Harpagon by the familiar device of double entendre (III, 7). The beginning of IV prolongs this tone as the anxiety-reassurance ritual of I, 1 is re-enacted by Cléante and Mariane. At the same time they entreat Frosine, now converted to their cause, to find a way out of their predicament.

The antithesis between the good and the bad son is also more elaborate than it was in *Tartuffe*. One of the distinctive traits of the play is rivalry between father and son and for the same girl. Yet the Oedipal confrontation here seems to move away from anger at thwarted love to a mutual, almost instinctive hostility. Cléante's rage against his father, Harpagon's ire toward his son transcend their rivalry to become, in one case, a primitive loathing and in the other, an emasculating exercise of authority. No confrontation between son and father in Molière reaches such heights of acrimony and aggressiveness as does Cléante's onslaught in II, 2: 'Ne rougissez-vous point ... de sacrifier gloire et réputation au désir insatiable d'entasser écu sur écu, et de renchérir, en fait d'intérêts, sur les plus infâmes subtilités qu'aient jamais inventées les plus célèbres usuriers? ' This hatred reaches its apogee in the bitter verbal encounter of IV, 5, all the more dramatically effective since it follows an apparent reconciliation:

HARPAGON
Je t'abandonne.

CLÉANTE
Abandonnez.

HARPAGON
Je te renonce pour mon fils.

CLÉANTE
Soit.

HARPAGON
Je te déshérite.

CLÉANTE
Tout ce que vous voudrez.

HARPAGON
Et je te donne ma malédiction.

CLÉANTE
Je n'ai que faire de vos dons.

We have here, as in *Tartuffe*, a form of symbolic murder. But while Damis went out meekly without a word, Cléante's brazen mockery both strengthens the impression of hatred and mitigates the demonic side of Harpagon. The father flails about impotently while the determined youth stands his ground. The paternal curse that had left Damis wordless triggers here an attitude of visceral defiance. Cléante embodies the comic *élan* thrusting forward to a happy resolution. His stance here recalls Elise's cautious disrespect in a lighter register: 'Je ne veux point me marier, mon père, s'il vous plaît' (I, 4).

While the bad son carries rebellion to the moral limits of comedy, the good son, Valère, turns out to be much more than his namesake in *Tartuffe*. Far from being the one-dimensional paragon of magnanimity who tries to save Orgon from arrest, the Valère of *L'Avare* shows only the outward appearance of loyalty; we know that in reality he is blatantly deceiving the miser. His flagrant hypocrisy and articulate cynicism would be shocking if they were not redeemed by being in the service of love.

Valère is, moreover, but one member of a team of tricksters who gull Harpagon and mock him behind his back (and to his face, when they can get away with it). Even the miser's son confronts his father twice with galling *faits accomplis*: the 'collation' he has ordered and the present to Mariane of a diamond ring pulled from Harpagon's finger (III, 7). The phalanx of this team, however, is formed by the auxiliaries. La Flèche throws out pointed asides at the audience while he is being searched by Harpagon (I, 3) and delivers eloquent broadsides against the miser among which the famous 'le seigneur Harpagon est de tous les humains l'humain le moins humain' (II, 4). And it is he who engineers and perpetrates the crucial stratagem of the play. Even though the theft of the *cassette* does not in itself save the situation, it does provide Cléante with the weapon for winning Mariane in the end.

Harpagon's go-between, Frosine, is converted to the lovers' cause and falls into the *soubrette* role. She symbolizes inventiveness and optimism more than effectiveness, for she never manages to put into operation her elaborate false *marquise* ruse (IV, 1). But even while still on Harpagon's side she plays outrageously on his vanity. Her transparent hypocrisy accounts for the humour of her memorable scene with him (II, 5).

The ease with which Harpagon is taunted and tricked puts an aura of vulnerability about him and diminishes the terror he would like to project. One can take too seriously his satanic self-image; for he is more like a bogeyman, or, in seventeenth-century comic typology, a braggart soldier, full of ranting and bombast but weak and ineffectual. Only twice does he momentarily get the better of his aggressors. Although he tricks his son into confessing his love for Mariane (IV, 3), even this triumph is short-lived as La Flèche makes off at the same time with the *cassette*. And he childishly discharges his spleen against those who tell him the harsh truth by taking a stick after Maître Jacques for imprudently repeating neighbourhood gossip.

Like *L'Ecole des femmes* this play, then, is a long aggression against the blocking character. Even those scenes with Harpagon where he is not gulled comment tellingly on his vice. In his first appearance on stage, before La Flèche's mocking asides, Harpagon expresses to us his grotesquely distorted view of the world. His much-commented demand to see 'les autres' after examining La Flèche's first pair of hands (I, 3) is more than a comic quip imitated from Plautus. It takes us to the heart of his perception of reality, to his vision of a tentacular monster probing into his treasure – a characteristic which will reach hallucinatory proportions in his 'Au voleur!' monologue (IV, 7). Harpagon's paranoia carries him to disquietingly epic extremes and constitutes a prime example of 'statements pushed beyond their meaning and exaggerated to absurdity by the passion of the utterance' (Moore, *Molière* 61). After stating his wish to put his entire household, including himself, to judicial torture ('faire donner la question à toute la maison: à servantes, à valets, à fils, à fille, et à moi aussi' [IV, 7]), he now demands detention of all his suspects, that is, 'la ville et les faubourgs' (V, 1). He seems to see himself as a wrathful God wreaking punishment on a cosmic scale for a crime with no parallel in his imagination.

Even the intrusion of caprice into the action – the sudden, unexpected turns which underline the contingent nature of the comic plot – are linked to character. Just as the sporadic fermentations of Argan's body send the 'malade imaginaire' hurriedly into the wings when we least expect it, Harpagon's anxieties have their own rhythm as he twice rushes off into the garden to check on his treasure (I, 5 and II, 3).

What sin, once again, does Harpagon commit to deserve such sustained ridicule? At one level, of course, avarice. His 'manière austère,' his 'rigoureuse épargne,' his 'tyrannie' are roundly condemned in I, 1 and mocked throughout the play. In its archetypal dimension, moreover, this conduct brings still more opprobrium upon it. Sterile and unproductive, miserliness stands in direct contrast to the life-giving and prodigal vitality that comedy is meant to celebrate (Lawrence 19). Small wonder, then, that we get the impression of a 'force of evil capable of blighting life itself' (Hubert 207) and that linked to this moral sterility we find the physical degradation epitomized by Harpagon's 'fluxion.' But Harpagon is not solely an *avare* like the Euclio of Plautus's *Aulularia*, a miser with the outward appearance of pauperdom. Someone concerned only with getting and not spending would not own a private *hôtel* with all the attendant symbols of status like numerous servants and transportation fit for a gentleman; nor would he offer formal dinners complete with fine cutlery and glass. When Cléante accuses his father of dishonouring his 'condition' (II, 2) he implies that Harpagon's social level demands a certain standard of conduct. As a member of the upper bourgeoisie he would be in that grey zone where wealth and titles mingled.

Harpagon, however grasping, does have a sense of the proprieties. The cost of status symbols is kept to a strict minimum, but Harpagon accepts it: he would rather have a starved nag than no horse at all. Indeed, the full comic force of his character surges out of his attempts to get the maximum of appearance out of a minimum of reality, to project an impression of largesse while trimming expenses where they supposedly escape notice. His comic contradiction lies in 'the discrepancy between the public image of himself which he so ludicrously strives to impose on others, and the reality of his sordid avarice and usury' (Hubert 211). The briefing Harpagon gives his household in III, 1 drives home this clash of illusion and reality. In what may be taken as the comic epitome of Harpagon's attention to appearances, he has the servant whose breeches are worn out in the seat stand against the wall, and the one whose jacket is stained hold his hat in front of him. What better emblem for the whole world of the miser: a brightly coloured headpiece covering a greasy blemish.

Out of a grudging recognition, then, of what is expected of a man in his social position, the miser refuses to present to others the full reality of his petty vice. Nor will he admit it to himself. When Cléante and Maître Jacques on separate occasions put his true nature squarely to him, he flies into a rage. As he beats his hapless cook-coachman, he can only say, 'apprenez à parler' (III, 1); that is, learn to lie. Maître Jacques thus discovers the converse of Valère's profession of hypocrisy. If 'les plus fins toujours sont de grands dupes du côté de la flatterie' (I, 1), it is always dangerous to tell unpleasant truths even to the most stupid.

Thus we laugh both at the transparent futility of Harpagon's efforts to ape gentlemanly munificence and his bad faith in refusing to face his own nature, in seeing himself motivated by 'charité' (II, 2) and not lust for gold. But Molière's supreme talent as a creator of character brings the comic fault to its richest expression in the portrayal of love. It is difficult to imagine a Tartuffe not obsessed with desire for Elmire, an Alceste without his quarrelsome affection for Célimène, or a Harpagon without his bizarre intention to wed Mariane. This love interest, however, makes no sense with respect to Harpagon's avarice. The young girl and her mother are destitute and alone with no promise of what Harpagon should logically be looking for; a generous dowry and attractive 'rentes.' Indeed, the union with 'une certaine veuve' (I, 4) which he proposes for his son is more in tune with his own acquisitiveness. Harpagon's hope to acquire 'quelque bien' through this marriage seems quite illusory, more an automatic afterthought than genuine expectation. Incongruous as the conclusion seems, we must assume that Harpagon is genuinely in love, as much as a grasping man of sixty can be.[18] Once again we are far from Plautus's miser; by giving Harpagon – as he had with Tartuffe and Alceste – an emotional attachment at odds with his basic aspiration, Molière opens up whole new comic vistas in his hero.

Until now the foolish lovers have all been in the *barbon* category; the Sganarelle of *L'Ecole des maris*, Arnolphe, Tartuffe are too old to rival with young love, but not old enough to be physically decrepit. Harpagon is Molière's only fully-fleshed version of the *senex iratus*, the quarrelsome, petulant old man of the traditional comic typology. In place of the *barbon amoureux* we find a *senex amans* where the contrast between age and affection reaches its most comic extreme. To aspire to love at sixty, Harpagon must deny his years with the same bad faith that made him refuse to admit his miserliness. Although he wears old-fashioned clothing (Frosine ironically praises his 'fraise à l'antique' [II, 5]), he glories in the image of youthful vigour and promised longevity that Frosine deftly builds around him. The same vanity which rejuvenates him makes him see true youth as prepuberty beardlessness and effete slavery to fashion: 'avec leur ton de poule laitée,' he sneers, 'et leur trois petits brins de barbe relevés en barbe de chat, leurs perruques d'étoupes' (II, 5).

This is no doubt the key to his love for Mariane. A widower infatuated with himself, convinced of his unflagging virility, would want to hold back time by marrying a young and attractive girl. But appearances belie this self-image: Harpagon is beyond the age and powers of love. Mariane's physical revulsion as she meets her fiancé – 'Ah! Frosine, quelle figure!' (III, 4) – bears witness to the miser's decrepitude, accentuated ironically by the eyeglasses he wears to conform to Mariane's supposed predilection for 'les nez qui portent des lunettes' (II, 5). Being physically deficient, he must also be morally unfit for courtship. In comedy, the mysteries of refined wooing are revealed only to the young. Harpagon can but ape externals, as in his lame travesty of the witty compliment: 'Vous êtes un astre, mais un astre le plus bel astre qui soit dans le pays des astres' (III, 5). It is Cléante who gives his father an object lesson in *galanterie* by providing a 'collation' and by urging upon the girl Harpagon's diamond ring.

In Harpagon's case, then, *vieillard amoureux* is an oxymoron which underscores rich comic contrasts. In *L'Avare* there is the same degree of incongruity between Harpagon's aspirations in love and his grasping character as there is between Alceste's desire to win Célimène and the petulant and insulting way he goes about it. If an 'amoureux' cannot be 'atrabilaire,' still less can he be 'avare.' True love is impulsively generous, affectionate. No present can be fine enough for the lady, no entertainment worthy enough. Avarice is only another sickness of self-love, more calculating and debasing than the will to power of a Philaminte or the jealous outbursts of an Alceste.

Harpagon fails in love for the same reasons as Arnolphe: the self-seeking egoist has no place in the regenerated world of the dénouement. On the contrary, his fault must be exorcized, so that the norm which it defies can be all the more enthusiastically celebrated. Harpagon's avarice, his tyranny and crassness all imply a contrary ideal, just as the physical, moral, and intellectual prison Arnolphe builds for Agnès evokes by contrast the school of confidence and selfless emancipated love from which Agnès emerges with Horace into the new society. The miser, like his predecessors, is a kill-joy at odds with normal standards of amusement and self-indulgence. Cléante wants to respect the norms of fashion, which his father reduces to their cash value: 'Je vais gager qu'en perruques et rubans, il y a du moins vingt pistoles; et vingt pistoles rapportent par année dix-huit livres six sols huit deniers, à ne les placer qu'au denier douze' (I, 4). He is utterly blind to his children's human dimension; they become ciphers in the money game. More generally, Harpagon perverts the highest aristocratic ideal: magnanimity both in its moral and monetary sense. A man of his financial status should have no concern about money whatsoever. Cléante's indignant appeal to his father's pride summarizes the chief moral blemish in the play: 'Ne rougissez-vous point de déshonorer votre condition par les commerces que vous faites? ' (II, 2) But Cléante is there to define true generosity and consideration, and Anselme arrives at the end of it to redeem the corrupted ideal. He gives in without quibbling to Harpagon's cascade of exactions; for him, a true *généreux*, the joy of a reunited family is all.

The fact that Harpagon's faults have been thoroughly denounced in the course of the play helps explain the mildness of the exorcism element at the end. Harpagon is defeated and humiliated; his hold over the family has been broken. One might even say that the family itself has collapsed to re-form in another. The miser loses Elise and Cléante to Anselme's newly discovered children, Valère and Mariane. At the same time all four lovers acquire a mother in Anselme's wife, Mariane's mother. Harpagon's power is seen as a passing shadow, a momentary disturbance of social harmony, comparable on a moral level to the shipwreck that broke up Anselme's family in the first instance. Like *L'Ecole des femmes*, *L'Avare* illustrates the ternary rhythm of comedy, the recovery of an original harmony and perfection after an intermediate phase of ritual bondage.

Harpagon, however, is spared the humiliating retreat of Arnolphe. Instead, the lost *cassette* severs him from human reality. Society's place will be somewhere off-stage; the world in front of us is now cold, lifeless, and metallic. The reunited family is imbued with the vision of the soon-to-be-found mother; what glows in Harpagon's mind is the image of more gold to be extorted from Anselme, and of the only form that woman can ever take in his vision of the world as objects to be amassed, 'ma chère cassette.'

Like Argan and Monsieur Jourdain, Harpagon is protected from the sense of defeat by his very mania. But while the other two join the triumphant family, imparting joy to it in their own happiness, however illusory, Harpagon stands alone. Society has not expelled him, it has left him behind.

LE MALADE IMAGINAIRE

Le Malade imaginaire and *Le Bourgeois gentilhomme* stand as Molière's supreme realizations in the new genre of the *comédie-ballet* fashioned by Molière out of the dominant performing arts of the time. Whatever depth of turpitude and cynicism each work plumbs, the final curtain brings a benign and cheerful mood. A colourful ceremony spun out of song, dance, and spectacle removes us from the realities of medical charlatanism and social pretentions to a land of playful fantasy, tolerant enough to accommodate the greatest fools.

As well as affinities of mood, these *comédies-ballets* share important archetypal characteristics. At the centre of the action is the familiar heavy father, the domestic tyrant making and breaking marriages as he pleases. But while Argan and Jourdain function in essentially the same manner as Arnolphe, Orgon, Philaminte, and Harpagon, they differ radically from them both in the way they are individualized and in action and mood. Each occupies the centre of the stage as if the world existed principally for their beguilement. They are spectators and participants at once, craving both the right of passive amusement and active interference. Argan's 'chaise,' emblematic of this solar position, reminds us of our own 'fauteuil d'orchestre'; we are indulgent to these amiable buffoons in part because they are devalued projections of ourselves. Although on a less sophisticated level, they take the same delight in entertainment and spectacle as we do. But Argan and Jourdain wish to control as well – not with the calculation of Harpagon or Orgon's rage, but by immediate fiat and peevish temper. These two are driven by the pleasure principle in its purest, most infantile form: they demand instant satisfaction and, if frustrated, they break into petulant anger.

Their desire to enjoy passively a world organized around them and created for them, together with their whimsicality, betray a profound, infantile narcissism. Alongside the mature heavy fathers of other plays Argan and Jourdain reflect the ulitmate deflation of paternal authority (Mauron, *Psychocritique* 107). They are children waiting to be pampered, entertained, given shiny new clothes, tucked in with pillows and blankets. As in the world of children, objects are the primary reality.

This infantilism is accompanied in each case by a strong female figure. Madame Jourdain, the mother of the threatened daughter, is resolutely on the side of the lovers and stands up vigorously to her husband.'Much more nefarious is Béline's effect on Argan; 'la seule épouse vraiment perfide du théâtre de Molière' (Gutwirth 119), she seeks to dispossess children of a first marriage and maintains her hold over Argan by reducing him to a passive, whimpering cry-baby.

It is no surprise that the danger represented by Argan and Monsieur Jourdain as blocking characters is minimal. Their very childishness – whether in bright-eyed enthusiasm or in foot-stamping rage – precludes any real threat to the love plot. Because they are incapable of deliberate and systematic action, the traditional settling of accounts between children and parents is never reached. The plot develops rather around the passive protagonist seated in the middle of the stage: a series of scenes that follow in a delightful, easy-going spirit of improvisation, that are filled out with the free play of verbal patterns and stage business. Both comedies are full of patter, give-and-take dialogue, repetition (eg, the scenes between Argan and Toinette in *Le Malade imaginaire* and the *dépit amoureux* episode of *Le Bourgeois gentilhomme*). The cumulative effect is a delightful impression of gratuitousness; the action bounces along on its own momentum, pulsating in harmony with the internal rhythms of each scene, bringing together in poetic coherence word, song, and sight.

Of the two, *Le Malade imaginaire* is more serious both in its functional and thematic development. Argan is bent upon marrying his daughter off to Thomas Diafoirus, while Monsieur Jourdain simply forbids his own to marry a commoner, without having a specific husband in view. Jourdain's rather innocuous social pretentions bring on stage relatively harmless predators — tailors, fencing teachers, and the like; but the doctors that have attached themselves leech-like to Argan's hypochondria represent the power and terror of death. While both characters are 'vaches à lait' (*Bourgeois* [III, 4] and *Malade* [I, 2]), there is no common measure between the character of the milkers in each case.

As with the earlier comedies, the love plot of *Le Malade imaginaire* weaves two threads in moral opposition: the romantic element which anticipates the reversal, and the grotesque counterpoint of an incongruous rival which links the love plot to the world to be exorcized. After setting a buffoonish tone in the first two scenes of the play, Molière changes his comic register to underline the tenderness and ardour of young love. Both Angélique and Cléante are together during most of II, and, although they are never alone on stage to speak openly of their love for one another, Cléante manages by his 'opera' (II, 5) to make his affection known and to receive Angélique's pledge of love. And later, while we do not actually see them, the substance of their tête-à-tête is described with charming naïveté by Argan's younger daughter Louison (II, 8). Once again we have an image of passionate, forthright, selfless love between civil and wellborn people.

In contrast stands the ridiculous Thomas Diafoirus who shares with Tartuffe, Trissotin, and Harpagon common traits as rival to the main love interest. Each prolongs the humorous society and its moral turpitudes, and their inability to cross the stage to the audience's side comes out nowhere more strongly than in their courtship patterns, their efforts to ape the gentle art of *galanterie*. Thomas presents yet another travesty of the normal suitor. Tartuffe's lust, Trissotin's pedantry, Harpagon's rapacity, Thomas's 'lenteur à comprendre' (II, 5) all augur ill for a successful career in amorous civility. What we see on stage confirms our expectations.

Molière makes no secret of his caricatural intention; in one of the few moral judgements contained in his stage directions he labels Thomas '*un grand benêt, nouvellement sorti des Ecoles, qui fait toutes choses de mauvaise grâce et à contre-temps*' (II, 5). Molière makes clear from the outset that what interests him here is the misfit, not the charlatan. In this respect *Le Malade imaginaire* is less a satire of medicine, than of social ineptness. Thomas's dullness, compounded by his crushing intellectual baggage, makes him a ludicrous intruder into the world of *honnêtes gens*. As suitor in II, 5, he unconsciously parodies each rite of *galanterie*. The amorous compliment becomes a stilted conceit reminiscent of Harpagon's 'astre' speech: 'Mademoiselle, ne plus ne moins que la statue de Memnon rendait un son harmonieux, lorsqu'elle venait à être éclairée des rayons du soleil: tout de même me sens-je animé d'un doux transport à l'apparition du soleil de vos beautés. [etc.]' His token of love becomes a thesis, a ponderous scholastic exercise. So grotesque is his notion of polite entertainment that he invites Angélique to a dissection. 'Le divertissement sera agréable,' Toinette comments; 'Il y en a qui donnent la comédie à leurs maîtresses; mais donner une dissection est quelque chose de plus galant.' Finally, his idea of witty repartee and debate is but the empty formalism of scholarly disputations with their *distinguos* and their *concedos*.

Argan's entire medical 'team' has been cast in this same mould. Monsieur Diafoirus's ceremonial salutation to Argan degenerates into ludicrous confusion as it collides with Argan's own compliment (II, 5). Worse yet, the doctor-father views love in strictly organic terms. When he praises his son's 'vertu prolifique' and his ability to 'engendrer et procréer des enfants bien conditionnés' he puts the institution of marriage on the level of animal husbandry. This is the 'back-side' of true civility: Béralde's devastating sarcasm to Fleurant, the apothecary who specializes in administering enemas, may be taken as symbolic: 'Allez, Monsieur, on voit bien que vous n'avez pas accoutumé de parler à des visages' (III, 4). This topsy-turvy world of heavy fathers, bondage, evil, and decomposition must once again be exorcized. This world has three components: Argan himself, the dour apostles of death and decay that pass for doctors, and his perfidious wife, Béline.

Argan embodies all the traditional attributes of the tyrannical blocking character: 'je suis maître dans ma famille pour faire ce que bon me semble' (III, 3). His rampant egoism comes out in the number of first-person forms he uses to justify his choice of Thomas as son-in-law: 'Ma raison est que, me voyant infirme et malade comme je suis, je veux me faire un gendre et des alliés médecins' (I, 5). That he is governed by avarice as well is proved in his detailed assessment of the material advantage of this marriage: Diafoirus will not only inherit all of his father's wealth but his uncle's, Purgon's, as well. Finally his temper tantrums testify to his irascible nature.

Beyond this stock of traits common to blocking figures — exaggerated here in the direction of infantilism — lies Argan's comic fault, hypochondria, which makes him vulnerable, in turn, to a more specific weakness, gullibility. Credulity stands comically in traditional tension with knavery: Orgon must have his Tartuffe, Philaminte her Trissotin, Argan his Béline and his Purgon. The knave's strength lies in his ability to see beyond surface gullibility to his victim's basically egotistic nature. Add the terrible weapon of a doctor – fear – and Argan's conduct becomes perfectly plausible. Purgon, and, to an extent, Béline, like Tartuffe, exploit the basic narcissism of their victim by furnishing an excuse for it. Argan wants to be coddled, he wants to be the centre of attention; what better way than through the ritual acts of medicine. Each treatment, conceived expressly for him, makes him a centre of attention: 'Mon lavement d'aujourd'hui a-t-il bien opéré? ' (I, 2). His illness, moreover, works symbiotically with his rage: 'Est-il possible qu'on laisse comme cela un pauvre malade tout seul? ' (I, 1).

His hypochondria seems so much a pose for that very reason – it is more a vehicle to justify his self-absorption than a mania in itself. He is willing to play the role of 'malade,' but when the costs rise beyond a certain ceiling his innate bourgeois common sense takes over: 'Ah! Monsieur Fleurant, tout doux, s'il vous plaît; si vous en usez comme cela, on ne voudra plus être malade' (I, 1). The same tendency explains Argan's fits of temper if his condition is questioned. In answer to Toinette's query: 'Est-ce que vous êtes malade? ' he can only splutter: 'Comment, coquine, si je suis malade? si je suis malade, impudente? ' (I, 5). Argan knows instinctively that his interlocutor is trying to trick him into betraying his *alibi*. Rather than set out on the perilous path of reasoning or specific elaboration, he shows his *mauvaise foi*, as does Harpagon, by taking refuge in a tantrum.

Medicine has enslaved Argan physically as well as morally. Béline's 'belle oraison funèbre' at the sight of her supposedly dead husband must hit the mark, however out of place it may be: 'un homme incommode à tout le monde, malpropre, dégoûtant, sans cesse un lavement ou une médecine dans le ventre, mouchant, toussant, crachant toujours' (III, 12). Argan's organism is wrecked by harsh emetics and enemas. His own proud totals bear witness to the violence he does on his body: eight medications and twelve 'lavements' in one month, twelve 'médecines' and twenty enemas the preceding month (I, 1).

Strangely enough, Argan is never bled, and yet he lives at a time when the universal remedies were, as the 'bachelierus' knows so well: '*clysterium donare, postea seignare, ensuitta purgare.*' The task of bleeding fell, of course, to the surgeon, as the other treatments to the apothecary. But while Monsieur Fleurant is very much in evidence, the surgeon does not appear in this or any other Molière comedy. Toinette does suggest surgical procedures in her role as doctor, and the 'bachelierus' of the final *intermède* is given the

> Virtutem et puissanciam
> Medicandi
> Purgandi

Seignandi
Percandi
Taillandi
Coupandi ...

But Toinette's buffoonish antics reduce her suggestion – absurd in itself – that Argan have an arm and an eye removed, to the level of a jest, while in the passage from the ceremony Molière is merely using poetic licence to paint in one ludicrous picture the whole medical team, or more precisely, the doctor with his two arms, the apothecary and the surgeon.

In any event, the surgeon's scalpel and the image of blood spurting out of a vein would introduce an element of the macabre out of keeping with the comic tone as it was then understood. Incision suggest *sparagmos* or mutilation, a feature more in tune, perhaps, with today's black comedy.

Of the three remedies, 'clysterium donare' dominates in the play. Enemas always outnumber other forms of treatment. A *clystère* is the first allusion to medicine in the play and becomes the emblem of medical tyranny; Fleurant, whose name suggests *flairer* ('sniffing'), brandishes one in III, 4, and the mock ceremony at the end includes eight 'porte-seringues.' Argan's frequent and unexpected trips to the *chaise percée* underline the unnatural fermentation of his body. Scatology points here not the life-possessing organism, but the body decomposing before it is dead. Argan's physiology is symbolic of the perverse desire of medicine to reduce health to impotence.

The essential contrast of *Le Malade imaginaire* is between the organism functioning in its normal rhythm – Argan is by nature robust, as his brother points out (III, 3) – and the same body where the same natural processes are forced and weakened through the ignorance of doctors and the slavishness of their dupes. We find here the same antithesis as in *L'Amour médecin* between real medicine with its deleterious effects and a mock medicine that heals. Toinette impersonates a doctor ('pour dégoûter [Argan] de son Monsieur Purgon' [III, 2]), while Béralde plays the role of healer in another way: he argues firmly and eloquently for the healthy body left alone to its own devices. His insistence that one do nothing when ill echoes of course commonplaces of the time and may well coincide with Molière's own beliefs. But Béralde is not advancing a thesis. The dramatic value of this position lies at once in the rhetorical flourishes with which it is elaborated – Béralde's tone is particularly vehement – and its relevance to the total structure of the play. The *raisonneur*, here, as in *L'Ecole des femmes*, is speaking to a particular point and a particular person. Just as Chrysalde would free Arnolphe from his obsession with cuckoldry (and not preach *complaisance* to the audience), so Béralde is attacking here a personal delusion. When Argan asks: 'Que faire donc quand on est malade? ' (III, 3) the brother's answer is intended for *him*. If he did nothing, took no medication, he would regain his health.

The final healer is the delightful mummery at the end of the play. To be sure, the charm of music and spectacle coincides with a savage attack on medicine contained in the macaronic Latin of the text. But this sardonic tone is always covered by the *élan* of the scenes and their archetypal implications. By becoming his own doctor Argan will regain his impaired life force. No longer will he need the Purgons and their ilk; he will find other, more innocuous justifications for his egoism – an egoism itself made harmless because true love has carried the day.

The mordant satire of the healing arts in *Le Malade imaginaire* has two facets.[19] Diafoirus and his son show an unconscious buffoonery that is quite inoffensive, while Purgon carries the terrifying bogeyman function of the type. Whatever the tone of their antics, however, the knaves in this play reign both by catering to the whims of the victim and by terrorizing him. Argan is caught in a far more deadly trap than, say, Philaminte or Jourdain. The pleasure of self-indulgence is contaminated by the fear of extinction. The doctors have mesmerized Argan into structuring his life to a rhythm of consultations and medications; he lives in abject fear lest the slightest derogation of any of these ritual acts bring calamity. If Madame de Sévigné's reaction is typical, this slavery is what the seventeenth century saw as Argan's ludicrous essence: 'Il était ... dans l'obéissance exacte à ces messieurs, il comptait tout: c'était seize gouttes d'un élixir dans treize cuillerées d'eau. S'il y en eût eu quatorze, tout était perdu' (Letter, 16 September 1676).[20]

The doctors use their chief weapon – the word – in the same contrasting ways. The savour of long, latinized words which Argan loves to roll around in his mouth: 'un julep hépatique, soporatif, et somnifère' (I, 1) turns readily into ashen-flavoured horror at Purgon's anathema (III, 5). But in both cases the word is empty, hollow – as the doctors in *L'Amour médecin* had already admitted in the intimacy of their consultation. Béralde hammers this point home: 'Toute l'excellence de leur art consiste en un pompeux galimatias, en un spécieux babil, qui vous donne des mots pour des raisons, et des promesses pour des effets' (III, 3). Theory replaces practice, the 'roman de la médecine' lays a deceptive veneer over harsh reality.

So compelling is the spell woven around Argan that object lessons, not reason, must be the ultimate weapon against the medical profession. Having failed in his debate with Argan, Béralde seizes the very next opportunity presented to him, Fleurant's unexpected arrival with Argan's *clystère*. In dismissing Fleurant with such contempt Béralde realizes he is provoking a confrontation with Purgon and hopes to prove to Argan that his fears are unfounded. Our last image of 'true' medicine, then, is the bogeyman at his most terrifying, making one final effort to prevail by fear. Passing himself off as the agent of 'an occult force or a vengeful deity having a will of its own' (Hubert 257), Purgon blows himself up to supernatural proportions and hurls at Argan a long and elaborate incantation that leaves the patient shattered: 'Ah, mon Dieu! je suis mort' (III, 6). But Argan quickly realizes that the curse has had no immediate effect on him and the spell gradually breaks down. Having done their worst to no avail, Purgon and his fellows leave the stage for good, to return only in the caricatured form of players singing macaronic Latin. The 'spécieux babil' has been transformed by melody and comic distortion into supreme entertainment. Hence, the doctors are not expelled in a formal sense by being tricked and humiliated; they have been devalued by their own conduct and by what has been said of them – whether by Toinette's mockery of Béralde's forceful eloquence. They carry away with them the terror by which they have ruled, the smell of decay which they have installed in the house. With the banishment of fear, medicine can become a game. There is almost a note of facetiousness in Argan's demand that Cléante become a doctor in order to marry Angélique, and he accepts with accommodating alacrity the suggestion that he become one himself. The simplistic idea that the medical gown confers the knowledge and status of the profession on the bearer appeals to his childlike side. After playing patient, he will now play doctor.

The true scapegoat in Le Malade imaginaire is Béline. Tricked into revealing her contempt for Argan and the real motives for her marriage to him (III, 12), she leaves the stage without a word, humiliated and undone. The crime that merits this punishment has several aspects. She, too, along with the doctors, has exploited for base purposes Argan's infantilism. Her simpering and saccharine ways reduce Argan to premature second-childishness. Such degrading endearments as 'mon petit fils' serve to give her a spurious maternal authority which she abuses flagrantly. In addition, she brings into the play a principle of social corruption parallel to the doctor's corruption of the body. A kind of female Harpagon, she is self-seeking, grasping, and devoid of humanity. She would have Angélique and Louison shut up in convents so that Argan's wealth would not pass into the hands of sons-in-law. She is even willing to pervert the law for her own ends. The sinister Notaire, symbolic of turpitude within the legal system, elaborates on ways to betray the interests of Argan's children. This perfidy too must be exorcized.

In a metaphysical sense, Béline stands as a symbol of sterility complementary to the death figures embodied by the doctors. She apparently has no children of her own (Argan bemoans the fact that he could have no issue by her, although the fault is apparently his) and, more significantly, is determined to prevent her two step-daughters from having any. Because she has thus attacked comedy in its very essence as a celebration of life, she must be excluded from it.

The dynamic principle in *Le Malade imaginaire* is the traditional one of trickery. Each member of the right society has his turn at promoting the cause of true love. Toinette, true to her function as helpful auxiliary, devises the stratagem that undoes Béline. Cléante impersonates a 'maître de musique' to gain access to Angélique and exchange vows with her. Finally, it is Béralde who contrives the trick and the entertainment that gives the play its festive, happy ending. Indeed, Béralde's role is probably the most complex of all: man of passionate eloquence, resourceful valet, good father, master of revels, he is a foil for all the evils we have seen: delusion, credulity, tyranny, and fear.

That all these stratagems meet with success accounts in part for the general tone of optimism in *Le Malade imaginaire*. There are, however, downturns in the mood – Argan repeatedly threatens to put Angélique into a convent and to disinherit her (I, 5, II, 6); but the closest we get to a point of ritual death is Angélique's renunciation of marriage as she laments over her father. The very fact, however, that Argan's demise is feigned – the only time in Molière that death is devalued in this way – puts the point of ritual death in an unusual archetypal perspective. This is a childish game of peek-a-boo, and Argan's triumphant resurrections prefigure the fantasy of the dénouement. Argan forgets his wife's perfidy with unreal haste and allows himself to be manipulated by Béralde with easy-going amiability. Freed from tyranny, his faults discharged upon the departed scapegoat and the now distant doctors, Argan can be absorbed without real humiliation into the 'right' world. He is duped, but painlessly; the spectacle is reality for him, an 'intermède' performed by 'comédiens' for us, but equally delightful for all. As Béralde assures Angélique, 'ce n'est pas tant le jouer, que s'accommoder à ses fantaisies' (III, 14).

LE BOURGEOIS GENTILHOMME

Prominent differences between *La Malade imaginaire* and *Le Bourgeois gentilhomme* are the importance of the love plot and the function of the main character within it. The romantic element here is subdued; there is not even a hint at it until the middle of the play, when Madame Jourdain advises her husband to 'songer à marier votre fille, qui est en âge d'être pourvue' (III, 3). When Madame Jourdain swears to aid the young lovers, the comic myth finally surfaces – in III, 7. A double plot obtains when Nicole, the *servante*, asks to be united to Covielle,

Cléonte's valet; and for the only time in this group of heavy father comedies, parallel love interests are placed in strong opposition of tone and diction. Whereas in *L'Avare* all the lovers were social equals, here master is set off against servant. Two views of love emerge, and the ritual of quarrel and reconciliation finds expression in two contrasting styles. However charming the *dépit* episode, however, it is the only time in the entire play – save at the dénouement – when all four lovers are on stage together. Until this point we have seen only Nicole; afterwards Covielle and his master return for the *turqueries* of IV and V. But there is no more talk of love, no more ardent dialogue, whether in anger or affection.

As the romantic element in the comic dialectic is subdued, we might expect a heightened anxiety to be caused by a more dominant blocking character. But Monsieur Jourdain is notably mild as a heavy father. Although determined to make his daughter a 'marquise,' he proposes no specific alternative to Cléonte and averts any threat of misalliance with the likes of Diafoirus, Tartuffe, or Trissotin. Jourdain's domestic tyranny appears only in veto form: he will not have Cléonte as his son-in-law.

In the absence of a struggle between 'blondin' and 'barbon,' Molière moves the action under two equally powerful impulses. We are intrigued, on the one hand, by a subtle system of comparisons and contrasts that points up the key moral issues of the play. The play has a linear aspect as well; a series of vignettes with Jourdain as protagonist shows up the various facets of his character and gives the work an engaging momentum that replaces the usual play of energies arising from the contest between the young man and the father.

As is to be expected in a comedy satirizing noble aspirations, the chief moral issue in *Le Bourgeois gentilhomme* is civility and its courtship form, *galanterie*. Like Tartuffe, Harpagon, and Diafoirus, Jourdain is an inept lover. His wooing of Dorimène, however, does not impinge on the main plot, nor does it look to marriage. In fact Jourdain has little genuine affection for his Marquise; she is rather a vehicle, interchangeable with any other, for the promotion of his noble self-image: gentlemen indulge in *galanteries*, so must he. The woeful results of this conduct are illustrated in every step of his courtship ritual. His love note ('Belle Marquise, vos beaux yeux me font mourir d'amour') is of dismaying banality, the normal rhetorical procedures suggested by the maître de philosophie pass his comprehension and degenerate into a farcical game of word scrambling (II, 4). His derisory conduct in Dorimène's presence amply fulfils our expectations (III, 16; IV, 1). His mechanical *révérence* forces her to back up; the gibberish of his compliment peters out in silence and is immediately put in perspective by Dorante's virtuoso piece on the standards of gastronomy required for a lady of distinction (IV, 1);[21] his banal flattery ('Ah! que voilà de belles mains') and lame efforts at repartee (underscored by Dorante's ironic praise: 'Il est homme qui a toujours la riposte en main') finish off the portrait of a foolish lover (IV, 1).

Jourdain's *galant* adventure with Dorimène establishes a strong contrast with normal patterns of civility. As we do not see enough of the young lovers to discover in their conduct an explicit model, it is Dorante's wooing of Dorimène which serves as a foil for Jourdain's absurd aping of courtly *galanterie*. Molière presents the two alone together twice (III, 15 and V, 2) and underlines in their refined and decorous banter a 'politesse mondaine' beyond Jourdain's ken. In this respect, Dorante must be viewed as far more than a swindler on the level of Tartuffe and Trissotin.[22] True, he cynically gulls the Bourgeois and treats Madame Jourdain with insulting arrogance. But with respect to comic norms, Jourdain is fair game; Dorante as a self-appointed 'maître de galanterie' is entitled to get as much out of him as do Jourdain's other teachers. The text contains a number of indications, moreover, that confirm the respectability of Dorante and his lady friend. The very first reference to him establishes him as a 'grand seigneur éclairé' but poor, in contrast to an empty-headed dupe with a full purse (I, 1). Dorimène too presents an image of distinction and does not share in whatever opprobrium Dorante might deserve for cheating Jourdain: she thinks herself courted by Dorante out of his own resources (III, 15 and 16) and merely entertained by the Bourgeois.

Most significantly, Dorante is unambiguously on the right side of the love plot. He admires Covielle's resourceful stratagems against Jourdain and makes his position clearly known to Dorimène: 'Il faut tâcher de servir l'amour de Cléonte ... C'est un fort galant homme et qui mérite que l'on s'intéresse pour lui' (V, 2). Finally, Dorimène's consent to marry him allows him to join the wedding party: together with Cléonte and Lucile, Covielle and Nicole, he and his Marquise stand at the core of the liberated, harmonious society created at the end of this play.

That Dorante's knavery, however cynical, is fundamentally benign in the moral world of *Le Bourgeois gentilhomme* receives further confirmation in his role as master of revels, one that is far more elaborate than is Béralde's in *Le Malade imaginaire*. He has used Jourdain's money to provide a sumptuous banquet complete with music and ballet, and the 'ballet des nations' is his undertaking (*loc. cit.*). Inasmuch as *Le Bourgeois gentilhomme* is a spectacular defence of entertainment, a comedy laced with song, dance, and ceremony, Dorante's role is absolutely central to the play's purpose. It is thanks to him as an imaginative creator of tasteful revels that singers and spectators can end the play with a joyous hymn: 'Quels spectacles charmants, quels plaisirs goûtons-nous! / Les Dieux mêmes, les Dieux n'en ont point de plus doux.'

Madame Jourdain is a curious amalgam of functions – killjoy and good mother, Elmire and Madame Pernelle rolled into one. She promotes the fortunes of the lovers, in the same way that Dorante stands in for the good father. And yet she is a railing, acerbic woman at odds with both poles of the dominant duality of the play: Jourdain's hilarious antics and Dorante's refined revelry. Her bluntness with her foolish husband balances her shrewishness, and her hostility towards Dorante is consistent with his insolence. But in both cases she is the enemy of play, the deflater of fantasy. She is right, of course, in her view of fools and knaves, but her attitude is depressingly negative: 'Je ne vois que chagrin de tous les côtés (V, 1). She disrupts the banquet of III-IV in a tactless, strident manner (IV, 2). Her railing, stubborn, and slow-witted nature comes out most sharply in the last scene when she nearly aborts the happy ending by opposing Lucile's marriage to the disguished Cléonte. Only when Covielle takes her aside and exclaims in an exasperated hyperbole: 'Il y a une heure, Madame, que nous vous faisons signe' (V, last scene), can the lovers find contentment.

This unseemly side of her bourgeois nature is seen as well in her tempestuous jealousy. In aristocratic society the marital status of the lady and her suitors in no way inhibited the spirit of ritualized courtship. In this world of mutual confidence, wifely jealousy was just as demeaning as husbandly distrust. But Madame Jourdain's humourless, low-class character renders her insensitive to his kind of play. Dorante's halfhearted (and sardonic) attempts at *galant* dialogue with her (III, 5): 'Je pense, Madame Jourdain, que vous avez eu bien des amants dans votre jeune âge' provokes a snarling outburst: 'Tredame, Monsieur, est-ce que Madame Jourdain est décrépite, et la tête lui grouille-t-elle déjà? '

Conjugal discord – the railing wife pitted against a slow-witted and tyrannical husband – furnishes, as in *Le Médecin malgré lui* and *Sganarelle*, still another vantage point from which to judge people of breeding, whether ardent young lovers or seasoned and deliberate suitors like Dorante. As if to evoke his earlier farce manner at the end of this sumptuous, courtly entertainment, Molière has Jourdain give his wife cavalierly 'à qui la voudra.'

Besides love and its social forms, there is another source of dramatic and comic interest of the play, the processional development of the action. What links the seemingly disconnected scenes of *Le Bourgeois gentilhomme* is the basic contrast they underline between the two sides of Jourdain's character. The Maître de Musique speaks of Jourdain's 'visions de noblesse et de galanterie qu'il est allé se mettre en tête,' aspirations far out of reach of his intellectual qualities: 'C'est un homme, à la vérité, dont les lumières sont petites, qui parle à tort et à travers de toutes choses, et n'applaudit qu'à contre-sens' (I, 1). As Argan was a slave to words, so Jourdain finds himself infatuated with show. Again like Argan, an innate narcissism reduces him to the level of a spoiled child demanding pampering and attention. When his new costumes fail to appear at the desired moment, he flies into mounting rage reminiscent of Argan's bell-ringing frenzy: 'J'enrage. Que la fièvre quartaine puisse serrer bien fort le bourreau de tailleur! Au diable le tailleur!' (II, 4)

With Argan it was, in Gutwirth's formula, 'l'amour de soi dans la fécalité' (p 118). For Jourdain it is self-love in ostentation; he wishes to 'show off' both in appearance and in conduct. As Argan needed a pretext to justify this fault — his 'maladie' — so Jourdain finds one in social pretention. Without his conviction that he is basically a *gentilhomme*, Jourdain's longing to draw attention to himself by sumptuous dress and skill in the arts would be mere self-indulgence; but he is already noble in his own mind and must naturally cultivate the attributes of nobility. Refusing to face any fact that would erode his sytem of self-justification, he takes refuge rather in *mauvaise foi*:

> MADAME JOURDAIN
> Descendons-nous tous deux que de bonne bourgeoisie?

> JOURDAIN
> Voilà pas le coup de langue?

> MADAME JOURDAIN
> Et votre père n'était-il pas marchand aussi bien que le mien?

> JOURDAIN
> Peste soit de la femme! Elle n'y a jamais manqué. Si votre père a été marchand, tant pis pour lui; mais pour le mien, ce sont des malavisés qui disent cela. (III, 12)

Any proof of his status is welcome: the escalation of compliments from 'mon gentilhomme' to 'Votre Grandeur' by the tailors at the end of II, the disguised Covielle's assurances in IV, 3 that Jourdain's father was a 'fort honnête gentil-homme.'[23]

This particular form of self-indulgence, however, makes him far less vulnerable than Argan. Those who take advantage of him rule only by pleasure, not by fear. Jourdain lives in a delightful imaginary world for which he is not paying too dearly. The doctors of *Le Malade imaginaire* lose their attributes of death-dealing terror to become in *Le Bourgeois gentilhomme* entertainers, participants in a vast masquerade which fills Jourdain with perpetual wonderment. The spectre of disease is banished, knaves become less knavish — whence the lighter, happier tone of *Le Bourgeois gentilhomme*.

In its most naïve and childlike form, ostentation becomes love of outlandish costume. Clothes make the nobleman, Jourdain seems to think; if he changes his dress often enough perhaps the longed-for transfiguration will occur. He is already sumptuously attired as he appears on stage for the first time,[24] but he undergoes two sartorial metamorphoses in the course of the play, each ritualized and accompanied by music. In the first (II, 5), four tailors ceremoniously remove his initial costume and invest him in the spectacular creation they have fashioned. This scene anticipates the great Turkish ceremony of the fourth *intermède*, where a change of costume symbolizes a change in rank. Jourdain is led on stage dressed '*à la turque*' to become a *mamamouchi*.

It is not enough to look the part of a gentleman. One's conduct, too, must bear the stamp of one's social distinction. So Jourdain sets about to master the abilities that surge up so spontaneously in men of quality. In this School for Gentlemen, a succession of tutors laboriously attempt to inculcate a modicum of proficiency in their pupil; and as with all educational programmes in Molière, this one sinks into ridicule. The masters, first of all, bring derision upon their specialities. Each sees his own art as the be-all and end-all of civilization; as the competition multiplies, the contest among areas falls from the decorous debate between the dancing and music teachers to the snarling dog-fight that embroils the whole teaching staff (II, 3). The tutor who first resorts to blows happens to be the philosophy teacher, who has just finished an eloquent lesson in equanimity and humility; this irony only devalues further the whole group of vain and vindictive profiteers. Each teacher's acrimonious pleas for the exclusivity of his own talent belie the very ideal of balance implicit in the life Jourdain is endeavouring to emulate.

The disciplines themselves tend to appear in a ridiculous light, particularly those of fencing and 'philosophie.' The Maître d'Armes comes across with great comic force as a robot whose jerky phrases ('Une, deux. Remettez-vous. Redoublez de pied ferme. Un saut en arrière') underline his puppet-like gestures (II, 2). Fencing seems the function of a clockwork mechanism; the only time emotion takes over it is to turn the master into a sanguinary bulldog. The philosophy teacher is blind to Jourdain's need for polish, not knowledge. Instead, the learning imparted is tainted with the most sterile and pretentious scholasticism. In such a school, even an intelligent Jourdain could become little better than an insufferable pedant.

That Jourdain's efforts have such insignificant and ludicrous results probably can be explained by the fact that they are efforts. In the well-bred, taste and ability are spontaneous, unlearned; noblemen are born, not made. That Jourdain's labours are proof of his own inferiority is underlined by both Dorante with his natural, self-assured art of living, and Cléonte who, although not a 'gentilhomme,' has the spontaneous distinction that makes him a morally superior man.

Of all the plays studied in this chapter, this farcical entertainment may well be the one in which the courtly ideal of the time emerges most explicitly. Here we find a full expression of an art of living that was repeatedly codified and consistently emulated among the élite: effortless versatility; proficiency in things intellectual, creative, and physical; ease in society, especially with members of the opposite sex – all this integrated into a balanced, harmonious whole where each talent, far from obtruding, appears only in fitting circumstances.

This ideal of *honnêteté*, even if it is apparent mainly by implication, pervades the whole comedy and accounts probably for the exceptionally benign and generous mood of dénouement. Harsh scapegoat rituals like those suffered by that other counterfeit nobleman, Pourceaugnac, would be out of place in a world where high-mindedness and tolerance prevail. The traditional *coups de bâton* are made painless by their function as ritual: ('*Dara, Dara,* / *Baston-nara* ... ' [IV, 5]). Jourdain is tricked only once, when he is made a *mamamouchi* and allows 'le Grand Turc' to marry his daughter. All the other characters, although they mock Jourdain in ironic asides, are careful to safeguard his illusions. Whatever exorcism there is in *Le Bourgeois gentilhomme* has taken place early in the play with the deflation of the teachers in I and II. The chief master, Dorante, has become the master of revels. No witch-like figure like Béline to expel here. The society that assembles to take in the final 'ballet des nations' comprises the largest, happiest, and most thoroughly integrated final tableau of any of Molière's comedies.

This chapter and the preceding one have sought to identify the tension which exists between the dialectical components of comedy. The comic myth presupposes a forward thrust embodied by young lovers to which is opposed another energy principle, that of the 'barbon' who must be 'berné.' In a broader sense this opposition expresses contrasting values. On the one hand a comic norm is always symbolized by the ideal young couple or couples and is almost always articulated in the play. We usually find here a socialized and humanized form of the pleasure principle: it is right for people of breeding to realize legitimate wishes.

The opposition to this norm presents two facets in Molière. In chapter 3 we studied plays in which the humorous society took the form of inimical precepts that constitute a general and diffuse danger to the 'right' world: corruption, bondage, death, or disease. These alien principles are devalued in the course of the play as ridicule is heaped upon their exponents. Trickery and baiting contribute to this process, which concludes characteristically in an exorcism, symbolic or otherwise.

In the plays just studied, the values betraying the comic norm are concentrated in a heavy father. Although he always embodies basic paternal despotism, his moral ambiance is usually much more complex, especially if he, in turn, is dominated by someone else. Molière's great blocking characters are far more than possessive fathers or rivals; they symbolize by their all-pervading influence a whole world to be rejected.

The actual form of the exorcism ritual Molière varied with his customary versatility. In the two *Ecoles*, a full-fledged scapegoat is expelled as a false father. In *Tartuffe* and *Les Femmes savantes*, the parental figures get off more lightly as punishment is heaped upon the knave who has taken unfair advantage of them. With the end of *L'Avare* the humorous society continued to exist in the solitary impotence of Harpagon, who is therefore neither triumphant nor defeated. In the two *comédies-ballets* we have just studied, finally, the father figure becomes part of the new society. As we move to an ever happier atmosphere, the exorcism element seems to recede more and more. The comic fantasy is so firmly entrenched in *Le Bourgeois gentilhomme* that no more victims, however guilty, are required.

The comic action need not be poised as neatly between the two poles of the comic dialectic as it has been up to this point. Either of the energy principles can pull the action toward it. It is possible to imagine a kind of comedy where the pressure of the reality principle seems to cause a partial collapse of the comic norm. The comfortable polarity of comedy slips away. We begin to question the hopeful message of the romantic dénouement, the brave new world of youthful love, happy marriage, and enduring harmony. The scapegoat's moral position appears more sound, he seems to deserve better. To this phase of comedy where moral and literary conventions blur into irony I shall devote the last chapter of this study.

The power of fantasy may be so compelling, on the other hand, that we lose the sense of the real world. We enter a luminous never-never land of romance where reality is so transfigured that it presents no threat. Such is the mood of the plays now to be studied. As *Le Bourgeois gentilhomme* comes the closest of all the heavy father plays to this atmosphere of untrammelled happiness, it furnishes a fitting transition to the following chapter.

5

Romance

The central theme of conflict and adventure imposes on romance what Frye calls 'a sequential and processional form' (p 186). Each exploit constitutes one episode in the hero's life; in the most literarily complete romance, these feats build up to a major conflict or *agon* ('the basis or archetypal theme of romance' [p 192]) which culminates in the exaltation of the hero. When romance is structured around the characteristic motif of the quest, it acquires narrative shape and direction. The hero undergoes a series of preliminary trials before the final ordeal by which he achieves his apotheosis. In this way, the plot, although episodic, acquires a measure of cohesion.

In the French seventeenth century, the novel, especially the 'grand roman,' best illustrates the total form of romance.[1] In *L'Astrée*, the determination of a lover to recapture the affections of his lady furnishes the quest element; manifold events which befall him and others, presented directly or in the form of *récits*, supply the narrative content, which can be spun out indefinitely. The hero or heroes go through 'one adventure after another until' – Frye's amusing point brings d'Urfé to mind – 'the author himself collapses' (*ibid*. 186).

The two settings to which this processional narrative form gives imaginative reality in the seventeenth-century French novel will help us understand other general characteristics of romance. D'Urfé's novel depicts the familiar idealized pastoral world of classical and Renaissance literature. Refined shepherds and shepherdesses pass from one adventure to another; a pattern of separation, disguise, misunderstanding, reconciliation spurs on an often flagging action. As for the heroic novels of Mademoiselle de Scudéry, they are no less sequential and idealized, save that the pastoral convention is generally replaced by the code and trappings of chivalry. *Le Grand Cyrus* and *Clélie* take place in an antiquity depicted as *le temps fort* of courtly distinction.

Idealization, a main component of romance, is reinforced in both cases

– pastoral and heroic – by the technique of distancing. D'Urfé situates his work in fifth-century Forez, the French counterpart of ancient Arcadia, while Mademoiselle de Scudéry takes us back to a time and place of recognized legendary superiority. In a further, and significant, effect of exoticism, both settings are non-Christian. The druids of *L'Astrée* have not yet been converted from a paganism analogous to that underlying the heroic novels. Romantic idealization, after all, suggests a make-believe land where the only moral imperatives are those of the courtly code in its heroic and amorous dimension; the dour strictures of the Christian ethic would function here as a kind of archetypal kill-joy.

In its haunting nostalgia, romance presents a symbolic paradise where man has not yet fallen or become conscious of his fall or the reasons for it. We slip over the harsh realities of man's baseness and corruption to 'some kind of imaginative golden age in time or space' (Frye, *loc. cit.*). D'Urfé shows us a world where love is so refined and exalted, people generally so high-minded, that a benevolent providence seems to preside over it, however painful the lovers' trials may seem. In Mademoiselle de Scudéry, the image of courtly perfection is even more immediate; distinguished, respectful suitors cluster around beautiful, refined ladies in the timeless rites of chivalry.

This remoteness in time and space represents a paradoxical effort to bring the action close to the reader and his view of himself as a member of a courtly élite. The relationship between the seventeenth-century novel and its readership clearly illustrates Frye's observation that 'in every age the ruling social or intellectual class tends to project its ideals in some form of romance' (*loc. cit.*). As the ideal is, by definition, what is not yet realized, the image cannot be contemplated as an unadorned reflection, nor can idealization function in the banal immediacy of contemporary time and place – the locus of imperfection. Thus the élite places its self-image at some distance, so that the reading of a novel can become a celebration of what the courtly society would like itself to be, a ritualistic recapturing of the *temps fort* which the fiction presents.[2]

Although the *mythos* as a whole is obviously best suited to narrative, romance can appear in drama either as a general mood of idealization or as an episode enacted from a particular story. Several segments of *L'Astrée* found their way to the stage in the seventeenth century, and Molière himself apparently drew the inspiration of *Mélicerte* from an episode of *Le Grand Cyrus*. Nor should we forget that the first great theatrical success in seventeenth-century France, *Le Cid*, is based on a major episode of the most memorable Spanish chivalric romance. Even where there is no direct romantic antecedent, as in most classical tragedies, the courtly ethic often obtrudes on the source, whether Roman or Greek. Cinna, a mere political intriguer in Tacitus, becomes in Corneille a medieval knight embarking on a dangerous adventure at the behest of Emilie, a courtly *belle dame sans merci*. Oreste, as Racine presented him to his audience, turns out to be a near-caricature of the passive, self-debasing lover bemoaning his lady's cruelty. Even the 'monstre naissant,' Néron, pays homage to Junie in the best manner of the respectful suitor. Whether in romance or in tragedy, then, the classical world viewed itself through the ideal of *chevalerie*.

Romance appears most forcefully in drama when the sequence enacted happens to be the major adventure, an *agon* which results in the apotheosis of the hero. The dénouement of *Le Cid* presents a transfigured Rodrigue (a metamorphosis underlined by the *nom de guerre* bestowed by the King) who has successfully overcome a series of internal and external obstacles. *Cinna* celebrates not so much its namesake's chivalric ideals as the major event in Auguste's life: his 'dernière victoire' over the base impulses of revenge.

The hero must have an antagonist worthy of his struggle; the more arduous the combat, the more glorious the victory. The enemy may be internalized, as when the two Augustes wrestle at the end of *Cinna*, or he may be presented as a true antagonist, as is the case with the Comte in *Le Cid*. In any event, 'the central form of romance is dialectical; everything is focussed on a conflict between the hero and his enemy, and all the reader's values are bound up with the hero' (Frye 187). We find, then, in romance a polarity strongly suggestive of the comic *mythos*. Indeed, comedy can be easily viewed as a down-to-earth, more socialized form of romance. The young man's determination to marry the girl of his choice constitutes the hero's quest, and the enemy which must be overcome takes the form of the heavy father or his surrogate.

Several criteria permit us, however, to establish a working distinction between comedy and dramatic romance, at least as we find it in Molière. The hero of romance is far more exalted in rank and in character than the usual bland comic hero. He is a prince with a sense of decorum suitable to his station, not a 'fils de maison' from the upper middle class. Impetuous though the romantic hero may be, his behaviour as a lover is marked by restraint, articulateness, and magnificence. For these reasons, the dialectic of romance is more pronounced and more clearly moral than social; since kings and princes touch on the divine, their antagonists must be presented in a demonic light. The struggle between the ardent young man of comedy and his *barbon* deals with only one question: whose norms should dictate society? The laws of probability are suspended but not the laws of nature. The hero in comedy is one of us and subject to our limitations; the miracle which allows him to triumph is not of his making. In romance, however, magic, both black and white, plays havoc with the natural order; superhuman virtue combats superhuman malevolence.

Not only is the moral polarity of romance on an epic scale, but the dramatic weight given to the two conflicting forces is the reverse of comedy. The latter depicts the movement from one society to another, a development fully realized only at the dénouement. The old régime of bondage holds the reins of power until the newly-formed, free society finally wrests them away. The ideal world toward which the play moves is there mainly in anticipation, in the confident expectation that 'blondin' will prevail over 'barbon'. It is true that Molière often gives the comic norm some textual explicitness. In *Tartuffe*, for instance, we infer the presence of a world of innocent social amusement relegated to the periphery of a sombre, joyless region – the stage – which ever threatens to extend its ominous influence. But the ideal may be presented only in a negative way, as an implicit contrast with the ludicrous or threatening actions of the humorous society.

In romance, the idealized society is before our eyes from the outset. Evil, when it exists at all, is well out of sight, as with the usurper Mauregat in *Don Garcie de Navarre*. When the enemy does find his way on stage, he serves only as an episodic, intrusive force like the magician in *Les Amants magnifiques*. So rarefied indeed is the courtly atmosphere in both *Les Amants* and its sister work, *La Princesse d'Elide*, that the enemy is commensurately degraded into an animal – a boar in both cases – which bursts into the picture only to be immediately slain. And, most significantly, the enemy is never a father; the paternal figures tend to be benign or inoffensive. Evil has a more general meaning, as befits a genre closer to cosmic issues than social ones.

In romance, finally, the hero is not the central figure and the sole concern of his beloved, as he tends to be in comedy. In *L'Ecole des femmes*, for instance, Horace has no competition among other eligible young men, nor does Agnès have eyes for any but him. On the other hand, the hero of chivalric romance tends to be but one competitor among many for a lady who makes a special point of showing no preference.

As a natural result, the antithetical force in romance shifts from the father figure toward the rival; the dynamic principle comes from within the idealized society itself, not from a struggle between two opposing units: what interests us are the demands made upon the lovers by the lady, the relative success of the suitors in fulfilling these demands, the ensuing episodes of jealousy, misunderstandings, separations, disguises to preserve reputation or decorum (women disguised as men, for instance) – in a word, the familiar stock-in-trade of the pastoral tradition.

In a court of love presided over by its princess, spectacle is at the very forefront. Heroes vie with each other in providing sumptuous entertainments for their beloved. The world of romantic fantasy, freed from human limitations, can be underlined by the most extraordinary scenic marvels and harmonic thrills. In no other plays by Molière is visual and auditory pleasure achieved at such a high level of artistic sorcery as in *Les Amants magnifiques* and *Psyché*.

Yet, spectacle is more than a matter of verisimilitude or magical ornamentation. By witnessing the same pleasures as those enjoyed by the idealized stage court, the onlooker brings himself closer to that ideal. Thus, spectacle, along with distancing, enables a closer identification between the élite audience and their near-perfect counterparts on stage, so that the celebration of commonly held values can be more intense still. Having penetrated through imagination into this fairyland, we express our exultation quite naturally in song and dance. In Frye's words, 'the more [comedy] rejoices in the free movement of its happy society [ie, the closer it is to romance], the more readily it takes to music and dancing' (*ibid*. 287). Thus the ballet sequences in Molière's romances are natural outgrowths of this sort of pageantry.

The predominance of spectacle can have important consequences for comedy as well. An articulated or structurally implicit vision of the ideal society need not be presented; spectacle is sufficient in itself to provide a positive moral focus for the courtly audience. Songs, dances, sumptuous décors, elegant and tasteful *intermèdes* represent clearly the discriminating milieu on the audience's side of the stage; the actual impersonation of that society is unnecessary. More attention can thus be paid to the antics of blocking characters; their power is basically harmless because of the unspoken presence of a dominant norm of refined entertainment. That is why farce seems in Molière such a natural counterpoint to the most elegant spectacle plays. In this light, the *comédies-ballets*, however strong the exorcism function, can be envisaged, from the standpoint of spectacle, as a species of romance. On the textual level, *L'Amour médecin*, *Monsieur de Pourceaugnac*, *Le Bourgeois gentilhomme*, and *Le Malade imaginaire* are scapegoat plays where satire, tempered to a degree by good-natured farce, points up and chastises humour types; the norm appears fully only with the emergence of the happy society at the end. But the ascendancy of the norm – a feature, we noted, in romance – is symbolized by the spectacle itself. In this sense, even the profoundly problematical *George Dandin* belongs, to an extent, to romance; it was first presented at Versailles with a counterpoint of song, spectacle, and dance.

In the plays we are now to consider, however, the romantic pattern is in the text itself, reinforced or not by spectacle. However diverse, they all have the characteristic elements in common: the traditional dialectic of comedy with its heavy fathers and grotesque rivals has disappeared. The obstacles to the resolution come from within the group of well-born lovers, so that the primary dynamism departs from the familiar *eiron-alazon* contest to dwell on the trials of young love caught up in its own complications. For those who persist in the outmoded position that Molière had no natural penchant for the *romanesque*, or who scorn the devices on which romance is based, these plays will seem contrived and flawed; but those who believe with Bray that Molière 'a eu toute sa vie un faible pour le précieux, le tendre et le romanesque' (p 268), that *la belle comédie* is no less significant than *la grande comedie*, will find in this chapter a rehabilitation of an important and unjustly neglected facet of Molière's art.

LE DÉPIT AMOUREUX

Despite surface resemblances with *L'Etourdi*, *Le Dépit amoureux* differs fundamentally from its buffoon-play predecessor. Mascarille does appear once again, this time as the servant of Valère; and the episodic valet of *L'Etourdi*, Ergaste, surges to the forefront here as Gros-René, the key auxiliary of *Le Dépit amoureux*. What counts in this play, however, is the parallelism between the fortunes of master and mistress, valet and *suivante*, not Gros-René's inventiveness and energy. Nor is the Mascarille of *L'Etourdi* recongizable in *Le Dépit amoureux*. His brilliant improvisations which had furnished the basic dynamism of *L'Etourdi* have turned into thick-headed obtuseness. Mascarille is baited and humiliated during most of the play, tormented by Eraste (I, 4), menaced by his own master (III, 7), slapped by Lucile (III, 9), faced with death by hanging (III, 10), and, as a final consolation, threatened with being broken on the wheel (V, 3). His innate cowardice only heightens the humour of these situations. In short, his bungling, faint-hearted character makes him a second *zanno*, a clear demotion from his status in *L'Etourdi*. While Mascarille does indirectly set the comic imbroglio in motion, he does so by muddleheadedness, not wit.

Le Dépit amoureux is therefore not a buffoon play. Nor does it adhere, for that matter, to the exorcism pattern. Even if the fathers, Albert and Polydore, appear the conventionally old, choleric, fearful, and gullible codgers of traditional comedy, they do not constitute obstacles to their children's designs. Whatever their faults, they are free from the traditional heavy father attributes of self-blindness and unreasoned despotism.

Jouanny hints at the real dramatic centre of the play when he implies that a more appropriate title would have been *La Fille travestie en garçon* (vol. I, p 119). Its actual title is certainly a misnomer; the *dépit amoureux* motif, however delightful, is an episodic elaboration upon the plot, an *hors d'œuvre* linked thematically to the main action but detachable from it (these scenes were very early amalgamated as a separate play).

An extremely complex imbroglio around Ascagne, the girl in man's garb, an imbroglio largely of Molière's invention,[3] forms the main dynamism of the play. Disguise of sex thus provides a high degree of comic potential, as it does in romantic comedy in general.[4] The piquancy of a woman acting a man's role is part and parcel of the comic situation, but occasionally special ironic effects heighten this impression. In II, 2, 'Ascagne' conveys her feelings to Valère who, in her words, 'Aurait, si j'étais fille, un peu trop su me plaire.' The conditional mode functions as a wink of complicity with the audience. With Frosine and ourselves as accomplices, she plays the game against Valère, who continues the banter, but in quite a different spirit: 'Ces protestations ne coûtent pas grand chose, / Alors qu'à leur effet un pareil *si* s'oppose.' This 'simple hors d'œuvre,' this 'curieux témoignage de mauvais goût romanesque,' as Jouanny would have it (note 180), is in fact a legitimate verbal prolongation of the total ironic situation, a way of underlining comically the play of reality and illusion that is at the dynamic centre of a play founded on disguise.

As the complicated action develops, the principals pass from wonderment to anger, to temporary relief, to renewed perplexity as they see their designs thwarted, not by domineering fathers, but by the misunderstandings that surge up in their own midst. One of the main by-products of these confusions is jealousy. As a fundamental dynamism of dramatic romance arises from real or imagined rivalry, unsure lovers are quick to view contentment in another suitor suspiciously, or to detect signs of favour from their beloved to others. Thus, Eraste is early tormented by Valère's smugness and suspects that he has Lucile's affection (I, 1). A tone of taunting repartee obtains when the supposed rivals meet:

ERASTE

Hé bien, seigneur Valère?

VALÈRE

Hé bien, seigneur Eraste?

ERASTE

En quel état l'amour?

VALÈRE

En quel état vos feux? (I, 3)

In the comedies studied in previous chapters, jealousy of this sort had little importance. The young man usually has no rivals among people of his own age and station; the only threat to his love comes from the humorous society, the Arnolphes and the Thomas Diafoirus. As the girl makes clear from the start her repulsion for any rival on that side of the stage, there can be no real cause for jealousy. On the other hand, Eraste's suspicions make perfect sense in terms of both the play's premises and the false appearances which result from the confusion.

In *Le Dépit amoureux*, then, the romantic plot provides its own tensions, suspense, resolutions; no alien world to be exorcized here. The ludicrous pendant Métaphraste could well have returned at the end of the play to remind us that comedy usually banishes representatives of a humorous society; but this character, the only potential scapegoat figure of the play, is not seen or heard after II. As the fathers quickly accept the situation imposed on them, the usual moral dialectic of comedy exists only in a vestigial and ornamental way. The right society is present from the start; if it is not in control, it is because internal divisions and confusions have temporarily fragmented it.

The strong romantic element in *Le Dépit amoureux* has important consequences for the tone of the play. The normal polarity opposing the high-flown romantic banter of the well-born principals and the ludicrous words and antics of the humorous characters tends to break down. Only two scenes draw derisive laughter: one presenting the pedant (II, 6), the other bringing together the fear-stricken fathers (III, 4). Otherwise, a formal, elegant, even studied diction suffuses the play.[5] This stylized repetition, for example:

> Quand tout contribuerait à votre passion:
> Mon père, les destins, mon inclination,
> On me verrait combattre, en ma juste colère,
> Mon inclination, les destins et mon père,   (III, 9)

or these well-wrought maxims:

> Quand l'amour est bien fort, rien ne peut l'arrêter,   (I, 1)
> Un cœur ne pèse rien alors que l'on l'affronte,   (II, 3)
> La douleur trop contrainte aisément se redouble.   (III, 5)

In counterpoint to these pithy generalizations we find a telling use of periodic construction as in Lucile's intricate *tirade* of II, 4 with its convoluted sentence structure and rhetorically emphatic 'dis-je.' The scenes involving the pivotal character of the romantic imbroglio, Ascagne, abound in taut, complicated set-pieces, such as Frosine's *récit* of II, 1. Frosine, moreover, is a *confidente* of Ascagne, not the mere *suivante* of conventional comedy. We are near the level of heroic comedy, and Ascagne is not too far removed from the Princesse d'Elide.

This high level of diction, while not underscored by derisive effects, is emphasized by another sort of tonal polarity. Instead of the typically comic dialectic between norms and derogations of them, we find two contrasting views of the norm. The trio Gros-René-Marinette-Mascarille is not ridiculous; these characters provide an ironic contrast with their masters both in their down-to-earth attitude and in the language they use to convey it. Gros-René cannot understand Eraste's doubts about Lucile: 'Pour moi, je ne sais point tant de philosophie: / Ce que voient mes yeux, franchement je m'y fie' (I, 1). As Eraste goes off full of trepidation to ask Albert for Lucile's hand, Gros-René and Marinette conclude their own marriage plans with dispatch:

MARINETTE
Et nous, que dirons-nous aussi de notre amour?
Tu ne m'en parles point.

GROS-RENÉ
                                Un hymen qu'on souhaite
Entre gens comme nous, est chose bientôt faite:
Je te veux; me veux-tu de même?

MARINETTE
                                Avec plaisir.

GROS-RENÉ
Touche, il suffit.   (I, 2)

Long before the *dépit* scenes with their juxtaposition of two levels of diction, opposing courtship patterns become explicit in the text (Eustis 79-82). The parallelism is broken only at the end of the play when Mascarille refuses to fight with Gros-René over Marinette. Although wifeless at the dénouement, he expects eventually to be well received by Gros-René's future spouse: 'De l'humeur que je sais la chère Marinette, / L'hymen ne ferme pas la porte à la fleurette' (V, 8). While the two well born couples exit into the world of eternal romance, we are left with an amusing vision of real marriage and the promise that it holds of a *ménage à trois*.

Le Dépit amoureux is more than an early concession by Molière to a 'penchant premier' for the *romanesque* (Jouanny, vol. II, p 117). Although he will never again draw this heavily on the romantic stock-in-trade, his next five-act play will take up again the essential themes of *Le Dépit amoureux*. In its stress on jealousy arising from misunderstandings, its use of disguise of sex, its high-flown diction, *Don Garcie de Navarre* both looks back to *Le Dépit amoureux* and points ahead in its heroic tone and chivalric mood to Molière's great courtly entertainments.

DON GARCIE DE NAVARRE

This heroic comedy is structured around Don Garcie's efforts to win Done Elvire. In typical chivalric fashion these efforts take the form of contests, of adventures, through which the hero attempts to make himself worthy of the high goal he has set himself. And contest implies adversary; Don Garcie will have to face the antagonists who, for one reason or another, want to impede his movement toward heroism. Three adventures against three enemies form the narrative frame of *Don Garcie*. The hero must defeat his political adversary, Mauregat, the usurper of Leon who has reduced Done Elvire, a princess of the same state, to a beleaguered exile behind the walls of her last redoubt, Astorgue (where the action takes place); he must triumph over his rival in love, Don Sylve of Castile, who, as a worthy knight, also serves the interests of Done Elvire. Finally, Don Garcie will have to face 'un obstacle plus fort' in Elvire's own words (I, 3), the demon within, jealousy. The major adventure of this quest thus takes place on the battleground of the hero's own self.

As seventeenth-century time conventions in serious drama all but precluded the processional character of romance, the major adventure of *Don Garcie de Navarre* exists in counterpoint with the minor ones, instead of in sequence to them. One subordinate act of prowess has already been accomplished before the play begins: Don Garcie has rescued Elvire from the clutches of the usurper (I, 1). The final battle with Mauregat furnishes an opportunity for the rival lovers to vie with each other, so that the love plot is resolved at the same time as the political one; finally, Don Garcie's struggle against his jealousy is the main, unifying theme of the play, a recurrent element of discussion and enactment from the first scene to the last.

A major consequence of this compression and the importance attached to Don Garcie's weakness is to throw more emphasis upon Done Elvire. The successive military trials of the hero are merely reported; the ordeal to which he submits in order to become a respectful lover takes place repeatedly before us, and his failures make Elvire all the more indignant and demanding. This image of the proud, uncompromising lady in the court of love recalls Emilie with all her high expectations of Cinna in Corneille's great play.

As the thematic material of romance in seventeenth-century France tends away from heroic prowess in itself to a more static picture of the courtly lady reigning over her admirers, the dynamic principle is less the knight himself than the lady. Thus Done Elvire receives with equal consideration Don Sylve, whom she admires, and Don Garcie, whom she loves (I, 1). To justify her refusal to give him definitive reassurance, she alleges maidenly decorum ('chez notre sexe, où l'honneur est puissant, / On ne montre jamais tout ce que l'on ressent' [I, 1]) and

Don Garcie's unreasonable weakness which makes him less than worthy of her esteem.

In all this, Don Garcie finds himself in the complex situation of being loved and not knowing it; he is beset time and again by false appearances which reinforce his doubts and arouse his jealousy in ever greater frenzies. Circumstances seem to conspire against him. His conduct may be unduly suspicious when Don Pèdre brings a note to Done Elvire (I, 3), or when he is given an ambiguous part of a torn missive from his lady (II, 4). But his supreme outburst of jealousy takes place when he sees his beloved in the arms of a *cavalier* (IV, 7). He can hardly be expected to guess that the gentleman in question is actually Ignès in male disguise, one of Elvire's Castilian friends who has sought refuge from Mauregat. He naturally blames fate for the succession of misunderstandings of which he is a victim and uses the only counter-weapon available to a knight who has failed his lady, *le chantage à la mort*: 'Cette épée aussitôt, par un coup favorable, / Va percer, à vos yeux, le cœur d'un misérable' (II, 6). Like Rodrigue he sees no way out of his predicament except to become an epitaph: 'Qu'elle puisse dire, en se voyant vengée: / "C'est par son trop d'amour qu'il m'avait outragée" ' (IV, 9).

While the contest for Elvire is waged for the most part in Don Garcie's heart, he does face one external obstacle during the action of the play. Don Sylve appears in III to throw the support of Castile behind the Leon loyalists in order to win Elvire for himself. Although he has only his lady's esteem, not her *inclination*, he is a rival to be reckoned with. His father had sustained the late King of Leon (presumably against Mauregat) until his death and had given refuge to the legitimate heir (Elvire's brother) after the tyrant's victory. In addition to this advantage of family obligation, Don Sylve has the same chivalric qualities, and to the same degree, as Don Garcie: 'Même éclat de vertus, joint à même naissance,' Done Elvire had already conceded (I, 1).[6] The only chink in the armour of this Castilian warrior (at least according to Elvire's exacting standards) is his ingratitude: he has betrayed his first love, Ignès, in order to woo Elvire (III, 2).

The two heroes are thus presented in a balanced way, each with his strengths and weaknesses. When they meet later in III, their rivalry is expressed in a proud verbal *agon*: 'le sort en notre bras / De tous nos intérêts videra les débats,' concludes Don Sylve (III, 4) as the two prepare to got out to do battle. The expected result, and, superficially, the logical one would be Don Garcie's victory. But the logic of the play is more complex, and, to our surprise, Don Garcie appears to have come out second best. Don Sylve is reported to have won the military contest by defeating Mauregat even before Don Garcie had left the walls. A consequence of this unexpected turn of events is Elvire's more compassionate attitude toward Don Garcie:

Votre sort dans mon âme a fait du changement,
Et par le triste état où sa rigueur vous jette
Ma colère est éteinte, et notre paix est faite.   (V, 3)

Fate has chastened Don Garcie. He has not only been humiliated by Don Sylve, but he expects to lose Elvire to him. For the rightful heir, Don Alphonse, is about to appear to claim his throne, and it is logical that the new king should give Elvire, his sister, to the warrior responsible for his victory.

The point of ritual death for Don Garcie occurs as Don Sylve appears in V, 5 ostensibly to claim his bride. In a persuasive entreaty, Elvire begs him not to force himself upon her and promises to choose 'une sainte retraite' (V, 5) rather than accept another's hand. All she can propose is a stoic renunciation for the three principals. But the situation is quickly righted: we learn that Don Sylve had no part in Mauregat's death, which had come about through a popular uprising. In a more important comic turnabout, Don Sylve announces that he himself is the Don Alphonse so long protected by Don Louis and finally revealed by him. Since he is, of course, Elvire's brother, he opportunely returns to his first love, Doñe Ignès.

Just as brother and sister embrace tenderly, Don Garcie happens upon the scene. The situation is the same as in III, when he had encountered Doñe Elvire embracing the *cavalier* that turned out to be Ignès. As he has no idea of the recent recognition that has made his rival his mistress's brother, he can only assume that the embrace signals a marriage arrangement. True, Elvire had warned him that she might be given to Don Sylve, but what disturbs Garcie is her look of happiness:

De grâce, cachez-moi votre contentement,
Madame, et me laissez mourir dans la croyance
Que le devoir vous fait un peu de violence.   (V, 6)

The stage is set for another jealous outburst, more degrading than all the others. But he overcomes 'Un transport don j'ai peur que je ne sois pas maître':

Oui, vos commandements ont prescrit à mon âme
De souffrir sans éclat le malheur de ma flamme:
Cet ordre sur mon cœur doit être tout-puissant,
Et je prétends mourir en vous obéissant.   (V, 6)

Thus, paradoxically, while thinking he has lost the military contest – to the last line he remains ignorant of the fact that Don Sylve is no more a victor than he – Don Garcie attains heroic status by winning the major adventure.[7] He rises above petty impulses of jealousy to become the perfect knight, a transformation Done Elvire herself confirms:

> De ce transport le soumis mouvement,
> Prince, jette en mon âme un plus doux sentiment.
> Par lui de mes serments je me sens détachée;
> Vos plaintes, vos respects, vos douleurs m'ont touchée. (V, 6)

Such key words as *soumis, plaintes*, and *respects* make clear that Don Garcie now embodies the ideal Done Elvire had so intransigently proposed for him: the respectful lover,

> Qui, plus que la mort même,
> Appréhende toujours d'offenser ce qu'il aime,
> Qui se plaint doucement, et cherche avec respect.
> A pouvoir s'éclaircir de ce qu'il croit suspect. (IV, 8)

Elvire's uncompromising position on jealousy seems to have won out. Early in the play she had criticized her *confidente*, Elise, for being too indulgent about this passion. For the maxim 'Et plus il est jaloux, plus nous devons l'aimer,' Elvire indignantly substituted: 'Et plus l'amour est cher qui lui donne naissance, / Plus on doit ressentir les coups de cette offense' (I, 1). Yet, in a sudden display of tolerance Elvire now relents: 'Jaloux ou non jaloux / Mon roi, sans me gêner, peut me donner à vous' (V, 6). Thus, as Don Garcie renounces jealousy, she accepts it. Like all *questions galantes*, this one seems to end unresolved; the stimulating presentation of contradictory attitudes, not their reconciliation, is the main interest of such themes.

One of the distinguishing traits of romance is its moral polarity. The contest between hero and antagonist opposes one set of values, to which we subscribe, against another, which we abhor. This contrast is particularly pronounced in *Don Garcie*, where the chivalric ideal is constantly celebrated. Heroic epithets set the tone very early: Elvire exalts the 'nobles travaux' of her rival lovers and Elise speaks of Don Garcie as an 'illustre amant' (I, 1). On the same level of diction but at the opposite end of the scale of values, the demonic world is also evoked by epithet: the 'traître Mauregat' and his 'lâche audace' (I, 1) take us far from the world of comic *alazoneia*; he is a chivalric Antichrist who calls forth hatred and indignation. Significantly he and the values he represents are far distant from the heroic world that we see before us. Mauregat and his henchmen throw but their shadow across the brilliant world of knighthood; the high-minded are in control, and Mauregat will be little more than a passing threat. So it is with this *mythos*; the heavy father becomes, in the antagonist of romance, a much more fearsome figure; but at the same time he leaves the stage and the function of direct, immediate menace, and becomes merely a remote foil for the values celebrated on stage and in the audience.

Mauregat is not the only villain of the piece, perhaps not even the most important one. Don Garcie's chief ordeal will be to master the demon within him. His jealousy is described both by himself and Elvire as a distinct, diabolical presence: 'ce monstre affreux / Qui de son noir venin empoisonne vos feux' (I, 3). This imagery of *dédoublement* and possession recurs time and again to stigmatize Don Garcie's weakness.[8]

The more imperious the hero's foible, the more it will affect his whole image. As Don Garcie falls prey repeatedly to his jealous instincts, the aura of heroic exaltation around him tends to erode. As a means of preserving the proper status of the protagonist, heroic drama sometimes externalizes evil impulses into an evil genius. Néron has his Narcisse, Phèdre her Œnone. So Don Garcie has his Don Lope, the cynical, self-seeking courtier who encourages him to drink of the poisoned cup of jealousy:

> Quand je puis venir, enflé d'une nouvelle,
> Donner à son repos une atteinte mortelle,
> C'est lors que plus il m'aime, et je vois sa raison
> D'une audience avide avaler ce poison.   (II, 1)

This insidious threat to Don Garcie's heroic image comes to an end, however, by IV when it is reported that he has banished Don Lope from his midst (IV, 1).

Inasmuch as the play concerns Don Garcie's conquest of jealousy, the internal antagonist and its outward manifestation are the most significant expression of anti-heroism. But as the plot also involves a political thread – the victory of legitimacy over usurpation – another good-evil antinomy runs in counterpoint to the first. The struggle between Mauregat and his adversaries has a geographical dimension: Astorgue, where the action takes place, is seen as an island of heroism surrounded by tyranny. The neighbouring states of Castile and Navarre have been instrumental in preserving this last redoubt of legitimacy and will play an important role in obtaining its final victory. The political polarity lies between the evil machinations of the tyrant and the rightful intrigues of the good genius of the play, Don Louis, an off-stage presence like Mauregat. His reassuring spirit hovers over *Don Garcie de Navarre* not unlike Charlemagne's over *La Chanson de Roland*. Early in the play we learn that this 'généreux vieillard' has been subverting Leon and raising a Castilian army to restore the legitimate monarch to the throne (I, 2). We are reminded in III, 2 that he is the preserver and protector of the young prince destined to replace Mauregat. Finally, at the dénouement, the image of Don Louis attains a kind of apotheosis: his strategic skill is largely responsible for the final victory over Mauregat (V, 5) and, above all, he has the key to the happy ending, the knowledge of Don Sylve's identity as the new monarch of Leon. This god figure, all-powerful, all-wise, stands in forceful antithesis to the evil and unfounded pretentions of Mauregat.

In its political aspect, *Don Garcie de Navarre* very much resembles the Elizabethan 'history play': the celebration of the continuity of the state and its values, or the presentation of 'an incident in the undying life of a society that meets good and evil fortunes on countless occasions but never concludes its quest' (Langer 334).[9] To make this ritual properly dramatic the state is shown as threatened, then triumphant. This species of romance comes close, then, to the ternary rhythm of comedy. A world of political legitimacy, heroic grandeur, and courtly love comes to an end with the death of the 'feu roi' of Leon. After a threatening period of usurpation and baseness, the destiny of the legitimate régime, personified by Don Louis, is restored in the guise of a young king; all is well, the brief perturbation fades into the past, a rejuvenated state reaffirms its rightness.

Romance in *Don Garcie de Navarre*, then, does more than legitimize the general values of the aristocratic spectators, their ideal of entertainment. It celebrates the divine rightness of that society's political organization. Consequently, the tone is high-serious; the destiny of a people symbolized by their leader is at issue, not the private frolics of the high-born. Just as *Le Dépit amoureux* pointed back to pastoral-type comedy, so *Don Garcie* exemplifies a long tradition of tragi-comedy; a love plot is tied to momentous political issues, so that the happy ending for the lovers confirms at the same time the foundations of a régime. Much of the negative commentary on this play can be attributed to a tenacious resistance on the part of critics to these basic generic conventions. Scholars seem bent either on stripping *Don Garcie de Navarre* of its heroic dimension – Done Elvire is 'une précieuse ... de la pire espèce' (Adam 272), 'silly,' 'ridiculous' in Hubert (pp 39-40); or, if they take the play seriously, they conclude that Molière was on the wrong track when he composed it (Gutwirth 72). Why may not Molière speak dramatically in any other voice but the comic? Few critics consider Racine's delightful farce *Les Plaideurs* as a false step on the way to *Phèdre*.

In the remaining plays of this chapter, the *temps fort* of romance recedes to its ultimate remove in time and place from reality. *Le Dépit amoureux* took place in the undetermined and presumably contemporary time of comedy; although its Italian setting introduced an element of exoticism, the effect of remoteness is slight, for we are still in the familiar world of *L'Etourdi* and *Les Fourberies de Scapin*. With *Don Garcie de Navarre*, we moved further back to the glorious and legendary era of Spanish chivalry. In *Les Amants magnifiques* we find ourselves in the distant and idealized Greece which had furnished the background for the aristocratic gambols in the novels of the time.

All the plays now to be studied remove the Court, moreover, from its palace-centred existence to a make-believe land of bucolic bliss. Hence, we are not surprised at the rather prominent pastoral element in them. Indeed, Molière wrote two pastoral plays, both for the *Ballet des muses* of 1666-7 where the playwright's task was to honour Thalia, the muse of comedy and the idyll. The second of these, the *Pastorale comique*, survives in such fragmentary form that it would be unwise to hazard any general remarks about its structure. *Mélicerte*, although still incomplete, lends itself better to archetypal scrutiny. Not only does it comprise two fully developed acts in verse, but our knowledge of its source, an episode in *Le Grand Cyrus* by Mademoiselle de Scudéry where a young shepherd and a young shepherdess, both in love, discover that they are high born, entitles us to make some comments on its curious archetypal features. The relationships in the court of love are reversed. The centre of amorous attention is a young shepherd, Myrtil, courted by two shepherdesses, Daphné and Eroxène, but in love with still another shepherdess, Mélicerte. In counterpoint with this high sylvan lyricism runs a somewhat buffoonish minor theme in the person of Myrtil's presumed father, Lycarsis. In both acts he plays the role of paternal tyrant, a function quite exceptional for the romantic genre. But the spectre of the heavy father quickly evaporates, and the mood of romance is further enhanced, as the unfinished play breaks off, by a vague prescience of a recognition that will place both Mélicerte and Myrtil among the high born.

In this movement from the pastoral to the heroic world, from the love trials of shepherds and shepherdesses to the high-flown amusements of noblemen at play, *Mélicerte* is strikingly unique. The pastoral world is usually set in counterpoint to the heroic world and distinct from it. Such is the case in the two *comédies-ballets* which will now be studied, plays so similar in their archetypal structure that it would be repetitive to examine them in separate essays.

LA PRINCESSE D'ELIDE AND LES AMANTS MAGNIFIQUES

Both works centre on a lady surrounded by a group of admirers who compete for pre-eminence. The Princesse d'Elide is besieged by a 'foule d'amants' (I, 1) represented on stage by three renowned Greek princes, Euryale, Aristomène, and Théocle. Similarly, Eriphile, the heroine of *Les Amants magnifiques*, is courted by three suitors; Iphicrate and Timoclès plead their cause openly and eloquently, while Sostrate, cowed by his comparatively low rank, is the brave, sincere, and respectful soldier who will finally be the victor in love.

The hero's quest thus pits him, not against an obstacle figure, but against some impediment within the love plot. Significantly, the parental figures in both *La Princesse d'Elide* and *Les Amants magnifiques* are paragons of tolerance and indulgence. Iphitas, the Princess's father, assures the girl that he does not intend to 'faire violence à tes sentiments, et me servir tyranniquement de la puissance que le Ciel me donne sur toi' (II, 4). The contrast between this profession of good fatherhood and the precepts of the normal blocking figures is so evident as to appear intentional. In *Les Amants magnifiques*, Eriphile's mother, Aristione, is even more emphatic in declaring to the rival lovers: 'Je me suis engagée à laisser le choix tout entier à l'inclination de ma fille' (I, 2). She is, as she herself says 'une bonne mère' (IV, 1), the archetypal good parent. In comedy this figure appears only at the end to right a disastrous situation; in romance he symbolizes during the whole action the secure reign of magnanimity and indulgence.

The dramatic interest of the play must arise from within the court of love itself. Euryale, who quickly emerges as the hero of *La Princesse d'Elide*, sets himself the formidable task of winning the love of a lady whose vehement contempt for love and marriage is only too often reiterated. Her arguments and her tone of voice anticipate strangely *Les Femmes savantes*: 'Ne devez-vous pas rougir,' she scolds her cousin, Aglante, 'd'appuyer une passion qui n'est qu'erreur, que faiblesse et qu'emportement, et dont tous les désordres ont tant de répugnance avec la gloire de notre sexe? J'en prétends soutenir l'honneur jusqu'au dernier moment de ma vie, et ne veux point du tout me commetre à ces gens qui font les esclaves auprès de nous, pour devenir un jour nos tyrans' (II, 1).

Since a head-on assault on this citadel of feminine pride would be no more successful than the contest of *galanterie* in which he is already participating, Euryale resorts to dissimulation. The device that furnishes the title for the Spanish source of this play – *El Desdén con el desdén* – becomes the dynamic principle of the action. Euryale's ploy of pretending to scorn the princess succeeds, as her curiosity and hurt crystallize into love. A last resurgence of pride and decorum prevents her from openly avowing her passion at the end of the play, but a triple wedding is clearly in the offing: the defeated suitors will console themselves with Aglante and Cynthie, two ladies of the Court.

Sostrate, the hero of *Les Amants magnifiques*, has a harder lot. His chief obstacle, as he says, lies in 'la bassesse de ma fortune.' When to this problem are added two others: 'la concurrence de deux princes' and 'le respect inviolable' that he owes his beloved (I, 1), his quest does appear doomed to failure. But in his very despair he is the perfect lover. Incapable of Euryale's shamming, he embodies the respect, sincerity, passivity, and deference that Elvire had demanded of Don Garcie. The courtly ethic as it concerns the suitor presents an inherent paradox. Too much aggressiveness takes him beyond the limits of proper respect and subservience, while no action at all leads to complete passivity and loss of dramatic momentum. Hence, some initiative must often come from the lady's side. Fortunately, Eriphile loves Sostrate and attempts to force him out of his timidity without encouraging him to disrespect or betraying her own sense of decorum (III, 1). And when she believes she is to be married off to another, she herself declares her love to Sostrate (IV, 4), who proclaims jubilantly: 'Je m'en vais mourir après cela le plus content et le plus glorieux de tous les hommes.' A better fate awaits him, however. A timely feat of heroism convinces Eriphile's mother that her daughter's *inclination* is well placed, and Eriphile, encouraged by her mother's blessing, gives her hand to a bewildered Sostrate. Yet, the final mood of *Les Amants magnifiques* is less happy and accommodating than that of *La Princesse d'Elide*. Instead of being rewarded with other ladies of the Court, the unsuccessful lovers are left frustrated and resentful: 'Peut-être Madame, qu'on ne goûtera pas longtemps la joie du mépris que l'on fait de nous.' But a hint of reconciliation is present as the entire group goes off to witness 'la fête des jeux pythiens' (V, 4).

The romantic plot, impelled forward by parental benediction, forms the locus of interest in both romances. This rarefied atmosphere of distinction and harmony almost reaches the cloying stage: 'une sorte de perfection sucrée,' in Jouanny's words; 'tout s'y déroule pour le mieux dans le meilleur des mondes' (vol. II, p 377). The alien world, the antithesis of courtly elegance, is represented only in a degraded, vestigial way by the sudden and momentary intrusion of wild boars. These beasts, while they do not appear on stage, are emblematic of the ugliness, violence, and savagery which stand in unspoken contrast to the beauty, cultivation, and civility which imbue the plot.

They also serve to emphasize another sort of polarity in each play, the easy heroism of the hunters who dispose so effortlessly of these terrifying beasts, and the down-to-earth world of the jesters, Moron in *La Princesse* and Clitidas in *Les Amants*. Each recoils in fear before the wild intruder: 'Où pourrai-je éviter ce sanglier redoutable?' exclaims Moron (I, 2) as he takes refuge from the off-stage hunt. He escapes this threat only to confront in the second *intermède* a bear who actually comes on stage. The jester's horrified reaction to this unexpected guest, before it is killed by hunters, is in the best tradition of the cowardly valet. Clitidas narrates a similar experience with the 'fort vilain animal' (V, 1) of *Les Amants*. He is able to tell only part of the story to Eriphile 'car un peu de poltronnerie m'a empêché de voir tout le détail de ce combat.'

Such mirth-provoking elements are not out of place in romance. Fools and jesters may play their role in the archetypal structure of the genre by being 'licensed to show fear or make realistic comments' (Frye 197). We have already seen striking examples of this first privilege. Both Moron and Clitidas are court jesters whose wisdom under cover of wit is much appreciated. As Euryale says of Clitidas: 'Malgré l'emploi qu'il exerce aujourd'hui, / Il a plus de bon sens que tel qui rit de lui' (I, 1). Both characters disguise their intelligence in teasing banter as they reason with their respective mistresses. As they serve the love interest, moreover, they join the function of the comic auxiliary in other plays. In *La Princesse*, Moron carefully nurtures the heroine's budding love (III, 3) and urges Euryale to play his role to the end no matter how painful; it is he as well who makes the Princess face up to her new passion: 'dans toutes vos actions il est aisé de voir que vous aimez un peu ce jeune prince' (IV, 5). Her rage at Moron's impudence is only a face-saving gesture; a monologue in the next scene makes it clear that Moron's remark has begun its work: 'De quelle émotion inconnue sens-je mon cœur atteint? ... n'aimerais-je point ce jeune prince?' (IV, 6). In like manner, Clitidas in *Les Amants* forces Sostrate to admit his passion for Eriphile in the very first scene, and in the next act he cleverly draws out her love for him (II, 2).

These two jesters provide, then, comic relief to the high-flown talk and distinguished conduct of the principals, while furthering at the same time their love interests. Although Moron has a far more copious role than Clitidas – he appears in nearly all the *intermèdes*, where he endeavours to win the shepherdess, Philis – the two have nearly identical functions.

With minor differences in emphasis both plays are built on essentially the same premises: the court of love with its disdainful lady, its circle of suitors, magnanimous parental figures, aristocratic games, cowardly but witty jesters, and the short-lived, symbolic intrusion of the demonic in the grotesque form of wild animals. Two features set the two plays apart, however: the role and nature of the *intermèdes*, and the presence, in the main plot of *Les Amants magnifiques*, of Anaxarque, the astrologer.

It may be, as Jouanny suggests (vol. II, p 379), that Molière wished to give voice to the general skepticism felt in his time about astrology and its practitioners. But Anaxarque's role goes beyond purely historical considerations, and he obviously brings about in *Les Amants* the same kind of polarity that we noted in *Don Garcie de Navarre*. Instead of a contrast between legitimacy and usurpation we find here an apostle of black magic, spurious knowledge, and diabolical machinations who stands in moral contrast with the exalted courtly values of romance. He plays the rival lovers, Iphicrate and Timoclès, one against the other and accepts presents from both. More importantly, he perverts the role of spectacle by contriving to have Vénus appear *dans une machine* (IV, 1) in order to trick Eriphile's mother into giving her daughter's hand to the suitor whose interests he is serving. Instead of allowing Aristione to marvel at how well artifice suggests reality (as she does with the other spectacles offered her), he wishes to pass it off *as* reality. Illusion has become deceit.

It is fitting, then, that Anaxarque should suffer the scapegoat's fate, although in a vague and distant way more suited to romance. We are told that the two deceived lovers have set upon the astrologer inflicting 'quelques blessures dont on ne sait pas bien ce qui arrivera' (V, 3). We are too close to comedy for death to be seemly in it, while the demonic aspect of Anaxarque's personality deserves more than humiliation or some *coups de bâton*. The ambiguity of his fate thus preserves the mood of the play.

However much the world evoked in *La Princesse d'Elide* and *Les Amants magnifiques* bears a heroic stamp, we are in another phase of chivalry compared to the war-like atmosphere of *Don Garcie*. Sostrate's conquest of the Gallic invaders of Greece is far behind in time (I, 1). The protagonists have won the right to relax, to enjoy other activities more suitable to the mood of 'désœuvrement azuré' (Gutwirth 73) which highlights both works. *La Princesse* begins and ends with a eulogy of love and amorous pursuits, while an atmosphere of *galanterie* dominates in both. Each takes place, as well, against a backdrop of play. The hunt, an aristocratic relaxation *par excellence*, is accompanied by more organized and ceremonial games. Iphitas, the Princess's father, has convened the finest flower of Greek youth to participate in 'jeux renommés' (I, 1) in the hopes that his disdainful daughter might find a suitable husband. *Les Amants magnifiques* builds up to the concluding sixth *intermède* 'qui est la solennité des jeux pythiens.' Here, sporting activities take the stylized form of ballet sequences and occur before us instead of off-stage as in *La Princesse*.

The main form of relaxation, however, is spectacle, dazzling entertainment for eyes and ears. Both plays emphasize *divertissement* for ourselves in the audience and our heroic and idealized counterparts on stage. The identification between the two audiences, however, is far less marked in *La Princesse*. Only two interludes occur before stage spectators;[10] the others take place as separate entertainments for us, although linked to the main action through the character of Moron. They form, essentially, a pastoral play in small segments set in counterpoint to the exalted main action. Expectedly, the jester intrudes a buffoonish and parodic tone into the pastoral fiction:

Bois, prés, fontaines, fleurs, qui voyez mon teint blême,
Si vous ne le savez, je vous apprends que j'aime.

Philis est l'objet charmant
Qui tient mon cœur à l'attache;
Et je devins son amant
La voyant traire une vache.
Ses doigts tout pleins de lait, et plus blancs mille fois,
Pressaient les bouts du pis d'une grâce admirable.   (*intermède* II, 1)

After the lyrical invocation, the jarring allusion to rustic reality sets the tone for all the scenes with Moron (who eventually loses his beloved to his rival, Tyrcis). The pastoral world is presented in a middle status, stylized enough to retain the lyrical overtones of antiquity despite an occasional effect of comic contrast, and idealized enough to make the realities of shepherding distant and grotesque; yet its inhabitants are well below the noble protagonists of the main plot. They become rather their entertainers; Moron is already the court jester, and the final pastoral provides the Princess and her group with a beautiful song.

Les Amants magnifiques is the apotheosis of spectacle. All the *intermèdes* take place before the stage audience and are contrived for them. The pretext for this lavish display was provided by Louis XIV himself who set the theme for the play: 'deux princes rivaux, qui ... régalent à l'envi une jeune princesse et sa mère de toutes les galanteries dont ils se peuvent aviser' (*avant-propos*). Chivalric competition moves from the battleground to the athletic field and finally to the stage where the chief spectator in the audience, Louis XIV, found his idealized extension: the play begins and ends with a sumptuous interlude glorifying the King first as Neptune and then, with twofold appropriateness, as Apollo (the Dieu Soleil of the Pythian games). With the exception of the third, the middle interludes are simpler, consisting of mime and dancing. But the third *intermède* is a veritable play-within-a-play, or rather '*une petite comédie en musique*' which, after a prologue by 'la nymphe de Tempé,' becomes a pastoral. The buffoonish element remains in the conventional guise of two satyrs who, rejected by their ladies, take consolation in a drinking song. We find as well the conventional themes and lyricism of this bucolic setting: the pangs of unrequited love, the harshness of cruel shepherdesses, and their final generosity in accepting the affection of their respectful suitors. After a *dépit amoureux* scene, all the actors intone the usual hymn to love and pleasure:

En aimant, tout nous plaît dans la vie;
Deux cœurs unis de leur sort sont contents;
Cette ardeur, de plaisirs suivie,
De tous nos jours fait d'éternels printemps:
Jouissons, jouissons des plaisirs innocents
Dont les feux de l'amour savent charmer nos sens.   (*intermède* III, 5)

Les Amants magnifiques is the romantic counterpart of *Le Bourgeois gentil-homme*, an exalted hymn to love and spectacle with the romantic playworld of ancient Greece replacing the farcical antics of Monsieur Jourdain in his native Paris.[11] Romance can take only one higher form after this lavish self-glorification: when our alter egos on stage become the gods themselves.

PSYCHÉ

The answer to the rather otiose question of *Psyché*'s authorship depends on the critic's perspective. For the purposes of the archetypal approach, concerned as it is with the total design of the work, the relationships among the characters, the broader plot conventions that inform it, the most significant portion of the work belongs to Molière who, in the words of 'le libraire au lecteur' 'a dressé le plan de la pièce, et réglé la disposition.'

At first glance the social setting of *Psyché* resembles that of the two comedies just studied. A girl, high born and beautiful, but filled with disdain for men ('cette humeur farouche,' as Psyché herself labels it [III, 3]), is persistently wooed by countless suitors. This 'foule d'amants' (I, 1, IV, 1) – cf. *La Princesse d'Elide* – are represented on stage, once again, by two respectful lovers, Cléomène and Agénor. Like the Iphicrate and Timoclès of *Les Amants magnifiques*, they do not allow their rivalry to destroy their enduring friendship. We note also a good-father figure in 'le roi,' admirably devoted to his daughter's welfare.

An atmosphere of relaxed amusement reigns as well. The serious business of war is well in the background – there is only a passing allusion to the combat that welded the two suitors together (I, 3). Hunting is again a chief pastime (I, 1). But a world of difference exists between *Psyché* and the romances just studied. A sustained, hyperbolic tone suggests that we are in a more grandiose realm. Psyché has put 'tant de cœurs près du trépas' (I, 3), her 'éclat' has spread 'jusqu'aux deux bouts de monde' (II, 3). Indeed her charms have drawn Venus's own son into her orbit of admiring suitors.

Until now the hero of romance has been depicted in what Frye calls the 'high mimetic mode': he is 'superior in degree to other men but not to his natural environment' (pp 33-4). Idealized as he is in his moral qualities and heroic prowess, he cannot suspend the normal laws of nature. There are two directions away from this central position which Frye considers characteristic of the epic, and which, by its moral polarity, tends to overlap with romance. In the 'low mimetic mode' we find the hero of ordinary comedy who is 'one of us: we respond to a sense of his common humanity' (p 34). Although Molière's typical lovers are idealized in terms of physical attributes and courtship techniques, they are still youthful projections of ourselves, human in their bumbling impetuousness and impulsiveness.

In *Psyché*, however, we transcend Molière's typical world of romance with its exponents of valour in war, prowess in games, and courtly respect in love. With Amour's passion for Psyché the supernatural takes over, and the natural order breaks down in the face of the gods' whims. The courtly premises quickly dissolve and are to be replaced by a cosmic struggle between capricious, all-powerful forces which metamorphose the scene. Gone is the stable bucolic world of the preceding romances, projected briefly into *Psyché* with the 'lieu champêtre' of the Prologue. The scene changes at will, palaces fade into rocky landscapes, splendid edifices are replaced by the terrifying flames of the under-world. Metamorphosis is no matter here, as it was in *Les Amants magnifiques*, of stage magic to entertain a bemused court. The spectacle that was captivating but comfortable illusion for the on-stage audience is now make-believe only for us, the real spectators. Psyché and her companions witness a bewildering array of worlds in movement and experience the full gamut of reactions from rapt delight to abject dread. The sumptuous settings, spectacular machines, and magic-like scene changes no longer provide a reassuring play-within-a-play for the partici-pants. This shifting and blending of images is their *reality*; hence the more serious tone, the more pronounced emotional contrasts of *Psyché*. The first interlude, for instance, takes place in a funereal atmosphere with dirge-like songs, and the fourth depicts 'les Enfers' where nearly the whole of the last act is set with its mood of death and eternal grieving. Jocularity is non-existent. Although Zéphire, Amour's servant, reminds us distantly of Moron and Clitidas and anticipates the Mercure of *Amphitryon*, only in III, 1, the last segment actually written out by Molière, does he have a real speaking role, and then only to convey discreet, smiling irony in place of the farcical antics of his predeces-sors. His comment on Vénus's jealousy is a good example of this elegant humour, so similar to that of *Amphitryon*:

> Bien que les disputes des ans
> Ne doivent point régner parmi les Immortelles,
> Votre mère Vénus est de l'humeur des belles,
> Que n'aiment point de grands enfants.

Such moments of gentle irony disappear completely in Corneille's uniformly serious tone.

Amour, then, is the master-magician of the play, the *demiourgos* who con-jures up dazzling worlds out of nothing. His chief advantage in being able to interfere with the natural order is that he can set his own rules for the game of love. He does not have to compete on the same footing with mortal suitors, whence his cruelly cavalier stratagem of the false prophecy in order to have

Psyché for himself. In a bit of dramatic irony which looks forward to *Amphi-tryon*, Amour admits that the whole device was divine whim. Disguised as an unnamed prince, he tells Psyché:

> C'est l'Amour qui, pour voir mes feux récompensés,
> Lui-même a dicté cet oracle
> Par qui vous beaux jours menacés
> D'une foule d'amants se sont débarrassés,
> Et qui m'a délivré de l'éternel obstacle
> De tant de soupirs empressés. (III, 3)

Amour's divine charm brings about an important change in tone. The previous heroines, Elvire, the Princesse, and Eriphile, have an imperious sense of feminine *bienséance*. Their maidenly pride forces them to keep even favoured lovers at a distance. In *Psyché*, however, the compelling attraction of a godlike lover breaks down this reserve and replaces it with a subtle sensuality. Mesmerized by the sight of her abductor Psyché murmurs with innocent abandon:

> A peine je vous vois, que mes frayeurs cessées
> Laissent évanouir l'image du trépas,
> Et que je sens couler dans mes veines glacées
> Un je ne sais quel feu que je ne connais pas.
> J'ai senti de l'estime et de la complaisance,
> De l'amitié, de la reconnaissance;
> De la compassion les chagrins innocents
> M'en ont fait sentir la puissance;
> Mais je n'ai point encor senti ce que je sens. (III, 3)

As John Lapp puts it, 'Cupid plays the magician's role, not only building lavish palaces at will but constructing in Psyché emotions she had never known' ('Corneille's *Psyché* and the Metamorphosis of Love' *French Studies* 26 [October 1972] 400.)[12]

Amour has no obstacles before him. Psyché has succumbed to his charms, he has the power to give her, and obtain from her, the ultimate in happiness. His only concern is to possess Psyché in his own right, not out of dutiful deference to a god: 'Je ne vous veux, Psyché, devoir qu'à mon amour' (III; 3). That is the simple human weakness – vanity – by which Molière explains the mysterious strictures of the original legend. Psyché should trust her lover without trying to ascertain his identity, and when she forces the issue she prevents him from wooing her as he would – whence her punishment.

In the previous romances we have studied, the obstacle through which the story is developed lies in the society of the lovers. Even in *Le Dépit amoureux*, the principle of the imbroglio can be traced to Dorothée-Ascagne, her mysterious background and secret marriage. With *Psyché*, however, such impediments early disappear by reason of the play's very premises: the heroine yields immediately to an all-powerful lover who imposes only one condition upon her, a condition which does not stand in the way of the consummation of their love. As the dramatic movement must then come from the outside Molière retains the elements of the comic myth present in this original legend, where two external obstacles impede permanent happiness: Vénus, Amour's implacable mother, who thus becomes a heavy father figure in the play;[13] and the two envious sisters who function as scapegoat characters.

The Prologue, written by Molière, tells of Vénus's grievance against Psyché – whose beauty has made men forget the Goddess of Love herself – and her plans for revenge. Her son, Amour, is under orders to infect Psyché with his most poisonous arrow: 'Du plus bas, du plus vil, du plus affreux mortel / Fais que jusqu'à la rage elle soit enflammée.' But by a twist of fate it is Amour himself who is love-struck as he seeks to fulfil his mission. Although angered from the outset at this turn of events, Vénus does not return in person until the end of the fourth act. Molière, closely following Apuleius, brings in the other principle of opposition at this point. Psyché's two sisters, Aglaure and Cidippe, have been set from the start in moral opposition to Psyché, whose innocent love and solicitude for them only underscores more sharply her perfection, their perfidy. But this effect of contrast becomes a functional element in IV. In the interval between the preceding act and this one they have witnessed their sister's blissful existence in the 'bienheureux séjour' Amour has provided for her. Envious, they prod Psyché about the identity of her lover, hold up the spectre of flightiness and infidelity on his part, until the alarmed Psyché disobeys Amour's stricture. This betrayal of confidence causes her lover to disappear and her happy world to evaporate before her eyes. The change of scene is emblematic of her fall from grace: she finds herself in an ominous '*vaste campagne*' (IV, 3) which metamorphoses at the next *intermède* into Hell.

A downturn so strongly marked visually and verbally is bound to make the point of ritual death especially poignant. In a vague and foreshortened version of the ordeals imposed on Psyché in the legend, Vénus sends the girl into Hell to fetch her a box from Proserpine, which, upon being opened, causes Psyché to fall into a death-like faint. In the meantime Amour returns to her, thinking her punished enough for her distrust. But Vénus will not lift her spell. The ensuing stalemate between mother and son necessitates Jupiter's intervention. Arriving in the suitably spectacular manner of a celestial good father, '*en l'air sur son aigle*'

(V, 5), he sets the situation right. By executive fiat he makes Psyché immortal, thereby cancelling out Vénus's last objection that a marriage between her son and a 'misérable mortelle' degrades her. So the same divine powers that sowed confusion and dissension bring 'order out of the apparent chaos of metamorphosis' (Lapp 396), and by the same easy expedient of the gods: by decreeing that it be so. 'Jupiter vous fait grâce, et ma colère cesse. / Vivez, Vénus l'ordonne; aimez, elle y consent,' proclaims the Goddess of Love as she revives Psyché for eternity (V, last scene).

Until now Molière has followed the original rather closely. His chief departure from his model, interestingly enough, concerns the sisters. According to Apuleius, they are already married at the outset (a fact which makes their perfidy more gratuitous) and undergo no punishment as a result of their pettiness and wrongdoing. Following through, perhaps, the comfortable and schematic polarity of the beginning, and wanting to tie up loose ends as seventeenth-century French dramaturgy dictated, Molière has the two sisters taken straight to Hell for their evil acts. As Psyché is told:

> Vos envieuses sœurs ...
> Pour vous perdre se sont perdues;
> Et l'une et l'autre tour à tour,
> Pour le prix d'un conseil qui leur coûte la vie,
> A côté d'Ixion, à côté de Titye,
> Souffre tantôt la roue, et tantôt le vautour. (III, 2)

This allusion to two exemplary and horrible punishments accorded to the great sinners of Hades puts an epic dimension to the girls' wrongdoing, a fitting demonic contrast with the heavenly apotheosis just described.

Psyché began in the realm where all the other romances of this chapter took place in their entirety – the human world of ladies and lovers. But we were quickly removed to the marvellous and terrifying domain of the supernatural where scenes are conjured up and dissolved at the whim of a god-magician. Spectacle has left the ropes and pulleys of human contrivance to reach its ultimate glorification where divine beings are stage managers. The *mythos* of romance reaches therefore its highest expression in *Psyché*. After the humble comic setting of *Le Dépit amoureux*, after the heroic but mortal world of Don Garcie's Spain, after the playland of Greek antiquity, we find ourselves at the ultimate remove from reality and thus at the ultimate idealization. The élite of Louis' time could go no further in self-flattery, in its exalted stage image of itself. Like Psyché, the Court has become immortal.

6

Irony: Beyond the Comic Myth

The final chapter of this study will be devoted to that small group of comedies by Molière which do not embody the comic myth. They represent the extreme of reality, or 'irony' in Frye's system, just as the works analyzed under the rubric 'Romance' deal with the extreme of fantasy and idealization. Molière's usual way of developing comedy, we recall, implies a balance between the two poles of the comic dialectic, desire and repugnance; we witness a tension between two forces, the self-affirmation of the lovers and the contrariness of the obstacle figure, before the plot is finally resolved. That balance, however, can be tipped in two ways: the wish-fulfilment function of the romantic plot can all but squeeze out the realities that comedy is meant to exorcize, so that the desirable society is in control throughout the action instead of triumphing only at the end; this is the world of romance. But the reality principle, too, can dominate to the point that the comforting idealizing process of the comic fantasy becomes inoperative. We are left only with what is, and instead of euphoria we feel anxiety and repugnance.

The nightmare component of Molière's typical comedies, before it is banished in favour of the happy ending, is the society in ritual bondage to the blocking character. In the works we shall now study this image of a fettered and foredoomed humanity becomes a dominant and final one. Eternal bliss fades into unending slavery, a spirit of vindictiveness replaces the forgiving and tolerant mood of normal comedy. *George Dandin* comes immediately to mind: there is no exit into fantasy for the mismatched couple, a kind of original sin is being punished in a psychological hell with no promise of a comic redeemer.

That the end of *George Dandin* seems a bitter comment on the fairy-tale formula of comedy: 'they lived happily ever after,' suggests another dominant trait of the plays we are about to analyse: parody. The theme on which *Le Mariage forcé* is based – 'future husband flees girl, father insists on wedding' –

must be seen as a sardonic inversion of the comic *mythos*: 'le blondin berne le barbon.' The fact that the comic myth has been so treated is a comment in itself on the assumptions implicit in the myth. Each of these 'ironic' plays calls into question one or more romantic clichés. The vision of eternal love projected into an unchanging future turns into endless questing, the paling of all attachments, the transitoriness of human emotion. Stasis in fantasy dissolves into the mobility of real life and its rhythm of relentless change.

The present series of plays can be conveniently and meaningfully grouped according to the way they deal with the comic myth. A first category transforms the idealized comic union into the down-to-earth marriage of real life with its different order of complexities. *Les Précieuses ridicules* presents this marriage as intention, *Le Mariage forcé* depicts it as prospective fact, and in *George Dandin* we see it in its full, life-long essence. The three plays form, then, a kind of composite drama of married bondage which parodies the purpose of the young lover at the beginning of comedy, the bliss he anticipates at the end of it, and the eternal freedom and happiness which is his lot for the future.

That very life force which comedy celebrates, libido as humanized and idealized by the comic myth, can be shown as well in a realistic aspect. The energy by which society is renewed and transformed into a stasis of contentment takes the form in *Amphitryon* of casual sexual dalliance by a flighty and self-indulgent lord – gone is the one-and-only-love theme of comedy. The disruptive, asocial nature of this drive is expressed in the havoc Jupiter wreaks on Amphitryon's marriage, which degenerates from a honeymoon to acrimonious squabbling.

Finally, the two five-act plays in this category, *Le Misanthrope* and *Don Juan*, both among Molière's greatest and most perplexing creations, carry the questioning of comic patterns to their logical extreme; 'each portrays a violent onslaught against the claims and values of civilized society,' to quote Brody's perceptive comparison; 'each is concerned with the questions raised by the assertion of a powerful individuality in the fact of the collective will' ('*Don Juan* and *Le Misanthrope*,' 568-9). We anticipate, then, that both aspects of the comic polarity – intruder versus norm – will be blurred into uncertainty. The scapegoat, that character whose antics normally feed our sense of superior complacency, becomes less reprehensible; the heavy father's sermonizing ceases to be tyrannical prattle. The frank laughter we directed at Arnolphe seems unjust when Alceste is the victim of it, and with Don Louis' eloquent condemnation of his dissolute son we are at the farthest remove from Harpagon.

In a more subtle way, each play parodies as well a narrative movement. The premises of *Le Misanthrope* point toward the multiple marriage ending of ordinary comedy while the development and the dénouement belie these expectations. *Don Juan* presents a powerful and effective inversion of romance: a scapegrace hero embarks on a dubious quest to find his would-be apotheosis in eternal damnation.

As defined here, irony will refer to Frye's ironic *mythos*, the vision of experience which is at once a generic form in its own right and a questioning of the other *mythoi* in his system, especially of romance.[1] Implicit in this notion of irony is a form of tension which results from any parody: a convention is alluded to, but shown at the same time to be inappropriate to the actual circumstances. We experience a suggestive clash between two levels of meaning, one explicit – what is actually happening in the play – and the other, our perception of the conventions to which the action obliquely or directly refers. It is in this context that we can briefly mention Molière's two 'treatise plays,' *La Critique de L'Ecole des femmes* and *L'Impromptu de Versailles*. In that they are not constructed on the comic myth, they obviously belong among the plays discussed in this chapter. Yet they stand apart in being the only plays by Molière not built on any fictional plot whatsoever. They are meant – on the surface at least – to reproduce two 'real' situations: a free-wheeling *conversation mondaine* in a drawing room setting, a *tranche de vie* showing the behind-the-scenes activities of Molière's troupe. This absence of narrative convention means that these works cannot have the same ironic force as the others to be discussed: there are no specific devices to be parodied or inverted. We are far from the world of bondage of *George Dandin* and the intriguing riddles of *Le Misanthrope*. But what is interesting about both *La Critique* and *L'Impromptu* is the subliminal presence of convention in the very form of the plays and the sudden intrusion of convention at the dénouement. Thus, while we take in the animated discussion of *La Critique* and the rehearsal scene of the *Impromptu* – actions that should be devoid of obvious literary shaping – a comic structure begins more and more to be felt.

At the beginning of *La Critique* we have a typical *salon* scene: as the habitués arrive one after another, the conversation grows more and more animated. Wit, irony, vehemence – the ingredients of stimulating discourse – win our adhesion; indeed we could well remain throughout the play with this conversation structure, this high-level *badinerie* seasoned with wit and buffoonery to alleviate the tendency to be over-serious. But soon the spirit of comedy begins to mould this realistic situation. Two camps quickly emerge which correspond to the *eiron-alazon* dichotomy: Climène, the Marquis, and Lysidas undergo the familiar process of caricature, while the reasonable people – Dorante especially – show the common sense of the true *eiron*. The contrast between the two groups is further heightened by Elise's mocking support of the *alazones*. A comic rhythm soon takes hold of the action, too, as the dialogue becomes more and more stylized. The pattern:

LYSIDAS: [criticism of *L'Ecole des femmes*]
THE MARQUIS: [crowing agreement with Lysidas]
CLIMÈNE: [brief approbation]
ELISE: [ironic echo of the other two]

is repeated six times after a similar, less obvious pattern of three repetitions as the habitués try to draw out Lycidas (6). These effects, so reminiscent of some of Molière's most comically stylized scenes (Purgon's anathema in *Le Malade imaginaire*, to name only one), erode the impression of a natural conversation in a *salon* setting.

A more general periodicity emerges toward the end of the play as the marquis breaks up the discussion into farcical absurdity. The *fou rire* which seizes him when he repeats '*tarte à la crème*' and his deafening singing (6) bring the conversation twice to a halt. With these buffoonish antics the pretext of a real conversation suddenly melts away, as if the comic spirit had intruded so strongly that its presence could not be ignored. At the end of the Marquis's song, Uranie says: 'Il se passe des choses assez plaisantes dans notre dispute. Je trouve qu'on en pourrait bien faire une petite comédie, et que cela ne serait pas trop mal à la queue de *L'Ecole des femmes*.' This remark betokens a sudden distancing effect. The characters look upon the events they have been through as scenes in a play and thus become roles which they are willing to contribute to the reconstruction of the action: 'Je fournirais de bon cœur mon personnage,' declares Elise. Now that we are fully in the domain of dramatic convention the question of a dénouement arises. The usual ones – 'mariage,' 'reconnaissance' – obviously do not fit this 'petite comédie.' With an effect of whimsy truly in the spirit of the normal comic reversal, Galopin arrives to announce that dinner is served (7). With the most ancient dénouement of all – the feast – the play ends.

This contrast between a supposed *tranche de vie* action and the presence – covert or acknowledged – of devices normally appropriate to fictional comedy is less marked in *L'Impromptu*, perhaps because the whole play is about theatrical convention, especially the fundamental one of impersonation. We constantly oscillate between the actors – so splendidly individualized – and the roles they are endeavouring to adopt. Yet formal conventions do make themselves felt. The frenetic atmosphere of the rehearsal calls, so to speak, for the arrival of a *fâcheux*, an importunate bore who both slows down the action and heightens the tone of irritation (2). We are taken back momentarily to the buffoon comedies based on a contest between energy and counterforce. Molière is the *meneur de jeu*, the driving force behind the play, the pulsating strength that keeps his ship on course; so he must have his final downturn, his point of ritual death in the best comic tradition, before the play can end happily. He loses control of his terrified players, who learn that the King has arrived to witness the new play and realize they must act without knowing their parts. Catastrophe and humiliation close in with the nightmarish repetition by various 'nécessaires' of 'Commencez donc.' But Molière's frenzied bewilderment is finally put to an end by a gratuitous lifting of the threat, again in the best tradition of the comic myth. A tolerant and merciful monarch in his role of good father allows Molière to play any comedy he might have instead of the new one. Molière's grateful exclamation: 'Vous me redonnez la vie' (11), underlines the sudden euphoric mood that concludes what was ostensibly a rehearsal but which turned out, like *La Critique*, to be a comedy after all.

These tangential remarks in no way, of course, exhaust the richness of these two plays or their significance as historical documents. What has concerned us is their position in an archetypal view of Molière. While not probing the basic comic conventions that we shall now analyse, questionings that go to the very heart of the genre, they are prime examples of the irrepressible force of Molière's comic spirit.

LES PRÉCIEUSES RIDICULES

The outraged departure of La Grange and Du Croisy from Gorgibus's house at the beginning of the play reminds us of the reason for their coming in the first place: to claim the two 'précieuses' as brides. The premises of this farce thus contain an allusion to the comic story. But this intimation of a double romantic plot – two young men aspiring to win two young ladies – quickly dissolves into what turns out to be an inversion of the same story. The formula boy-wants-girl-father-objects is turned upside down; the prospective lovers are quickly repelled by one another, and the father demands that the marriages take place.

More significant, however, is the transformation wrought upon the moral polarity of the comic myth. Gorgibus has all the traits of the traditional blocking figure: authoritarian ('je veux être maître absolu' [4]), egotistical (he has contracted the marriages in terms of his own values, namely the wealth which these 'Messieurs' possess), vulgar in speech and tastes, and choleric. But the romantic antithesis to this authority principle is now non-existent. Gone are the idealized youths aspiring to an eternal romantic union; La Grange and Du Croisy have come to conclude a normal marriage contract for the time – an agreement among parents which the children accepted unquestioningly. This very fact removes them from the world of romance and *précieux* banter – whence La Granges' unflattering remarks about *préciosité*.[2] There are no sentimental attachments whatsoever on any side; indeed, the future husbands had apparently not yet set eyes on their wives-to-be. The 'amants rebutés,' moreover, seem to have been content with this arrangement until they were ill treated. Gorgibus reminds his rebellious daughter and niece: 'Vous avais-je pas commandé de les recevoir comme des personnes que je voulais vous donner pour maris?' (4). Thus the father's choice, usually inimical to the romantic interest of Molière's typical comedy, is here implicitly accepted as the right one. La Grange and Du Croisy do not criticize Gorgibus's marriage plans, only the incredible incivility of the two 'précieuses.'

We are now in the domain of the 'reality' marriage depicted in comedy as actual fact, whether it be the reserved, decorous relationship which unites Orgon and Elmire or the more characteristic acrimony between Monsieur and Madame Jourdain and between Sganarelle and his wife in *Le Médecin malgré lui* and in *Sganarelle* itself. Romantic marriage on the other hand is never actually presented; we see young husbands- and wives-to-be, never a couple wed. It is as if the vision of a married couple at the end of comedy – united by bonds of love in an enduring relationship of harmony and equality – would so clash with the real view of marriage that the comic fantasy would be threatened.

Through its wish-fulfilment nature romantic marriage escapes a fundamental problem inherent in any relationship between the sexes. Mademoiselle Molière alludes to it teasingly in *L'Impromptu*: 'C'est une chose étrange qu'une petite cérémonie soit capable de nous ôter toutes nos belles qualités, et qu'un mari et un galant regardent la même personne avec des yeux si différents' (1). Human relationships are in a state of constant flux; the alluring lady of mystery is no longer the same, once possessed. And when possession is eternalized by sacrament, the erosion of ardour may be the more rapid. But the comic fantasy simply denies all this by asserting: they lived happily ever after.

In real life, however, the institution of *galanterie* allowed courtship to continue outside of and beyond marriage, as a social game (in theory at least) built ultimately upon the model of courtly love. But there is no escape for the *précieuses* into the *salon* life of the seventeenth century. Molière wastes no opportunity to underline their fundamental stupidity and vulgarity, traceable in large part to their provincial origin. The hinterland which produced la Comtesse d'Escarbagnas and Monsieur de Pourceaugnac would do no better with Cathos and Magdelon. The girls, moreover, are unable to make the elementary distinctions between play and reality. Their explanation for their discourtesy betrays at once their obsession with escaping the realities of their station: 'La belle galanterie que la leur! Quoi? débuter d'abord par le mariage!' (4) In refined society, of course, a suitor may indeed go through some of the courtship ritual of *galanterie* before the final matter of marriage is brought up; but in the 'précieuses" bourgeois world, such conduct from a future husband would probably have been thought of as affectation. Whatever the case, Cathos and Magdelon move quickly to the outer limits of foolishness by insisting that the real courtship must in every point correspond to the models they have gleaned in novels. Magdelon details in a long speech each step in the eventful course between love at first sight and happily-ever-after marriage, each vicissitude in the quest of the lady by the hero: 'Voilà comme les choses se traitent dans les belles manières et ce sont des règles dont, en bonne galanterie, on ne saurait se dispenser. Mais en venir de but en blanc à l'union conjugale, ne faire l'amour qu'en faisant le contrat du mariage, et prendre justement le roman par la queue!' She continues the same tone in her final entreaty to Gorgibus: 'Laissez-nous faire à loisir le tissu de notre roman, et n'en pressez point tant la conclusion' (4).

In a word, they want their own life to be a fiction, subject to the elaborate rituals of amorous civility as codified in the pastoral and heroic novels of the time. Instead of being content to project these experiences into social games, as did the élite of the *salons*, they want to live them with La Grange and Du Croisy. They want to become Polyxène and Aminte for the *état civil* instead of in the literary games of fashionable get-togethers. In short, they long for a romantic marriage with all the trappings in their everyday lives, whereas they scarcely have the distinction for a bourgeois union.

The real tone of *préciosité* is thus beyond their ken: refined wit, good taste, a sense of elegant play. The distance between these grotesque caricatures and the *précieux* world to which Molière gave voice in his courtly *divertissements* is so great as to invalidate completely the claim often made that Molière was attacking distinguished society in this play. There is no reason why we should not take Molière's word for it: 'les véritables précieuses auraient tort de se piquer, lorsqu'on joue les ridicules qui les imitent mal' (*Préface*).[3]

If Cathos and Magdelon are unable to put romantic fancy in its proper place, they surely will not distinguish between the genuine *bon ton* and an outrageous counterfeit. They are in rapt enthusiasm before the antics of the two valets who treat us to a systematic parody of the ideal of courtly distinction. Military prowess becomes the ludicrous braggadocio of 'il commandait un régiment de cavalerie sur les galères de Malte,' the display of wounds and quips about 'demi-lunes' and 'lunes.' Amorous civility is degraded into the grotesque *galanterie* of such phrases as 'je dis que nos libertés auront peine à sortir d'ici les braies nettes' (11). What passes for literary distinction is contained in Mascarille's *impromptu* and commentary (9). Finally, the 'cadeau' or refined entertainment a *galant* gives to his lady turns out to be farcical ball where bourgeois neighbour ladies dance to the tune of 'violons de village' (12).

This high-spirited fun comes to an end, of course, with the return of La Grange and Du Croisy (13). Instead of the usual comic reconciliation and final collective tableau we witness a dispersal heavy with punishment. The valets are ceremonially stripped and leave the scene with their masters. It remains for Gorgibus to drive home the 'précieuses' final humiliation and to drive them out with blows at the same time: 'Allez vous cacher, vilaines; allez vous cacher pour jamais' (17). Thus, we witness a scapegoat ritual unrelieved by any parallel romantic fulfilment.[4]

Even if the normal comic dialectic disappears in *Les Précieuses*, the sense of a moral norm does remain. Well deserved chastisement implies some ethical standard, although it need not be elevated necessarily to a social ideal or fully articulated. Right, here, takes the form of the righteous anger which justifies the 'pièce sanglante' (16) La Grange and Du Croisy perpetrate on the girls. Wrong is in its traditional comic guise of stupidity and self-blindness, ripe for some exemplary humiliation. Comic polarity thus recaptures its elemental farcical essence: the conflict between *eiron* and *alazon*, trickster and fool.

That the 'amants rebutés' vent their spleen on the two valets who have simply carried out their orders may seem unjust in moral terms. But we must take Mascarille and Jodelet as buffoon figures who accept with relative equanimity the ups and downs of their destiny. Both have relished this charade. Mascarille, above all, has had an unanticipated opportunity to indulge a particular fancy of his: 'faire l'homme de condition' (1). While they are at first distressed at the blows they receive (13), they accept their demotion lightheartedly with Mascarille's mock-heroic lament: 'O Fortune, quelle est ton inconstance' (15).

The dominant presence of these amiable buffoons, together with a morally reassuring dénouement, mitigates the lack in *Les Précieuses ridicules* of a romantic plot. On the other hand, the dispersal of the final scenes removes the possibility of marital bondage. All parties have escaped an undesirable union, and the trick, however painful to digest at the moment, will soon be a thing of the past.

LE MARIAGE FORCÉ

If parody constitutes a key aspect of Frye's ironic genre, this play constitutes a simple and straightforward example of it. Not only is the comic myth itself turned topsy-turvy, but the action alludes derisively to a basic component of romance, the quest. Drawing upon that great exponent of the mock epic, Rabelais, Molière fills out the rather thin plot of his *Mariage forcé* by enacting Sganarelle's repeated and fruitless attempts to seek enlightenment on the question: should he marry? His several consultations furnish a major thread in the play. His entreaties for guidance, especially with the pedants (4, 5), are answered

by meaningless verbal elaborations which illustrate, as Hubert remarks, 'the use-
lessness of discourse' (pp 88-9). Add to this the fact that Sganarelle has no free
choice, that he is moving not towards an unexpected revelation but inevitable
disaster, and we understand the full extent to which the quest motif is degraded
in this play. Faced in the end with the rather hollow option between marriage
and death at the hands of his future wife's brother, he prudently chooses the
former, thereby making retrospective mockery of his elaborate efforts to attain
wisdom. All in all, he has but ascertained his destiny, and at the end he has
accepted it willy-nilly.

The love plot itself recalls the pattern of romance. The suitor and his beloved
have agreed to marry, and the father is only too happy to sponsor the forthcoming union. But we are, of course, far from the world of courtly harmony and
distinction, the dénouements of *La Princesse d'Elide* and *Les Amants magnifiques*. Under this appearance of concord lies a truculent critique of the comic
myth and its romantic aspect. Sganarelle and Dorimène have agreed to wed, not
out of mutual love, but for crassly personal and egotistic reasons. Sganarelle
leaves no doubt as to his down-to-earth view of marriage: 'Outre la joie que
j'aurai de posséder une belle femme, qui me fera mille caresses, qui me dorlotera
et me viendra frotter lorsque je serai las, outre cette joie, dis-je, je considère
qu'en demeurant comme je suis, je laisse périr dans le monde la race des Sganarelles, et qu'en me mariant, je pourrai me voir revivre en d'autres moi-mêmes,
que j'aurai le plaisir de voir des créatures qui seront sorties de moi, de petites
figures qui me ressembleront comme deux gouttes d'eau' (1). We see at a glance
the various forms of Sganarelle's self-seeking expectations: the satisfaction of
instinct, the indulgence of narcissistic whims, the desire to propagate children
merely as multiple copies of himself. His remarks in 2 to Dorimène only under-
score these aspirations: 'Vous allez être à moi depuis la tête jusqu'aux pieds, et je
serai maître de tout: de vos petits yeux éveillés, de votre petit nez fripon, de vos
lèvres appétissantes, de vos oreilles amoureuses, de votre petit menton joli, de
vos petits tetons rondelets, de votre ... enfin, toute votre personne sera à ma
discrétion.' One can scarcely imagine a more ludicrous fusion of lust and
gluttony.

At this point the action could take the familiar turn of the comic genre.
Sganarelle, after all, is cast really as a typical rival lover, a more ridiculous
Arnolphe. All we need to complete the pattern is the intrusion of a young man
with whom Dorimène would be in love and whom she would finally marry over
her father's objections and to Sganarelle's discomfiture. Half of this hypothetical
development does take place; her 'amant,' Lycaste, will appear toward the end
of the play. But the most significant element of this romantic extrapolation
– the prospective dénouement – is utterly lacking. Far from craving a happily-

ver-after marriage, Dorimène is quite content to wed the buffoon hero of the play. She is disarmingly frank in her reasons:

> Je crois que ... vous ne serez point de ces maris
> incommodes qui veulent que leurs femmes vivent comme
> des loups-garous. Je vous avoue que je ne m'accommoderais
> pas de cela, et que la solitude me désespère. J'aime le
> jeu, les visites, les assemblées, les cadeaux et les
> promenades, en un mot, toutes les choses de plaisir, et
> vous devez être ravi d'avoir une femme de mon humeur.
> Nous n'aurons jamais aucun démêlé ensemble, et je ne vous
> contraindrai point dans vos actions, comme j'espère que,
> de votre côté, vous ne me contraindrez point dans les
> miennes. (2)

In the romantic world of comedy, this *profession de foi* we could take at face value. The guiding precept of comedy is, after all, the victory of the pleasure principle. What makes this demand for freedom and equality spurious in this context, however, is that true love, and the confidence it carries, is not there to validate Dorimène's claims. Under cover of what is a reasonable rejection of male tyranny in marriage, Dorimène is cynically seeking *carte blanche* for licence. Jouanny is quite correct in labelling Dorimène's speech as 'l'envers du programme que l'Ariste libéral de *l'Ecole des maris* offrait a Léonor (acte I, scène II)' (note 670). We are dealing with two different worlds. Ariste's assumptions are valid in a realm of well born lovers consumed with respectful, selfless, and enduring passion; in the society dedicated to cynical self-serving of *Le Mariage forcé*, Dorimène's words have a suitably hollow ring. In the romantic world *cocuage* is impossible; so here it is inevitable. The girl herself leaves again no room for doubt on this score as she talks to her *galant*, Lycaste: 'Je vous considère toujours de même, et ce mariage ne doit point vous inquiéter: c'est un homme que je n'épouse point par amour, et sa seule richesse me fait résoudre à l'accepter' (7). After Dorimène's sardonic speech guaranteeing Sganarelle's death in six months, the future corpse happens upon the scene, and Lycaste addresses him with thinly veiled sarcasm: 'Monsieur a toute la mine d'être un fort bon mari. Oui, Monsieur, je veux faire amitié avec vous, et lier ensemble un petit commerce de visites et de divertissements' (7). The double-edged adjective *bon* underlines the young man's expectations: dalliance with his beloved and social pleasures paid for out of Sganarelle's purse. Thus the 'visites' and 'divertissements' proposed by Lycaste are far removed from the legitimate *galanterie* valued as a social ideal.

Le Mariage forcé presents rather a degraded and caricatured vision of a man-woman relationships. Marriage is a prostitution for Dorimène, an invest ment in pleasure and dishonour for Sganarelle: courtship becomes promiscuity The cutting irony of the curtain line spoken by the father: 'Allons nous réjoui et célébrer cet heureux mariage' (10) seems a deliberate parody of the last word of a romantic dénouement like Jupiter's summons to Amour and Psyché 'Venez, amants, venez aux Cieux / Achever un si grand et si digne hyménée' (V last scene). One cannot imagine a more total collapse of the comic fantasy.[5]

GEORGE DANDIN

With the deñouement of a typical comedy, the young lovers step out into the ideal world of happy, harmonious marriage, sustained by unchanging love. A the curtain falls on *Le Mariage forcé*, its characters find themselves transported as it were, to the woodland setting of *George Dandin*. Names have changed Lycaste is now Clitandre, Dorimène has become Angélique, the buffoonis Sganarelle has taken on the traits of a surly peasant, the Sotenvilles now play th role of Dorimène's father. *George Dandin* picks up where *Le Mariage forcé* leave off; we witness a marital bondage all the more ritual in that it has been made law by a ceremony from which there is no return. The forced marriage in prospec has become a harsh reality, and the *insouciance* of the bridal pair has turned int hostility and recrimination.

Behind these broad analogies lie profound differences, particularly in motiva tion. Sganarelle's rather naïve desire to be coddled and to perpetuate his rac becomes the foolish and disastrous aspiration to a higher social class. Wit Dandin, *alazoneia* takes on the basic meaning it has in the *Tractatus Coislinianus* he is an 'impostor,'[6] a would-be gentleman with rough hands, dirty fingernails and coarse ways. As this error belongs to the past, the dominant mood of *George Dandin* is remorse. The exclusion suffered by the blocking character in tradi tional comedy is by comparison more merciful, because it is momentary and (fo us at least) quickly forgotten. Here, punishment is forced inclusion and con tinued humiliation. The collapse of the romantic fantasy results in a heightened sense of reality, of slavery in a dialectical relationship with desire. And as the comic fault is sealed in the past, exorcism has become expiation. In *George Dandin*, the moment of painful enlightenment that is the lot of the usual block ing character has been extended into an enduring continuum of time. A victim of a kind of moral *sparagmos*, the fool must eternally suffer the awareness of his foolishness.

That belated wisdom cohabits in Dandin with the memory of folly explains the distinctive *dédoublement* of this main character and the constant dialogue that goes on within him. The 'je' of 'Je suis là-dessus savant à mes dépens' stands ı permanent opposition to the 'vous' of 'George Dandin, George Dandin, vous ʋez fait une sottise la plus grande du monde' (I, 1). His only consolation is to ıvorce himself from the fool by assuming him to be another person and to give ent to his hostility against that other George Dandin. His self-hatred goes to the ᵪtreme of self-violence: 'je me donnerais volontiers des soufflets' (I, 3).[7]

Yet this is only one moment in his psychological dynamism. If repeated ιumiliations force him to verbal self-punishing, he also knows the poisoned ᴵelight of momentary triumph when his hostility is directed against others. The nechanism on which the play is based brings inevitably to mind the wild oscilla- ions between exultation and masochistic rage experienced by Arnolphe in ᴵ'Ecole des femmes. As Hubert notes (p 191), the irony of the two situations is 'ery much the same: Dandin has a trump card – Lubin's indiscretions – which is ιaralleled by Horace's bubbling confidences to Arnolphe. As a result of this ιoreknowledge, both Dandin and Arnolphe crow their imminent victory only to ιe dashed to defeat by the quick-wittedness of Angélique on the one hand, ʌgnès on the other. The pattern is repeated 'selon un rythme obstiné et fatal' Jouanny, vol. II, p 184), which only enhances this impression of a perverse ᴵestiny unleashed against hapless protagonists.

In L'Ecole des femmes, however, the presence of a romantic interest and the ᵌnergy that guides it to fulfilment mitigate this impression of machine-like recur- 'ence. We are really dealing with the two symbolic projections of the comic ᴵialectic, the 'right' force which impels us forward to a renewed and regenerated ιociety – a force conceived as a single thrust – and the countermovement of the ιlocking character spending itself on the futile circles of the wheel of fortune. In ᴰandin there is no such contrast. The wheel of fortune moves three circles and he action is over for us. Nor is there a reversal to bring the cycle to a true halt, ιs happens in L'Ecole des femmes. Dandin will have his ups and downs ındefinitely.

Hence, punishment has two facets in George Dandin – the painful but comic ιnagnorisis which is his continuous conscious state during the play ('que mon nariage est une leçon bien parlante à tous les paysans qui veulent s'élever au- ᴵessus de leur condition' [I, 1]), and the specific humiliations which the play's nechanism inflicts on him. The first is an awareness within, the second a flaying ᶠrom without which only reinforces Dandin's general feeling of expiation. As if ᵗo humble him further, the action underlines punishment in terms of physical ιction or attitude: at the end of I he stands with head bowed to Clitandre, as II ᴵraws to a close he receives the blows ostensibly meant for Clitandre's shoulders ʹII, 8) and as the final act ends we find him on his knees before his wife.

Punishment in comedy is always justified; there is always a comic fault com- mensurate with it. Dandin is guilty of social climbing, a foolish aspiration ιeyond his station – his 'original sin,' in short. But is wrongdoing only retrospective here, or is there a justification for chastisement within the play as it unfolds before us? The key to this question lies in the character of Angélique. She is in essence a married Dorimène: in her cynical frankness toward her husband, in her unabashed deceitfulness, in her availability to amorous entreaty. And yet, there is an absolutely essential difference which puts each woman in a separate world. Dorimène could have escaped marriage with Sganarelle but chose to accept him as a cover for her flirtations. Angélique has been sold to Dandin, and against her will. When Dandin reminds her of her marriage vows, she retorts: 'M'avez-vous, avant le mariage, demandé mon consentement, et si je voulais bien de vous? Vous n'avez consulté, pour cela, que mon père et ma mère; ce sont eux proprement qui vous ont épousé' (II, 2). Marriage, forced upon Sganarelle and accepted freely by the wife-to-be in the previous play, is imposed here upon the wife and contracted willingly by the husband. This reversal of roles makes of Angélique a victim like her husband, but she has the luxury of being able to blame others for her plight.[8]

Angélique is firmly enmeshed in a reality marriage of the time, exiled from the world of romance to which she would have aspired as a lover in a comic plot. She is wed, moreover, to a husband whose traits place him squarely in the repugnance phase of the comic dialectic: the jealous, possessive, spiteful, violent 'mari loup-garou' whom comedy is meant to gull and humiliate, a peasant version of Arnolphe: 'Je vous dis encore une fois que le mariage est une chaîne à laquelle on doit porter toute sorte de respect.' And when Angélique coolly stands up to him, he threatens to 'accommoder tout son visage à la compote, et le mettre en état de ne plaire de sa vie aux diseurs de fleurettes.' Such is his anger that it literally drives him off the stage (II, 2).

Dandin holds the *barbon*'s view of marriage as subjection, solitude, and symbolic death, for which the romantic plot furnishes an antithesis and an escape. Like Agnès, Angélique is perfectly right in rejecting this vision of joyless, solitary bondage in favour of something more in harmony with the seventeenth-century ideal of civility. As the realm of romantic wish-fulfilment is closed to her, her recourse must be in social life and its normal concomitants of *divertissements* and *galanteries*. This, for her, is life: 'Je vous déclare que mon dessein n'est pas de renoncer au monde, et de m'enterrer toute vive dans un mari,' just as Célimène refuses to 'aller [s]'ensevelir' in Alceste's isolation. Continuing the imagery of death and the implicit comparisons with the austerity and joylessness of convent life, Angélique adds: 'C'est une chose merveilleuse que cette tyrannie de Messieurs les maris, et je les trouve bons de vouloir qu'on soit morte à tous les divertissements, et qu'on ne vive que pour eux. Je me moque de cela, et ne veux point mourir si jeune' (II, 2).

Far from being a 'monstre d'égoisme' (Jouanny, vol. II, p 185), Angélique views marriage in the light of the norm so often articulated or implicit in

Molière's comedies. She merely aspires to what it is Agnès' lot to realize: a relationship based on confidence where social pleasures are accepted as a fitting pastime. When Dandin asks: 'Quel personnage voulez-vous que joue un mari pendant cette galanterie?' Angélique's answer states the comic ideal of tolerance and generosity: 'le personnage d'un honnête homme qui est bien aise de voir sa femme considérée' (II, 2).

Were we in the domain of 'normal' comedy, then, the functions of this play would be clear and reassuring. Like Sganarelle in *Le Mariage forcé*, Dandin embodies the traits of a foolish rival lover, an exponent of crass and selfish views of marriage. Angélique's liberal precepts, reminiscent of Ariste's in *L'Ecole des maris*, as well as her youth and beauty, put her in the function of the young beloved. Clitandre, an ardent, courtly *galant*, could well be the *jeune premier* of the romantic plot. After marvelling over his love note, Angélique exclaims: 'Que dans tous leurs discours et dans toutes leurs actions les gens de cour ont un air agréable! Et qu'est-ce que c'est auprès d'eux que nos gens de province?' (p 210). Seducer or not,[9] Clitandre is evidently meant to embody the good breeding of the Court in contrast to the crassness of provincial life. The caricatural point of reference for Clitandre is the Sotenville family with its mechanical punctiliousness, its pretentions to distinction, its narrow and prudish idea of virtue.[10] Ironically, however, they function with Clitandre and Angélique as the agents of Dandin's various humiliations.

The structure of this play would be totally predictable if the normal comic dialectic prevailed; but *George Dandin* is 'a drama of courtly love seen through the reverse side of the glass' (Lawrence 45). The reality principle predominates, Angélique is already married to a coarse, stubborn, and egotistical peasant. Thus, all the romantic functions come under the harsh, ironic light of reality. The *barbon* has won. The embittered beloved is trapped, the suitor reduced to cynical subterfuge; normal decorum breaks down: we behold, as Adam perceptively suggests, 'une *Ecole des femmes* où Horace serait un fourbe, et Agnès une vicieuse' (p 370). The married couple will live unhappily ever after; Angélique will insist on the social freedom she deserves, Dandin will expect peasant-like devotion and subservience from her. Each has carried into the misalliance his own world irreconcilable with that of the spouse. With the trust necessary for marital fidelity lacking here, *cocuage* is again inevitable. Dandin's jealous temperament will drive Angélique into the arms of Clitandre and others like him, although Angélique, in what appears to be a sincere reassurance, implies that she is above anything beyond harmless flirtation ('rendez grâces au Ciel de ce que je ne suis pas capable de quelque chose de pis' [II, 2]).

We behold, then, a total inversion of the comic myth: loathing, not love, links man and woman, marriage is present bondage instead of future bliss; parental authority, represented here in the ludicrous Sotenville couple, has prevailed in its most crass form. Even the energetic forward thrust of comedy has been tamed to a sterile, predetermined, cyclical movement. And in a genre whose purpose is to celebrate life, the last words sound a vague threat of suicide: 's'aller jeter dans l'eau la tête première' (p 234).[11]

George Dandin, then, brings to an ironic apotheosis the reality marriage. But marriage itself is institutionalized libido, the id tamed by sacrament. In Molière's comparatively decorous comedy, desire among lovers is never depicted as pure instinct, but as a drive to be fulfilled and validated in the marriage bond. Consent to the wedded state, whether real or idealized, already implies a socialization of desire, the ritual celebration of an institution symbolizing order and social renewal. While the plays about real-life marriage show the dark side of the marital bond and the constraints it imposes, the theme of social order remains, even if that of social harmony is called into question.

Pure libido, the drive to satisfy sexual instinct with no ennobling motives like the young lovers' honourable intentions, must then appear in a profoundly ironic light. Uninhibited desire is a challenge to order, a principle of social disruption. In this context two plays by Molière may be considered as critiques of the same libido that is normally sublimated and socialized by the comic myth. Amphitryon portrays desire as dalliance, disrupting to the victimized family but partly justified in the final analysis by godly superiority; with Don Juan, the hero's flightiness raises so many moral questions that the entire play becomes, along with Le Misanthrope, one of Molière's most problematical.

AMPHITRYON

The mood of Amphitryon calls to mind that of Psyché. Both plays were created in the Salle des Machines of the Tuileries; the possibilities for a breathtaking variety of visual marvels account in part at least for the theme of magic in each play. We find ourselves again in a shifting, perplexing, spellbinding theatrical realm under the control of some deity-magician who suspends at will the laws of nature, holds back the dawn, fashions new shapes for himself according to his caprice, knows everything without and within the minds of mortals. The intrusion of Jupiter and Mercure in the human world has the same effect as that of Amour: an obscure and awesome feeling of divine mystery dangerously close and little concerned with its impact upon mortals.[12] Constantly recurring words like songe, magie, folie, mystère, reinforce this powerful poetic impression of a world suddenly wrested from the natural order.

Amphitryon also shares with Psyché a mood of sensual self-indulgence. The exquisite ironies of the Prologue, the amiable banter and cynicism of Nuit and Mercure, project into the main action a compelling mood of dalliance and voluptuousness. Alcmène's ecstatic evocation of Jupiter-Amphitryon's ardour

(II, 2) reminds us of Psyché's disarming declaration of her passion to Amour. This breakdown of normal feminine decorum – Psyché is overwhelmed by the presence of a god, Alcmène sees no reason for restraint in the presence of her husband' – explains the peculiar, yet discreet, sensuality of both plays.

Behind these surface resemblances, however, lie fundamental differences which put the two works into separate archetypal worlds. The story of Amour and Psyché is a grandiose and ultimate passion, the one-and-only event of their lives. Psyché was a disdainful young princess until she was subjugated forever by Amour's charms; similarly, he never felt love before his first view of Psyché. Their future life will be the absolute apotheosis of the comic marriage: while an effort of the imagination is needed for us to assume that the typical human lovers of comedy will live happily ever after, a god and a recently immortalized young lady are perfectly at home in their realm out of space and time.

Amphitryon on the contrary, recounts a casual episode in the amorous career of a self-indulgent immortal. Jupiter has been 'taureau, / Serpent, cygne' (*prologue*) before his present disguise as Amphitryon, and other metamorphoses will follow. We behold here 'le comédien fait dieu, le Mascarille de la haute mythologie' (Jean Rousset, *L'Intérieur et l'extérieur* [Paris 1968] 144). The unforgettable poetry of the play dignifies and immortalizes what is basically a king's one-time visit to the bedchamber of a lady-in-waiting, a visit, moreover, under false pretenses. We see here a libido – never permanently satisfied, always trying to escape its own erosion, egotistical, deceiving, and disruptive – raised to the level of eternal omnipotence: 'Si déguisé qu'il soit par l'espèce de jeu brillant qui enveloppe toute la pièce, le désir d'illimitation divine parcourt d'un bout à l'autre la comédie d'*Amphitryon* (Bénichou 164).

Gods and kings are above our petty moral reactions to such self-indulgence. 'Un partage avec Jupiter / N'a rien du tout qui déshonore,' the husband is rather cavalierly told (III, 9). An undertone of cynicism established from the beginning of the play disturbs our tranquil acceptance of divine whim and throws an even more problematical light on libido. Nuit and Mercure are aware of their dubious status as go-betweens, but with heavy irony bordering on sarcasm Mercure assures her: 'Lorsque dans un haut rang on a l'heur de paraître, / Tout ce qu'on fait est toujours bel et bon' (*prologue*).

Amphitryon is a self-mocking justification of godly caprice in general. Because 'l'amour ici ne m'offre aucun plaisir,' Mercure contents himself with other whims like baiting Amphitryon and Sosie:

> Cela n'est pas d'un dieu bien plein de charité;
> Mais aussi n'est-ce pas ce dont je m'inquiète,
> Et je me sens par ma planète
> A la malice un peu porté. (III, 2)

Such is his dubious excuse for adding to the confusion already forced upon the Amphitryon household by Jupiter's dalliance. His cruelty to Amphitryon's hapless servant goes far beyond the need to keep him out of the house. Sosie becomes a scapegoat figure. In two long scenes (I, 2 and III, 6) he is beaten by his alter ego and robbed of his name and identity. The misunderstandings created by Jupiter and Mercure give rise to harrowing scenes between master and valet (III, 2 and III, 4). To be sure, Sosie is a typical valet, cowardly, vain (II, 1), concerned with his creatural comforts ('Le véritable Amphitryon / Est l'Amphitryon où l'on dîne' [III, 5]). But the combination of his own weakness and Mercure's bullying lessens the notion of comic justice; we seem dangerously close to *sparagmos*, that world of gratuitous and mutilation which is the ultimate expression of the ironic genre.

The play is built, then, on two versions of godly caprice set in ironic contrast and juxtaposition: Jupiter's amorous dalliance is expressed by his high-flown love dialogues, while Mercure's truculence and Sosie's desperate physical and verbal dodging give rise to a different, more laughable kind of diction. The amorality of this aspect of the story is mitigated, in the eyes of some critics,[13] by an allegedly favourable picture of marriage presented by Alcmène. She does resist Jupiter's attempts to separate 'l'amant' from 'le mari' – that is, to individualize himself with respect to Amphitryon and thus possess her, as Amour wished to do with Psyché, in his own right. Jupiter is finally forced to admit to the husband: 'Alcmène est toute à toi, quelque soin qu'on emploie' (III, 10). But if these two roles are bound together in Alcmène's own mind, to us they appear distinct. Jupiter is the ardent, eloquent lover who astounds Alcmène with the intensity of his feelings: 'Jamais votre amour, en pareille occurrence, / Ne me parut si tendre et si passionné' (II, 2) is her summary of Amphitryon-Jupiter's visit. In two long, poetic scenes (I, 3 and II, 6), he marshals all his seductive powers, even that last resort of the courtly lover, *le chantage à la mort*. Amphitryon, on the other hand, appears in only one scene with his wife (II, 2), and he is very much 'le mari'; their conversation degenerates quickly into suspicion and acrimony. The rest of the time Amphitryon is more concerned with his marital honour than his wife's feelings. Whatever sympathy he deserves, he reduces himself to the role of suspicious and egotistical husband in a surprising speech to his friends *after* he has found out that Alcmène has been duped in a situation for which she has not the slightest responsibility:

> Ah! sur le fait dont il s'agit,
> L'erreur simple devient un crime véritable,
> Et sans consentement, l'innocence y périt. (III, 7)

Because he is dishonoured, Alcmène is guilty.

The down-to-earth exchanges between Sosie and Cléanthis do not stand in the usual comic contrast with the main couple. In such plays as *Le Médecin malgré lui* and *Sganarelle* the reality marriage with its discord forms an amusing commentary on the romantic plot which will end in the usual promise of marital harmony *in aeternam*. In *Amphitryon*, we have two pictures of the reality marriage: the heroic and impassioned quarrel of a young married couple, the sardonic exchanges of a lower-class pair made cynical by fifteen years of acrimony (I, 4). This second system of ironic contrasts, founded on parallel misunderstandings provoked by Jupiter and Mercure at both conjugal levels, forms an unflattering view of marriage, just as the first conveyed the cavalier side of caprice.

The final scenes accentuate the irony underlying these systematic ambiguities. On a superficial level Jupiter appears to set things right: the misunderstandings are cleared up, and we learn that he is leaving a worthy souvenir of his visit – the embryo that will become Hercules. But Alcmène's silent shadow and Amphitryon's wordless presence bid us look beyond Jupiter's spectacular departure. Instead of the eternal concord promised by the comic myth, we find, in this ironic inversion of convention, a suggestion of continuing bitterness. How can the spouses be truly reconciled after this unsettling episode of which there will be an eternal reminder? The honeymoon intensity of Amphitryon's love is a thing of the past; lover and husband can never co-exist again. Jupiter's victory is complete after all. That dissension and disruption are the price of this triumph is of no consequence; desire as godly caprice can have no second thoughts.

LE MISANTHROPE

In none of Molière's plays is the traditional vision of comedy questioned with more irony and subtlety than in this masterpiece. The initial situation seems to hint at a conventional development and dénouement: 'Célimène a deux amants, Alceste et Oronte: au moins, comédie de rivaux. La présence d'une cousine, Eliante, et d'une amie, Arsinoé, ainsi que d'un ami d'un des rivaux, Philinte, laisse présager une comédie non à deux couples, mais à trois, c'est-à-dire un harmonieux arrangement final et un triple mariage au dénouement' (Guicharnaud, *Aventure* 347). A comedy in the pure romantic tradition seems to await us, an example of the *comédie d'intrigue* founded on rivalries and misunderstandings which evolved out of pastoral and which was so successfully practised by Corneille and Rotrou in the 1630s. This schema does not even allow for a blocking character, a fact in keeping with the traditions of romance where the principle of opposition comes from among the lovers themselves.

At the very outset Molière questions comic convention by steering us into ostensibly familiar territory, only to jolt us with the unknown. It becomes apparent, as the drama takes hold of us, that the action, far from creating the typical imbroglio, will be slight, linear, based on a simple pattern of repetition.[14] Copeau caught this simplicity in his deliberately understated résumé: 'C'est un Monsieur qui veut parler à une dame et qui n'y arrive pas.' Five times Alceste arrives in Célimène's house to have it out with her. Four times various intruders frustrate his hopes. Twice he leaves the stage on his own: at the end of I he is overcome with rage at Oronte, and III concludes with his departure from the stage with Arsinoé to examine the alleged evidence of Célimène's perfidy and to accept, if he wishes the all too apparent favours Arsinoé has in mind. Twice Alceste is forced to leave; at the end of II the *Maréchaux* have summoned him to settle the Oronte affair, and IV concludes with the vague legal threat so clumsily announced by Du Bois. This build-up of harassment and frustration makes an ironic reference to the comic rhythm itself. The confident buffoon, thrusting ahead out of sheer vitality no matter how many *contretemps* intrude, becomes the sour and petulant misanthrope at odds with the *fâcheux* which surge up in his path.

Like the mechanism of *L'Ecole des femmes*, and unlike that of *George Dandin*, a dénouement does bring the action of *Le Misanthrope* to a halt. However, the very ending seems a parody of the traditional comic reversal of *L'Ecole des femmes*. The happy tableau grouping the greatest number of characters possible in a final euphoria degenerates in *Le Misanthrope* into a gaggle of spiteful mediocrities who burst in upon Célimène and confront her with the evidence of her double-dealing. The contrast with the forgiving mood of the usual tableau is driven home with the image of a 'procès' (Guicharnaud, *loc. cit.*) presided over by a triumphant hypocrite who is both accuser and judge; for it is Arsinoé, ironically, who enables the action to break out of its futile circles and reach a solution of sorts from within.

A mood of sombre dispersal sets in after Arsinoé and the irate suitors leave, a mood not unreminiscent of Racinian tragedy with its successive exits. The departures, however, point ahead not to the finality of death, but to a social form of that finality: Alceste's 'désert.' Célimène's enigmatic departure is followed by that of Alceste, who storms off toward his self-hating solitude. Only Eliante and Philinte remain behind to fulfil in a strange, muted way the romantic premises of traditional comedy.[15] Eliante accepts the other's decorous affection, while Philinte is content to be second best. The void left by Alceste becomes our final impression as Eliante and Philinte themselves leave the stage: 'Allons, Madame, allons employer toute chose, / Pour rompre le dessein que son cœur se propose,' a curtain line standing in stark contrast to the 'sweetness and light' variety typical of romantic fulfilment.

The singularity of this ending strikes home all the more when we recall that the comic dénouement, in its full splendour, celebrates a social ideal. The desire pole of the comic dialectic triumphs as our vision of harmony, order, and regeneration. The norm in this regard is high standard of civility in the form of elegant play; the anti-comic role is that of the kill-joy, the censor. Once again, Ariste's tolerance in Léonor of all the customary varieties of social life and entertainment comes to mind, as does the *salon* hidden in the wings of *Tartuffe*. The first complaint registered against the hypocrite is his censoriousness, his suppression of innocent social pleasures. The polarization of comedy, in short, results in an idealization of society and its proponent. Elmire, the lady of the *salon* in *Tartuffe*, is depicted as the epitome of elegance, decorum, self-control – the sort of woman we can imagine easily fending off compliments from her *galants*, holding her own in a contest of repartee, commenting tastefully on a play or poem.

The *salon* comes to centre stage in *Le Misanthrope*, and Célimène is no less worthy of her central position in it than Elmire. She reminds us of the proud princess of romance surrounded by admiring suitors whom she decorously keeps at a distance – even her preferred one – and who do her every bidding in the hopes of the slightest favours.[16] Her charm, wit, poise make of her, no doubt, the figure most closely approximating the ideal of the *salon* lady, admired, courted, longed-for – the symbol of 'la promesse du bonheur, la recherche frémissante du plaisir' (Gutwirth 88). But the spell she works does not blind us to the underside of the brilliant world which surrounds her, a world founded on empty euphoria kept alive by role-playing, social accommodation, and futile pastimes. No exit here into idealizing fantasy: we face the hard choice, put so well by Guicharnaud, 'entre un monde glacé, où déambulent de jolis sourires sans passion, et l'éclatante jungle qui se manifeste à la fois sur scène et dans les coulisses' (*ibid.* 461). For we cannot forget the off-stage faults of the institutions which prolong this courtly society. Whether Alceste is right or wrong in his lawsuit, justice is still bought, not rendered; and it is the job, ironically, of the chief *sage* of the play, Philinte, to encourage Alceste to influence those who will judge his case: 'Mais qui voulez-vous donc qui pour vous sollicite?' 'Aucun juge par vous ne sera visité?' (I, 1). A Court laced with pretentiousness, corruption, and self-interest is represented on stage by the two vain and vindictive *marquis*, Acaste and Clitandre.

Célimène's own failings, finally, furnish a constant counterpoint to her qualities. This drawing room princess plays her lovers against one another not out of womanly decorum but to live in a state of perpetual, ego-satisfying intoxication. She is self-centred, hypocritical, devoid of fellow-feeling, and given to petty and degrading gossip. Indeed, the idealizing force of comedy has been so impaired in this picture of society that Célimène undergoes a humiliation analogous to expulsion, the normal fate of the blocking character standing in the way of the social ideal. The come-uppance she suffers at the hands of her former suitors comes from a basic *hubris* in her character, a more dignified version of the *alazon*'s comic fault; she intended to keep all her *amoureux* at bay indefinitely by playing them off one against another, and thought she could extend her circle of *médisance* in all directions with impunity. And so she is rejected by a society not worthy of her. If there is a tragic figure in *Le Misanthrope*, it is probably she (Guicharnaud, *ibid.* 473).

Do the faded surrogates of the young lovers, Philinte and Eliante, redeem this fallen ideal? They are the *honnêtes gens* of the play, after all, people of common sense and realistic expectations. But tolerance of wrongdoing is acknowledgement of its existence. While the dialectic of desire and repugnance implies the exorcism of evil, Philinte's smiling, passive shrug in the face of corruption consecrates the reality principle. Society is portrayed here in a fall from grace, the Republic viewed from the Empire, a moment of effete corruption seen from 'Cette grande roideur des vertus des vieux âges' (I, 1). The censor in this play seems to be right. For once the idealistic premises of comedy are questioned, we must re-evaluate our opinion of the *alazon* standing in opposition to it. By and large, Alceste's strictures on society are validated by that very society as we see it on stage.

Yet, we are in the domain of great theatre and great comedy, where characters are much more than embodied precepts, more than ideas in a moral allegory. Molière knew, as Moore has so convincingly demonstrated, that comedy arises out of inner contradiction, the comparison between what characters say and what they do, between their *persona* and their inner being (eg, the violent clash between Tartuffe the ascetic saint holding a handkerchief before Dorine's bosom, and the animal slavering over Elmire). Such contradictions, although less extreme, invalidate Alceste's self-righteous pronouncements: 'his views, his doctrines, are in sharp contrast to his nature, his mood, his real situation' (Moore, *Molière* 50). First of all, there is his utter dependency on the very society he detests; he needs its attention and recognition and leaves it only under duress or when it has finally failed to satisfy his absolute demands.[17] A suggestive clash between precept and conduct fills in the picture; in his encounter with Oronte Alceste falls short of the high principles he has just so rashly enunciated: 'Je veux qu'on soit sincère et qu'en homme d'honneur, / On ne lâche aucun mot qui ne parte du cœur. (I, 1). He skirts the issue of the sonnet, as Brody says, 'with all the artful circumspection of a practiced courtier' ('*Don Juan* and *Le Misanthrope*' 571); his repeated 'Je ne dis pas cela' collapse into a brutally sudden and devastating outburst: 'Franchement il est bon a mettre au cabinet' (I, 2). His criticisms, while put crudely and simplistically, turn out to be well founded.[18] But once again, he invalidates his strictures by proposing as a model a no less conventional and cliché-ridden song from Henri IV's time which he considers a pure expression of love. Only, its archaism and his conservatism blind him to such a degree to these defects that he recites the song a second time in a ludicrous outburst of enthusiasm.[19]

The most telling commentary on his comic inconsistency, however, is his willingness to sacrifice his most cherished principle before the onslaught of passion. When he enjoins Célimène to be insincere: 'Efforcez-vous ici de paraître fidèle' he reminds us of the beleaguered Arnolphe giving Agnès *carte blanche* to cuckold him; but while the heroine of *L'Ecole des femmes* has no idea of the privilege given her, Célimène flings his self-righteousness back in his face: 'Je voudrais bien savoir qui pourrait me contraindre / A descendre pour vous aux bassesses de feindre' (IV, 3).

Nor should we forget the traditional subtitle of *Le Misanthrope*: *L'Amoureux atrabilaire*. Alceste suffers from an excess of black bile, the humour in classical physiology which produced that state of profound sadness known as melancholia. But the symptoms of this condition went beyond the passive, despondent immobility which we would today call depression. The atrabilious had an active state distinguished by antisocial behaviour, as disruptive as their withdrawal was disturbing. Thus, Alceste is 'un personnage partagé entre les rentrées en soi-même et la lutte coléreuse contre autrui' (Guicharnaud, *ibid.* 353); he oscillates between a desire to escape into brooding solitude (whether in his 'désert' or in 'ce petit coin sombre, avec mon noir chagrin' [V, 1]) and his uncontrolled outbursts of rage against 'mes bons amis de cour' (II, 4) and against Célimène herself.

We cannot dignify the misanthropy of this humour character by making it a reasoned, deliberately taken position, because he has no alternative to being what he is: 'Je ne suis plus à moi je suis tout à la rage' (IV, 3). Behind all his moral indignation, moreover, lies a hidden 'amour de soi': his self-righteous strictures go back to a basic egoism, his vehement generalities about vice-ridden humanity stem from personal hurt. And, as a crowning element of inner contradiction, this misfit is in love, and with a woman who embodies all that he hates in society. Such a passion clashes with his atrabilious nature, since the social form of love, a form he execrates, is *galanterie* (cf. Philinte's solicitous courtship of Eliante and the latter's witty speech on how lovers idealize their ladies [II, 4]). Alceste's jealous and possessive nature would make his courtship techniques insulting and humourless no matter who their object.

Notwithstanding these shortcomings, Alceste does get his way in the end. By the time of his final interview with Célimène, he has accomplished the purpose he had assigned himself at the outset and which has been frustrated four times. He has finally had his *explication* with Célimène, the rival suitors have been eliminated (thanks to Arsinoé), and – most importantly – Célimène consents to marry him: 'Si le don de ma main peut contenter vos vœux, / Je pourrai me résoudre à serrer de tels nœuds' (V, last scene). Hence, the romantic suggestions in the initial dramatic situation return for a brief moment in the last scene. If Alceste were a normal lover he would gratefully accept a prize coveted so long by so many; we would have a conventional double marriage with a stasis of bliss for the future. But he is not a lover content to see his future wife gravitating freely in society. He places himself forever among the *alazones*, the censorious, possessive, blocking characters, by demanding of Célimène the same marriage Arnolphe demands of Agnès, Dandin of Angélique:

> Qui, je veux bien, perfide, oublier vos forfaits;
> ...
> Pourvu que votre cœur veuille donner les mains
> Au dessein que j'ai fait de fuir tous les humains,
> Et que dans mon désert, où j'ai fait voeu de vivre,
> Vous soyez, sans tarder, résolue à me suivre.

The formulation is different, to be sure, but the intention is the same: to be the sole human presence in the other's life,[20] to impose a hell of solitary austerity. Only at this price can Célimène redeem herself in Alceste's eyes. 'Elle sera,' in Guicharnaud's striking phrase, 'l'ombre d'Alceste, ou louve' (*ibid.* 463).

For this reason, Célimène's position makes perfect sense. She speaks the social norm, however immediately self-interested her remarks may be: 'Moi, renoncer au monde avant que de vieillir, / Et dans votre désert aller m'ensevelir!'[21] Alceste's absolute lack of humour puts in a favourable perspective the mood of elegant play that suffuses this exciting, if dangerous society which Célimène will no doubt reconquer after her momentary humiliation (Brody, 'Don Juan and Le Misanthrope' 575).[22] In this world of relativity and compromise, Alceste has given Célimène an unfairly radical choice between absolute acceptance and total rejection, between humanity, good and bad, and sterile solitude, between the enjoyment of her fellow men (and women) and a living death with a man whose churlishness as a suitor leaves little hope for his prospects as a husband.

Molière, then, captures in *Le Misanthrope* his society's contradictory image of itself, brilliant and vitiated, sophisticated and corrupt. The subtlety and ambiguity of this vision come out all the more forcefully when we remember the myth to which it alludes. The polarity of comedy makes it tend to avoid difficult moral issues, the grey world where right and wrong cohabit and intermingle. We escape in the one direction into romantic fantasy with an idealized society symbolized by the lovers, and on the other into the comic fault and its punishment. A more complex world is presented here: a world neatly poised between these usual comic extremes, a deflated but still attractive society set off against a scapegoat ennobled but still all too human.

DON JUAN

As most commentators have observed, the distinctive trait of *Don Juan* from the standpoint of plot development is its episodic construction. In no other comedy does the hero wander through a similar succession of settings, each with its particular cast of characters. The urban scene of Don Juan's stopover in I becomes the maritime and bucolic vista of the second with its amiable peasants; the woodland setting of III, peopled with hermits, thieves, and harassed travellers, is followed by the events that take place in Don Juan's own home in IV with its domestics and importunate visitors; finally, a vague landscape full of supernatural menace – spectres and talking statues – becomes the scene of Don Juan's exemplary punishment.

Each act is so self-contained in its geographical isolation that it can be thought of as a separate adventure. The first is concerned with one more amorous quest: Don Juan plans to abduct a 'jeune fiancée' while she is being entertained by a 'promenade sur mer'; still other seductions occupy him in the following act as he courts Mathurine and Charlotte; III centres on his encounter with Elvire's two brothers, after which we witness two episodes which could be entitled: 'En attendant le Commandeur' – the suspenseful fourth act culminating in the arrival of Don Juan's dinner guest, and the ominous events which lead up to the fatal handclasp of the dénouement.

Within this episodic structure, the principal element of continuity is, of course, Don Juan himself and his valet, Sganarelle, linked together by their perverse need for one another: '[Sganarelle] a besoin, pour s'épanouir, de suivre ce maître qu'il n'aime pas' (Guicharnaud, *ibid.* 188), while, in Moore's words, the master 'constantly needs and enjoys the company of the valet whom intellectually he despises' (*Molière* 123). Their meanderings, and their complementary and contrasting views of the events which befall them, give the play its essential forward motion. This thrust is made more compelling by the theme of pursuit. We are early made aware of Elvire's efforts to bring her husband to accept his responsibilities. When they are not on stage, her avenging brothers are in hot pursuit, just behind their quarry. To the suspense of the chase is added the glowering presence of the supernatural: the Commandeur appears in each of the final three acts, after being mentioned as early as I, 2.

This series of adventures linked by the processional movement of the hero harks back, of course, to romance and its episodic construction. Don Juan and Sganarelle bring to mind the travelling knight and his squire discoursing together, commenting variously upon the ever-new world they pàss through; Moore's allusion to Don Quixote is very much to the point (*Molière* 95). We need not summarize the various debates in which they indulge, the dramatic meaning of which Guicharnaud has fully analysed. These disputations — in which Don Juan so often plays the straight man to tease Sganarelle into outraged incoherence — form an essential continuity in the play, a continuity which complements their contrasting reactions to the events that occur: Don Juan's bravado, Sganarelle's cowardice before the statue; the former's callous indifference, the latter's mawkish fellow-feeling, regarding Elvire's eloquent speeches.

We are, moreover, in that special domain of romantic legend where the laws of nature are suspended. *Psyché* and *Amphitryon* come to mind, other works where the whims of supernatural beings create a shifting and confusing world. As in these plays, the creative efforts of the divine in *Don Juan* point toward spectacle. But instead of wonderful palaces and cloud-borne gods rising to the heavens, we plunge into a terrifying demonic realm: in addition to the brooding figure of the animated statue we see a grisly 'spectre' who becomes before our eyes a premonitory image of Time (V, 5).

The ominous role of spectacle and the supernatural in *Don Juan* is only part of a general questioning of the *mythos* of romance. Just as marvel and awe have turned into anxiety, just as the jaws of hell replace the luminous apotheosis of *Psyché*, the knight errant becomes a cynical, callous seducer whose heroic dreams parody the chivalric tradition of military prowess: 'J'ai ... l'ambition des conquérants, qui volent perpétuellement de victoire en victoire, et ne peuvent se résoudre à borner leurs souhaits. Il n'est rien qui puisse arrêter l'impétuosité de mes désirs: je me sens un cœur à aimer toute la terre; et comme Alexandre, je souhaiterais qu'il y eût d'autres mondes, pour y pouvoir étendre mes conquêtes amoureuses' (I, 2). This transposition of seduction for seduction's sake into the epic language of battle shows how far Don Juan has fallen from the noble ideal of warlike prowess and courtly respect for women.[23]

This debased vision of the romantic hero leads expectedly to an ironic view of the quest motif, the central one of the genre. In romance the hero goes from one victorious adventure to another until, with a major challenge, he reaches his high point of achievement, his apotheosis. *Don Juan* can be seen as a bitter comment on this rising movement. There is a marked slowdown in the action and a strong contrast between the 'dashing pace of a seducer' in the first half of the play and the 'besieged' hero of the second (Hubert 116-17). In actual fact, the quest exists as a motif only in the first two acts as the Don pursues first the 'fiancée' and then the peasant girls. These adventures, moreover, come to naught. Only here do we see Don Juan as legend depicts him: a buoyant, self-assured lady's man; even then, the image of a conqueror soaring from victory to victory is belied by actual defeat and flight.

In the remainder of the play Don Juan loses his sense of enterprise. When he is not playing games with his servant he is mainly concerned with escaping unpleasant situations. In III he is caught in the middle of the quarrel between Elvire's brothers; IV shows him dealing expeditiously with several *fâcheux* who intrude upon his privacy: Monsieur Dimanche, Don Louis, his father, Elvire, and the statue. The heroic impetus is spent; the counterforce has seized the initiative. Even the Don's hypocrisy in the fifth act is a ploy to escape his father's sermons and his wife's claims, and to allow him to be dissolute with impunity.

Ever more frequent warnings give the impression that time is closing in; Don Juan's carefree present is being eroded away. We foresee a heavy period of divine vengeance bringing time to a stop, rather than a divine providence about to open up an eternity of heroic bliss. As a last, powerful effect in this ironic view of romance, the apotheosis of the hero, his assumption into the timeless world of legend becomes the final vision of a miscreant burning in agony and pulled down into everlasting flames. Romance, 'nearest of all literary forms to the wish-fulfilment dream' (Frye, 186) becomes the nightmare view of human destiny.

The processional nature of the plot points, then, to a devastating parody of romance, a topsy-turvy, degraded version of the heroic world. In another way, as many commentators have pointed out, the restless rhythm of the action under-lines Don Juan's own character. As the plot must move from one centre of interest to another, so is the hero unable to remain still. His profession of faith is eloquently set forth early in the play: 'Quoi! tu veux qu'on se lie à demeurer au premier objet qui nous prend, qu' on renonce au monde pour lui, et qu'on n'ai plus d'yeux pour personne? La belle chose de vouloir se piquer d'un faux honneur d'être fidèle, de s'ensevelir pour toujours dans une passion, et d'être mort dès sa jeunesse à toutes les autres beautés qui nous peuvent frapper les yeux ... tout le plaisir de l'amour est dans le changement' (I, 2). Gone are the familiar romantic archetypes: the first love prolonged into eternity – that of Amour and Psyché; the 'happily-ever-after' stasis of young lovers. Indeed, the sense of fidelity and duration that underlies these bonds is expressed by Don Juan in the imagery of death ('s'ensevelir,' 'être mort'). Pleasure is not in perma-nence, or attainment, but in the hunt.

Yet, the hunt is an important element in romance; it is the amorous form of the quest motif itself. Don Juan has been punctilious in following the ritual of *galanterie*, as Gusman incredulously notes: 'tant d'hommages pressants ... tant de lettres passionnées, de protestations ardentes et de serments réitérés' (I, 1), a passage that foreshadows Don Juan's own description of the delight 'à réduire, par cent hommages, le cœur d'une jeune beauté' (I, 2). What astounds Gusman is not this love ritual in itself, perfectly in tune with romance whether in this serious register or in the ridiculous account of 'la belle galanterie' contained in *Les Précieuses ridicules;* what he cannot understand is Don Juan's rejection of the goal for which all this effort is expended: the chivalric ideal of fidelity to the lady thus conquered. In Don Juan the movement toward romantic fulfilment has become an end in itself; pleasure is in the process of conquest, not in the final result.[24] The more resistance Don Juan encounters and the greater the number of obstacles, the more ardent he becomes and the greater his pleasure. But this delight in the ritual of seduction does not, as Gossman seems to think (p 44), betoken a lack of sexuality. A civilized and refined aristocrat-lover, Don Juan knows the art of 'pacing' the amorous encounter to derive from it the greatest and most continuous delight.

Don Juan rejects, then, all the assumptions underlying the romantic union: first and last love projected into a future where tastes never pale. But he is not above using marriage, the form of romantic stasis, for his own ends, thus converting the image of permanence into a mere step in the process of seduction: 'C'est l'épouseur du genre humain,' warns Sganarelle (II, 3). Instead of resorting to disguise, as did Jupiter in *Amphitryon* and, for that matter, the hero of Tirso de Molina's *Burlador de Sevilla,* Molière's Don Juan blithely uses marriage for the purpose of the moment: to capture a new prey.[25] In this ironic view of romance, however, marriage is not an idealized form of wish-fulfilment, but a solemn sacrament, a bond consecrated by a supreme being. So it is by implication, for example, in *George Dandin;* neither of the unhappy partners is free to break the covenant (or even to separate without the agreement of the wife's parents). The sacramental nature of marriage is made explicit at the very beginning of *Don Juan,*·where Gusman speaks of its 'saints nœuds' (I, 1), and Sganarelle alludes to its 'mystère sacré' (I, 2). By perverting this solemn covenant, Don Juan by implication challenges all moral and religious beliefs; his contempt for this sacrament leads inevitably from lust to *libertinage.*

Unable to take refuge in romantic fantasy, the pleasure principle must clash head-on with its opposite, religious austerity and constraint. The conflict between aristocratic paganism and Christian imperatives, between self-indulgence and self-abnegation, is central to the understanding of the play (Bénichou 169-72). The pleasure-seeker must willy-nilly be a free-thinker in this ironic setting – although, as Brody puts it so succinctly, Don Juan is 'more concerned with freedom than with thinking' (*'Don Juan* and *Le Misanthrope'* 566).[26] And in a final debasement of romance, the link between the libertine and the blasphemer is further reinforced by the hypocritical poses Don Juan assumes in each domain. A faithless promise of marriage before the play begins finds its ironic fulfilment in a profession of religious hypocrisy of V. The high-minded, sincere hero of romance is thus reduced to a histrion belonging to '[la race] des Scapins' (Rousset, *L'Intérieur et l'extérieur* 144).

From a parody of romance we advance into an inverted and extended form of the comic myth.[27] The action which normally underlies comedy – the winning of the beloved – has already taken place. We are in the ironic counterpart of the 'happily-ever-after' period. Only, instead of being heavy bondage as in *George Dandin*, it is heavy freedom for both bride and groom. After her fruitless efforts to win back Don Juan, Elvire annuls her marriage by retiring to the convent from which she was abducted. In words made hollow by her enduring passion for Don Juan, she assures him: 'Pour moi, je ne tiens plus à vous par aucun attachement du monde; je suis revenue, grâces au Ciel, de toutes mes folles pensées; ma retraite est résolue' (IV, 6). That convent life, brought up so often as a threat by the heavy fathers of comedy, is freely accepted as a form of expiation further devalues the comic myth.

As for Don Juan, he escapes the bond because he never accepted it in the first place. But because he has committed an impious act demanding punishment, he is drawn willy-nilly into the nether world of damnation. As a result, *Don Juan* goes beyond *Le Misanthrope*, whose ambiguities, however intriguing, are revealed only in a 'métaphore humaine' instead of the 'métaphore quasi-métaphysique' of *Don Juan* (Guicharnaud, *ibid*. 343). Don Juan strays beyond the norms of society in his egotistical and disruptive pursuit of the pleasure principle. But by perverting a sacrament he defies the cosmic realm. The *agon* between man and the order beyond takes place against a background of divine imperatives which can be contravened only at the price of eternal torment.

The perplexities of *Le Misanthrope* are echoed here by our ambivalent attitude to this strange mixture of egoism, courage, common sense, and folly. Don Juan's tirade on hypocrisy rings true, cynical but lucid; his sarcastic remarks about medicine put him among such men of sense as Béralde.[28] Yet, in terms of the comic myth this play must be seen as a reversal of the normal polarity. The young man has become the *alazon*, the father the *eiron*. The traits of the blocking character – egoism, callousness, rejection of legitimate social norms, desire to have one's way with impunity – are transferred to the young man. Don Louis, despite all his sermonizing, turns into a noble, eloquent old warrior revolted by his son's frivolous life. The kill-joy's dour imperatives are validated here by the collapse of the comic norm, the degradation of the pleasure principle. Thus, when Don Juan exclaims to his departed father: 'mourez le plus tôt que vous pourrez, c'est le mieux que vous puissiez faire' (IV, 5), this parricidal wish, usually viewed lightly in comedy, becomes all the more repugnant since the Commandeur can be thought of as a father surrogate whom the hero has already slain. And the hypocritical pretense by which Don Juan deceives his father in V becomes in this inverted world a cruel joke, instead of a legitimate weapon against a paternal tyrant.

When Hyacinthe in *Les Fourberies de Scapin* laments the difficult course of her love and sighs: 'La douce chose que d'aimer, lorsque l'on ne voit point d'obstacle à ces aimables chaînes dont deux cœurs se lient ensemble,' Scapin responds: 'Vous vous moquez: la tranquillité en amour est un calme désagréable; un bonheur tout uni nous devient ennuyeux' (III, 1). This gentle debunking of a young girl's romantic illusions reaches its most powerful and unforgettable expression in *Don Juan*. The 'chaînes' of marriage are no longer 'aimables'; they are no longer even endured. The overriding quest for pleasure has reduced sacred vows to a mockery, one deception among many practised upon the intended victim. And in the final analysis, this devaluation of the romantic extreme of the comic myth is hardly counterbalanced by the ennobling of the realistic one. While Don Louis' heavy virtue can be seen as a heroic norm set against the reign of licence, this norm itself in retrospect seems hollow and meaningless. The last image we have of Don Louis is that of a lonely, credulous old man gulled by his son, and there is no attempt in the play to generalize or institutionalize this private symbol of right. 'With no divinely appointed King to mark the restoration of order, with no divinely sanctioned marriage to suggest human participation in God's victory, Don Juan's punishment and death are replete with irony' (Brody, 'Don Juan and Le Misanthrope' 567).

This blurring of norms. this settling of accounts where 'justice has not been served, wrongs have not been righted' (Brody, *loc. cit.*),[29] dislocates all the familiar features of comedy. The reversal is transformed from a miraculous surprise to a terrifying confirmation of expectations; it consecrates the defeat of the young man and the empty moral victory of the old one. Instead of Anselme's arrival as the long-lost good father, the dénouement brings forth an avenging *deus ex caelo*.

With *Don Juan*, then, we reach the final shattering of the comic myth. Comedy's underlying hymn to life is no longer heard. Sganarelle's easy-going libido in *Le Médecin malgré lui* becomes, at this final point, a principle of social disruption and cosmic defiance.

Conclusion

An archetypal approach to Molière implies that his plays should be treated as autonomous verbal and visual structures, examined as much as possible apart from the life, background, philosophy, or stated intentions of the author. His theatre has been viewed for the most part as if on the timeless living stage of enduring drama. By the same token, we have been little concerned with the creative process as such: the elements — literary, personal, historical — which went into the genesis and maturation of each comedy. The Molière canon has been seen as a series of finished products.

Nor have we endeavoured to detect and isolate an 'evolution' in Molière, a meaningful, sustained thrust forward. Even Guicharnaud, in positing for Molière a mid-career *mise en question* of traditional comic conventions, wisely shies away from concluding that there is a definite break, a new direction in Molière's theatre. Not only are the plays written after *Le Misanthrope* often marked by the same 'théâtralisme' as those penned before *Tartuffe*, but there is a 'renchérissement sur la mascarade proprement dite, sur le ballet, sur la farce' (*Aventure* 534). There is good reason to take Bray's word for it: 'il n'y a aucune évolution dans la carrière du comédien sinon celle d'une technique qui prend de l'assurance' (p 201).[1]

We have tried rather to consider Molière's works as a constant shifting and blending of patterns, a movement from one facet to another of a versatile, receptive, Protean genius. The plays analysed in each chapter of this study seem to belong to no particular 'period' — buffoon plays range from the early *Etourdi* to the late *Fourberies de Scapin*: the romances as well as the comedies suggestive of Frye's ironic *mythos* are similarly spaced out over his entire career. Molière's theatre does not seem to develop; it responds rather to a mixture of inner and outer stimuli: the caprice of creative instinct, the need to climb out of financial doldrums, or the imperatives of his demanding role as *fournisseur* for courtly entertainment.

I sought at the beginning of this work to persuade the reader that archetypal theory provided a useful and fitting tool for the analysis of Molière's comedies. Whether, at this final point, precept has survived practice, whether theoretical soundness has produced critical illumination is for the reader to judge. If he is a theatre-goer, he may be able to measure how much the emotional appeal I have posited for Molière's comedy has been actualized on his own direct experience. This is one of the possible tests for archetypal methodology: do our reactions confirm or substantiate the hypothesis of literary archetypes and their appeal for us? But beyond this subjective and personal encounter which escapes generalization, the final justification for an archetypal approach must lie in the degree to which, in this long itinerary through individual plays in various groupings, the reader has gained new insight into Molière's theatre as a whole.

In the broadest possible dimension, our analysis of basic archetypal patterns points to a tripartite division in Molière: romantic comedies (those embodying the comic myth, whether buffoon or exorcism plays), romances (the works discussed in chapter 5), and the ironic comedies just analyzed. These three categories correspond more or less to three of Frye's basic *mythoi*: comedy, romance, and irony. I have tried to avoid any *a priori* value judgements among these various categories, any assumptions that one group of plays is more authentically *moliéresque* than another. From the archetypal point of view, each play has its interest not only in its position in the generic plot concerned but in its unique structural pattern.

While avoiding any systematic 'thesis,' the foregoing chapters have nonetheless stressed the importance of the romantic element in Molière. As Baumal maintained a half century ago in his pioneer study *Molière auteur précieux*, critics have been all too prone to assume a 'genuine' Molière full of Gallic wit and realistic observation, as opposed to a restive Molière who catered only with reluctance to the *goût romanesque* of the time (p 49). I have tried rather to follow the trail blazed by Moore, Bray, Guicharnaud, and Lawrence who have laid particular emphasis on the importance of fancy, 'le chimérique,' poetic invention, and unreason in Molière. A more specific facet of the romantic Molière, and, I hope, a distinctive finding in this study, is the one that emerges from our analysis of the comic myth. We have noted that the action of Molière's comedies generally presents a world of ritual bondage, the reign of tyranny and egoism which comes to an end through the miraculous reversal which puts into power a 'pragmatically free society' symbolic of what we desire. And if the meaning of comedy is 'the establishing of a desirable society' (Frye 286), its significance must lie to a large degree in the reversal, the twist in the plot that allows the 'right' society to emerge. The dénouement, then, that very feature of Molière's dramatic art which so embarrasses certain scholars, carries in its luminous glow the central archetypal meaning of the comic *mythos*.[2] It is, in Frye's suggestive analogy with music, 'the final harmonic chord revealing the tonality under the narrative movement' (*loc. cit.*). The archetypal meaning of *L'Ecole des femmes* is the victory of the lovers and their allies over Arnolphe. The image of the heavy father may predominate as we leave the theatre, but our final picture as spectators still in our seats is the happy tableau from which Arnolphe has been banished. The vision of a simultaneous comic polarity is largely retrospective. What we experience as theatre-goers is the passage from one world to another, the triumph of romance over reality.

Molière's theatre has a profoundly romantic imprint, since the comic myth recurs in over two-thirds of his plays. If we add to romantic dénouement the many examples of *romanesque* themes in the context of his most 'realistic' theatre – the shipwreck motif of *L'Avare*, for instance – the role of fantasy becomes even more considerable. Most of Molière's comedies, moreover, belong to the fourth phase in Frye's schema, where the action is presented on two social planes, one of which is 'preferred and consequently in some measure idealized' (p 182), the other of which is momentarily in control as 'the ritual bondage of the humors' (*loc. cit.*). The romantic ending is prefigured in the course of the play by the presence, by direct statement or by implication, of a social norm. As we noted in *Tartuffe*, an ideal of salon society with its elegant and legitimate *divertissements* stands in explicit contrast to the kill-joy, perverted world of Tartuffe and his allies. In *Les Femmes savantes*, a standard of civility is clearly articulated by Clitandre and Henriette before they are given a chance, at the end of the play, to put it into practice. Even more explicit, of course, is the programme of tolerance and trust sponsored by Ariste in *L'Ecole des maris*, a point-for-point antithesis of Sganarelle's school for slavery, and the articles of faith for the new society formed at the end. This sense of a presiding norm in the course of the play is even more pronounced in romance, where it can take the simple form of tasteful spectacle.

In still another sense, then, Molière is romantic. The preferred world exists already in embryo form, a clear point of reference for us, so that the short-comings of the humorous characters' society can be underscored long before that idealized world is fully realized at the dénouement. Hence, that sombre, realistic comedy, *Tartuffe*, is doubly romantic: the young prevail with their promise of harmony and joy; but even before, we can see dimly in the wings the happy, if threatened, social unit presided over by Elmire.

The question of the comic norm in *Tartuffe* brings up the subject of Cléante and, more generally, that of the *raisonneur* in Molière's theatre.[3] Many explanations of the *raisonneur's* function have been offered: spokesman for the norm

(Guicharnaud, Gossman) 'fâcheux' (Gutwirth 158), a verbal foil for the foolish character of the play (Moore), an *eiron* who 'throws complex, spirited irony' against Arnolphe and his likes (Lawrence 33); or, in the now discredited view that placed Madame Jourdain and the Gorgibus of *Les Précieuses ridicules* on the same footing as Cléante, the voices of Molière's 'bon sens.' Indeed, the very existence of such a category has been flatly denied: 'Il n'y a pas de *raisonneurs* dans le théâtre de Molière.' But Bray's extreme position (p 28) applies only to the old-fashioned definition of the term. It is tempting indeed, in reacting against obsolete views, to hide behind what Gossman rightly calls a 'wall of estheticism' (p 243) and to deny or minimize the moral relevance of such characters. Yet, while Moore is surely correct in arguing that the *raisonneurs* 'ensure symmetry and roundness of comic presentation' (p 74), the fact that the opposite to excess is being pictured, a foil to the ridiculous, necessarily confers a kind of positive norm on what the *raisonneur* says. In fact Moore himself anticipates Guicharnaud and Gossman: if any point of view is presented, 'it is that of the average spectator for whom the show is devised' (*loc. cit.*).

We cannot deny the existence in Molière of characters who articulate eloquently and at length various moral positions that converge, in general, on a standard of *honnêteté* or civility. From the archetypal view, they may be seen as spokesmen for the values of the right society in opposition to the blocking characters. Such is certainly the case for the first, chronologically, of these characters, Ariste, as well as for the Clitandre of *Les Femmes savantes*. Yet the *complaisance* which Chrysalde urges upon Arnolphe seems intended less as a standard of conduct than as a vehicle for irony and as a means for freeing him from a dangerous obsession. Somewhat the same explanation was offered for Béralde. Still more problematical, of course, is the norm in *Le Misanthrope*: Philinte's passive acceptance of human evil can be thought of as a standard of conduct only in the vitiated society in which he moves.

To generalize about the exact function of the *raisonneur* is to invite trouble. Even Cléante's role raises problems in this regard, although in his moral alliance with Dorine he supports Lawrence's view that 'the *raisonneur* ... is a more sophisticated embodiment of the opposition traditionally offered by the servant' (p 32). His main function is to articulate a standard of religious conduct in opposition to Orgon's fascination with show and Tartuffe's vindictiveness against Damis. But this is part of a larger, less explicit norm: that of social life in general. While he is a friend of the lovers and pleads their cause, he propounds little that can be compared to Ariste's programme of freedom and trust. What he does say is fairly narrow in scope and developed at such lengths as to appear over-emphatic.

Must we conclude, then, with Hubert (p 93) that his presence flaws the play? Perhaps, to look at the question from another angle, we have been too long concerned with *what* characters like Cléante say, as opposed to *how* they say it. The appeal of the *raisonneur* lies not only in his conclusions but in the rhetorical skill by which he arrives at them. The ability to marshal proofs, present them in the most effective order, and dress them in the most persuasive figures was greatly admired in the seventeenth century; one of the most compelling aspects of the serious drama of the time was the manner in which the protagonists jousted verbally with each other. The domination of the set-piece in French classical drama ultimately goes back to such love for rhetoric. Since the *raisonneur*'s speeches are generally long and well constructed, it is possible that Molière was introducing into comedy a much appreciated element of serious drama, just as he incorporated in it the charms of the ballet.

Critics have generally failed to notice the link between one of the seventeenth-century meanings of the word *raisonner* – 'discuter' – and the traditional art of dialectics. Béralde, for instance, simply takes up the challenge thrown at him by Argan: 'Mais raisonnons un peu, mon frère' (III, 3); the latter wants a good argument, and he gets it. Thus the *raisonneur*'s real function may be to bring the set-piece into comedy, to use rhetoric effectively, to impress us more with his debating skill than with his ideas, perhaps even, as Lawrence suggests, 'to ... build up his arguments purely for the fun he gets out of seeing the protagonist react' (p 26). While he does slow the action down, he can be labelled a 'fâcheux' solely if the only desideratum in comedy is fast-moving action. But if we assume that Molière aimed at total comedy, a fusion of many elements of proven audience appeal, we can put Cléante and his eloquent fellows in a more favourable and positive light.

The ambiguity of the *raisonneur*'s role is one of several factors that lift Molière's theatre far above the category of mere 'naïve melodrama' (Frye 47) founded on a comfortable and simplistic moral Manicheism. The blocking character's fault justifies his defeat and punishment; the young win because they deserve to and because we wish it so. But that Molière was aware of the basic tenuousness of this polarity is amply evident, for *Le Misanthrope* and *Don Juan* constitute a critique of these very conventions. And even the comic myth plays escape from a rigid and unimaginative adherence to these formulas. The blocking character transcends very often the schematic flatness that the comic polarity would impose on him if a less perceptive playwright were at work. Arnolphe is perhaps the best example of 'a dramatic character at once both realistic and ridiculous' (Moore, *Molière* 17), a creation with human complexities, caricatured enough to elicit our laughter and mark firmly his *alazoneia*, but capable of giving his purse spontaneously to a friend's son. Argan and Monsieur Jourdain have winning qualities, too, whatever their foolish obsessions and general ludicrousness.

The lovers also are variously treated. The four young people of *L'Avare* are remarkably individualized: Valère's dissimulation stands in sharp contrast to Cléante's passionate directness; the instinctively wise naïveté of Agnès is unique in Molière's theatre; the decorous and restrained affection of Clitandre and Henriette, or the pathos aroused by Mariane in *Tartuffe*, are further variations in mood. Even the comic reversal can be presented to us with a nuance of irony. We have noted such phrases as 'la fin d'une vraie et pure comédie' to describe the ending of *L'Etourdi*, the bantering about how to conclude *La Critique de L'Ecole des femmes*. In *L'Ecole des femmes* itself there is a suggestion of parody in the series of couplets that apprise Arnolphe of the situation. The fact is that our theatrical perception is double when we witness a play based on fixed generic conventions. We enjoy the play as an individual vicarious experience while all the time perceiving in the back of our minds the recurrence of familiar devices which put a distance between us and the spectacle. Molière was astute enough to appeal not only to our spontaneous emotions as we witness the triumph of youth and love, but to that reflective part of us which intellectualizes a theatrical experience by comparing it to others already stored in our memory.

Within the archetypal dimension, then, Molière's theatre has an astonishing richness and complexity. The conventions of comedy are shaped into individual creations obeying the laws of their own inner theatrical coherence. While there are resemblances among lovers, blocking characters, auxiliaries, and the like, to organize our findings under such rubrics would have been to lose the sense of the profound uniqueness of each play. In addition, there is more in each work than a *rapport de forces* among the above-mentioned elements: plot development, the play of dramatic irony, the elaboration of spectacle can vary considerably from play to play. The same archetypal premises can develop in vastly different directions. No two plays are more dissimilar than *L'Ecole des maris* and *L'Ecole des femmes* in the banal dynamism based on trickery of the one and the powerful ironic structure of the other. Yet the underlying archetypal pattern is similar.

We perceive the full range of Molière's genius only when we go beyond the limits of any particular approach. A stage director looks for his own structures in Molière: mood, rhythm, visual and verbal dynamism. Close study of the text as literary form would yield still a different order of results. Yet, no matter how subtle the verbal patterns, no matter what elaborations astute stagecraft can invent, there must be a story. And as is the case with all narrative, that story must have an underlying meaning. Whatever the particular method we use, we proceed from *mythos* to *dianoia*, from plot to significance. The narrative content of comedy can be seen in a number of ways, but the recurrence of a particular story in Molière – a story for which a convincing archetypal basis has been established – has been our prime consideration in the foregoing chapters. Ahd the *dianoia* which informs this comic plot is an overall vision which varies as subtly from play to play as does the treatment of the comic *mythos* itself.

One is always tempted to forget the dangers of generalizing about such a varied theatre. Critics have been all too ready to propose an overall meaning for Molière's comedies on the basis of a few atypical works. The plays analyzed by Gossman, for instance, belong with one exception among the problematical ones studied in chapter 6; only *Tartuffe* fits in elsewhere, and it is one of the most ironic of Molière's exorcism comedies. This limited vantage point from Molière's 'problem plays' leads Gossman to hasty conclusions, eg, that Molière 'always tried to see things honestly and truthfully' (p 305). While Guicharnaud is more careful not to generalize sweepingly, the three works he probes and the point of view from which he studies them makes the reader consider them as a kind of triumphant moment of lucidity and artistic integrity in Molière's career.

When the whole of Molière's production is impartially examined a different order of generalization is more appropriate. If the majority of Molière's plays – including many great ones – embody the comic *mythos*, they must project to a large degree the optimism and idealism that suffuses that generic plot. It is likely, of course, that the dramatist had no illusions about the reality of the world around him; Brody is no doubt right in contending that Molière's 'natural impulse was to accept [vice and corruption], in the deep conviction of their inevitability and permanence' ('*Don Juan* and *Le Misanthrope*' 576). But Molière's theatre was for his contemporaries, and is for us, a way of abolishing chronological time and its distasteful realities, and of recapturing ritually and momentarily a golden age of harmony, order, and innocent pleasure.[4] Through its intense celebrative appeal, it calls out our recurrent yearnings and dreads and thus gives us the powerful vicarious experience that is ours as we respond to great works of art.

Notes

INTRODUCTION

1 For a brief, but comprehensive summary of the Cambridge 'view,' its exponents and their works, see S. E. Hyman, 'The Ritual View of Myth and the Mythic,' in *Myth: A Symposium*, ed. T. Sebeok (Philadelphia 1955) 84-8.

2 Other valuable books could be cited as well (eg, Philip Wheelwright's *Metaphor and Reality* [Indiana 1962]), but no work has had the general impact of *Anatomy of Criticism*.

3 Will G. Moore, *Molière: A New Criticism* (Oxford 1949). The major books which have followed in Moore's wake are: René Bray, *Molière homme de théâtre* (Paris 1954); Judd Hubert, *Molière and the Comedy of Intellect* (Berkeley 1962); Lionel Gossman, *Men and Masks: A Study of Molière* (Baltimore 1963); Jacques Guicharnaud, *Molière: une aventure théâtrale* (Paris 1963); Marcel Gutwirth, *Molière ou l'invention comique* (Paris 1966); F.L. Lawrence, *Molière: The Comedy of Unreason*, Tulane Studies in Romance Languages and Literature, No. 2 (New Orleans 1968); A. Eustis, *Molière as Ironic Contemplator* (The Hague 1973).

Other significant works on Molière have been published during the same period but are less relevant to the internal analysis that is our concern here. No background reading on Molière would be complete, for instance, without careful perusal of the pages devoted to him in A. Adam's monumental *Histoire de la littérature française au XVIIe siècle*, vol. III (Paris 1952). Other works worthy of note are Georges Bordonove's *Molière génial et familier* (Paris 1967), a well-written biography which avoids in general the excesses of the *biographie romancée* which so flaw J. Meyer's *Molière* (Paris 1963); a restatement by René Jasinski of the literary history view of the author (*Molière* [Paris 1969]), and Maurice Descotes' interesting study of literary reception (*La Fortune littéraire de Molière* [Paris 1971]).

4 From the publication of *Anatomy of Criticism* Frye's approach to poetics and criticism has attracted much attention in the Anglo-Saxon world, eg *Northrop Frye in Modern Criticism*, ed. M. Krieger (New York 1966). During the same period he has become more and more recognized as an important precursor of *structuralisme*. Curiously enough, however, he has made little headway in France despite the translation of *Anatomy* in 1969 and the similarities between his system and some aspects of *structuralisme* which I describe in Appendix B. For a significant example of French attitudes to Frye see T. Todorov: *Introduction à la littérature fantastique* (Paris 1970) 13-24. G. Hartman approaches the problem from a wider perspective in 'Structuralism: The Anglo-American Adventure,' in *Structuralism*, ed. J. Ehrmann (New York 1970) 137-58 (first published 1966). Frye's position in the whole complex of structuralist thought has been summarized, although rather inadequately, by R. Scholes: *Structuralism in Literature: An Introduction* (New Haven and London 1974); pp 117-39 contain, however, an excellent account of Todorov's objections. Another critique of Frye, on an entirely different basis, is contained in R. Girard, *La Violence et le sacré* (Paris 1973).

5 The latter, especially, seems to be at the fountainhead of a stream of myth criticism on Racine: Marc Eigeldinger, *La Mythologie solaire dans l'œuvre de Racine* (Neuchâtel 1969); Revel Elliot, *Mythe et légende dans le théâtre de Racine* (Paris 1969); and Bettina Knapp's avowedly archetypal study, *Jean Racine: Mythos and Renewal in Modern Theater* (University of Alabama 1971).

6 Developed in a later article: 'Pour une Sociologie des obstacles au mariage dans le théâtre français du XVIIe siècle,' *Dramaturgie et société*, ed. J. Jacquot (Paris 1968) I, 297-305

7 Henri Fluchère's recent article, 'Ploutos, Eros, Molière et les vieillards' (*Molière: Stage and Study: Essays in Honour of W. G. Moore*, ed. W.D. Howarth and M. Thomas [Oxford 1973] 117-31), has affinities with the archetypal approach but treats the concept of 'Eros' largely with regard to blocking characters. The question is a good deal more complex.

CHAPTER 1: COMEDY: THE ARCHETYPAL VIEW

1 'Tum quod in Tragoedia fugienda vita, in Comoedia capessenda exprimitur,' quoted in H.W. Lawton, *Handbook of French Renaissance Dramatic Theory* (Manchester 1949) 10. Mauron also acknowledges comedy's role in promoting 'le sentiment sacré de la vie' (*Psychocritique* 56).

2 Cf. the *premier placet* of *Tartuffe*: 'Le devoir de la comédie étant de corriger les hommes en les divertissant, j'ai cru que dans l'emploi où je me trouve, je n'avais rien de mieux à faire que d'attaquer par des peintures ridicules les vices de mon siècle' (vol. I, p 632). The argument of *La Lettre sur l'imposteur*, assumed by most scholars to reflect Molière's own ideas, turns also on the concept of *le ridicule*. For interesting modern exegeses of this work, see G. Poulet, 'Molière,' in *Etudes sur le temps humain* (Paris 1949) 79-88; and W.G. Moore, 'Molière's Theory of Comedy,' *Esprit créateur* 6 (Fall 1966) 137-44. The reader is also referred to C. Gutkind, *Molière und das Komische Drama* (Halle 1928) 85-111, and Hubert 106-12.

3 Cf. Baudelaire's distinction between 'comique absolu' and 'comique significatif' (*Essence du rire*) and Freud's 'esprit inoffensif' as opposed to his 'esprit tendancieux' as discussed in Mauron (*Psychocritique* 38-9).

4 Langer gives a good description of euphoric mirth (p 340).

5 As Jacques Leenhardt has observed, 'le groupe élabore, au fil de son existence, les moyens conceptuels qui permettent [au créateur] de résoudre, selon son originalité, les problèmes que lui posent la vie en commun et la confrontation avec le monde. Ces moyens conceptuels sont des systèmes de dogmes ou de mythes, des philosophies, que constituent ce que nous appelons des visions du monde' ('Psychocritique et sociologie de la littérature,' *Les Chemins actuels de la critique*, ed. Georges Poulet [Paris 1968] 270. The myth mentioned here is of course the historical one which gives story content to the *Weltanschauung* of the group.

6 In his recent book on *Le Langage dramatique* (Paris 1972), Pierre Larthomas deals in a different way with these difficulties by postulating in Molière 'deux dénouements: l'un de convention, obligé, l'autre chaque fois original, en accord avec l'orginalité de l'intrigue. Il faut bien qu'Octave épouse Hyacinthe et que *L'Avare* se termine par un double mariage; mais l'important est de savoir comment, par une dernière ruse, Scapin, que les deux vieillards veulent faire pendre, échappe à la potence, et quel sera, en face d'une situation qui rentre dans l'ordre, le dernier trait d'avarice d'Harpagon' (pp 128-9). The originality of Larthomas's position does not go very deep, however. The underlying tone of the above quotation betrays the same basic contempt for Molière's romantic dénouement as we have found elsewhere in Molière criticism. A later statement is even more explicit: 'les amoureux n'intéressent guère l'auteur; ils sont des fairevaloir, Valère pour Harpagon, Octave et Léandre pour Scapin' (p 129).

As regards the study of 'la réplique finale de chaque œuvre' which Larthomas advocates (*loc. cit.*), see Quentin Hope's perceptive article, 'Molière's Curtain Lines.'

7 Cf. E.B.O. Borgerhoff's forceful phrase: 'We ... have no right, in a sense, to demand at any point the plausible' ('Tartuffe,' in *Esprit Créateur* 11, No. 2 [Summer 1971] 17.

8 Cf. The term 'catastasis' coined by Scaliger (M.T. Herrick, *Comic Theory in the Sixteenth Century* [Urbana 1950] 119).

9 A point also made by Guicharnaud against those who refuse to accept the dénouement of *Tartuffe*: 'c'est ne pas jouer le jeu que [la pièce] demande' (*Aventure* 146).

10 For Frye, 'the contest of *eiron* and *alazon* forms the basis of the comic action' (p 172); see also Wylie Sypher, *Appendix to Comedy* [*An Essay on Comedy*, George Meredith; *Laughter*, Henri Bergson] (New York 1956) 228ff.

CHAPTER 2: BUFFOON

1 Hubert seems to take these scenes of domestic discord too seriously. He interprets the latter quote as showing that 'Martine wants to make sure her wife-beating husband will not return to pester her' (p 155). It would seem rather to be gruff but affectionate irony. Martine's conduct toward M. Robert would suggest that she finds Sganarelle's beatings not all that distasteful.

2 *Le Médecin volant*, a farce attributed to Molière and built upon a similar situation, goes much further along these lines. 'L'urine de l'egrotante' is brought on stage to be tasted, and the verb *pisser* is repeated with child-like delectation.

3 These roles, together with the importance of story-telling in the play, lead Hubert to argue that Molière 'has centered the entire play around the idea of literature, of literary creation, of appreciation' (p 233). I would see these features as belonging to the broader category of wit and affirmative energy. Thus the 'absurdity of the ending' (p 239) is less Molière's deliberate parody of 'bad' literature than a final culmination of the gratuitous impulse that carries the action along.

4 For a convincing explanation of Boileau's much discussed allusion, see Adam 386-7, n 3.

5 Cf. Hubert 232-3.

CHAPTER 3: EXORCISM: THEME AND VARIATIONS

1 For a further explanation of these ironic techniques and an example of their use, see chapter 3 of my study on Rotrou.

2 Hubert underlines with great perceptiveness the theme of musical entertainment in this *comédie-ballet*, especially 'the contrapuntal contrasts of which *bémol* and *bécarre* provide the musical keys' (p 160).

3 Cf. Bénichou: 'Molière ... a fait tourner le combat de la galanterie française et de la jalousie sicilienne à la gloire de la première et à la confusion de la seconde' (p 190).

4 It is impossible to accept Adam's high-serous interpretation of this buffoon: 'l'on parlerait volontiers du *bovarysme* de Sganarelle. ... Il s'en faut de peu qu'il ne soit tragique' (pp 267-8).

5 Hubert seems to assume that he actually has blue blood and lowers himself to act like a lawyer (p 202).

6 Curiously enough, the number of *fâcheux* (if one discounts those of the ballets and the off-stage theatre-goer) is exactly the same as that of the *contretemps* of which Mascarille is the victim in *L'Etourdi*.

7 Cf. Hubert 64.

CHAPTER 4: EXORCISM: THE HEAVY FATHERS

1 Eg, G. Michaut, *Les Débuts de Molière à Paris* (Paris 1923); Adam 277; Jouanny, vol. I, p 314

2 I would hesitate to label this contrast a 'paradox,' as does Lawrence (p 77). If the middle-aged Ariste is a champion of youth, it is in the traditional function of the good father, while Sganarelle is a typical *barbon*.

3 Contrary to what Hubert says (p 48) and Michaut before him (*Débuts* 124-5), Molière was not the first to use the word *école* in his title. Montfleury had got a *privilège* for *L'Ecole des cocus* some months before the first performance of Molière's play (see Adam 274).

4 Here is an example of what Adam calls, in a rare intuition of the archetypal basis of comedy, 'cet esprit moderne et mondain' of *L'Ecole des maris*, 'son optimisme essentiel, son principe qui est la foi dans la vie,' its faith in society as well: 'La vie sociale agit ... comme force libératrice' (p 276).

5 As Jouanny appears to suggest (vol. I, 316)

6 'Pour localisée qu'elle soit, la corruption n'en est pas moins la plus forte expression de la nature humaine dans la pièce' (Guicharnaud, *Aventure* 521).

7 Recent critics shy away from accepting this pathos at face value. Hubert proposes for Mariane a 'false *persona*' on the grounds that her blind obedience to her father is psychologically improbable and therefore a pose (pp 99-100). Similarly, Guicharnaud sees her elevated diction as something close to parody: 'elle tente d'élever à la hauteur de l'héroïsme romanesque son éducation de petite bourgeoise obéissante' (p 60). In both cases there is

too much stress on psychological verisimilitude. What is important is not Mariane's social class but her function in the play, a function that clearly justifies her high diction. And the speech of lovers in comedy, whatever their social origin, is usually elevated.

8 Cf. Guicharnaud *Aventure* 49-50.

9 Elmire's role has caused some perplexity in recent criticism. 'There is every reason to believe,' argues Gossman, 'that Molière wanted us to feel relatively uncertain about Elmire' (p 135). Guicharnaud attributes 'mauvaise foi' to her (*Aventure* 91-2) because she in effect laughs away threats to the social order. But is this not one function of the comic myth itself? It makes more sense to see her as an idealized version of *la femme du monde*, poised, self-controlled, having the best interests of her family at heart, and able and willing to use the social art of *galanterie* – play courtship that is by defini-tion hypocritical in the strictest sense – to support those interests.

10 This archetypal interpretation of the dénouement assumes for the immediate aftermath of the reversal a contrite and enlightened Orgon. That his fundamental character has not changed is very possible: 'Orgon est et sera toujours Orgon' (Guicharnaud *Aventure* 148). See also Gossman 142.

11 This interpretation runs counter to Hubert's opinion that Trissotin is 'some-what more clever' than Tartuffe (p 241).

12 That these are 'typically feminine expressions of enthusiasm' (Hubert 244) is open to doubt. The sexual identity of the speakers is not important; what is is the comic incongruity between tone and substance, between emotional response and ideological content.

13 M. Descotes, 'Molière et le conflit des générations,' *RHLF* (Sept.-Dec. 1972) 786-99

14 In Bénichou's interpretation of this couplet, 'Molière oppose [à l'absurdité d'un amour spirituel] non pas un juste milieu, mais la force entière de l'instinct' (p 197). There is more here than instinct, however – 'tout moi-même' is not only body. Bénichou sees moreover only a simple antithesis between disembodied affection and carnal love. Chrysale's point of view makes the system of comic contrasts much richer.

15 One must therefore dispute Bénichou's contention that 'tout le ridicule des femmes savantes est dans leur obsession d'égalité' (p 196). They do not aspire to equality – unlike Clitandre and Henriette – in their ideal of married love.

16 Hubert in his perceptive analysis of *L'Avare* emphasizes the fairy-tale aspect of this dénouement in particular (pp 216-17). His discussion of Harpagon's exclusion (p 214) also brings him close in this part of his book to aspects of archetypal methodology.

17 Even an anti-*romanesque* critic like Adam recognizes that 'les scènes entre Cléante et Mariane, entre Valère et Elise, sont essentielles à l'œuvre' (p 373).

18 For an example of a contrary view, see Hubert 208-9.

19 Hubert (p 255 *et passim*) suggests that the Faculty of Medicine may have been a convenient and safe metaphor for the Sorbonne and that Molière was directing his mockery, in part at least, against the hated theologians – a plausible hypothesis but not relevant to our purpose. See also Adam 395-6.

20 See Hubert (pp 261-2) for an interesting commentary on precise number references of this kind in *Le Malade imaginaire*.

21 For a perceptive exegesis of this set-piece in terms of the play's verbal structure, see Hubert 228-9.

22 Cf. Guicharnaud (*Aventure* 66) and also Gutwirth's attitude to this 'comte un peu véreux' (p 115), a character considered by Adam as a precursor of 'le chevalier d'industrie' (p 383). But Adam correctly sees Dorante as 'sympathique' at the end of the play (*loc. cit.*).

23 It is true, as Hubert contends, that Jourdain 'remains faithful to all the attitudes and habits peculiar to petty merchants' (p 229). But this fidelity is only on the level of reflex – like other Molière heroes, Jourdain must preserve his *alibi* by refusing to own up to his true nature.

24 For details, see Jouanny, n1492.

CHAPTER 5: ROMANCE

1 What is meant here, of course, is the run-of-the-mill, action-filled novel cast in the *roman à tiroirs* form with a happy ending. The shorter novel of the latter part of the century is in part a reaction against these conventions. *La Princesse de Clèves*, for instance, with its dénouement of separation and renunciation, might be considered in this context as an ironic version of romance not without analogies with the plays discussed in the next chapter.

2 This is a secular version of the ceremonial process described by Eliade. Following a different line of reasoning, J.P. Sartre evokes similar considerations in his definition of *classicisme*: 'il ne s'agit en aucun cas de découvrir des terres nouvelles à la pensée, mais seulement de mettre en forme les *lieux communs* adoptés par l'élite, de façon que la lecture ... soit une cérémonie de *reconnaissance* analogue au salut, c'est-à-dire l'affirmation cérémonieuse qu'auteur et lecteur sont du même monde et ont sur toute chose les mêmes opinions' (*Qu'est-ce que la littérature?* [Paris 1948] 117). Although intended for literature in general, Sartre's remarks are especially pertinent to the collective ritual act which is theatre-going.

3 It is misleading to blame the complexity of Molière's play on his source (eg, Hubert 9); since he added to it, Molière obviously did not consider his source complicated enough.

4 For the use of this device before Molière see Roger Guichemerre, *La Comédie avant Molière: 1640-1660* (Paris 1972) 84. A more detailed account of the effects it gives rise to in Rotrou can be found in my *Ironic Game* 54-6.

5 This interpretation runs counter to the trend, most apparent in Eustis (pp 101-37), to see a parodic intention in Molière's serious style. Hubert assumes that the spectator will evaluate the conduct and words of the lovers in *Le Dépit amoureux* from Gros-René's mocking point of view (p 9). But the elevated style is underlined by the lower one, not diminished by it. To assume that both perspectives are seen through one only is to destroy an essential notion of aesthetic balance.

6 Words reminiscent of the heroic equality Gormas sees in Rodrigue and Don Sanche at the beginning of *Le Cid* (vv. 25-8)

7 Hubert notwithstanding ('the Prince never does achieve this difficult victory over his instincts' 36), the text seems quite explicit.

8 The verbal analogies which link the behaviour of Mauregat and Don Garcie are perceptively studied by Hubert (pp 33-7).

9 Langer's discussion of heroic comedy (pp 334-8) is wide-ranging and provocative. Unduly influenced, perhaps, by Francis Fergusson's essay on *Bérénice* in his *The Idea of a Theater* (Princeton 1949), she contends that the 'stately Gallic classics' of Corneille and Racine belong to this kind (p 337).

10 In the fifth, the Princess, disturbed by her love for Euryale, interrupts two shepherdesses who discuss in song the pains and pleasure of love: 'Achevez seules, si vous voulez,' she tells them; 'je ne saurais demeurer en repos' (*intermède* 5). In the sixth and final *intermède*, a chorus of shepherds and shepherdesses, having heard the news of the Princess's conversion to love, arrive on stage to sing their joy before the assembled Court. Philis, one of the shepherdesses herself, vouches for them in addressing Iphitas: 'si ce n'est point un spectacle que vous méprisiez, vous allez voir l'allégresse publique se répandre jusques ici.'

11 In a rather different perspective Guicharnaud sees the spoken text as a partial 'démystification' of the spectacular elements in the play ('Les Trois Niveaux critiques des *Amants magnifiques*,' *Molière: Stage and Study* 21-42).

12 Lapp's perceptive article considers the work as part of Corneille's canon, to

be studied in the light of the playwright's other machine-plays — a valid perspective, although it tends to make Lapp underestimate Molière's part in the enterprise (cf. his assertion on p 395 that Corneille's verses surpass Molière's).

13 Or, as Lapp notes in his Cornelian interpretation, the assertion of male superiority (the 'maîtrise' of Doubrovsky) coupled with the theme of rebellious youth (p 403).

CHAPTER 6: IRONY: BEYOND THE COMIC MYTH

1 'The central principle of ironic myth is best approached as a parody of romance' (p 223).

2 As Bray observes (and as many more recent commentators forget), 'son rôle exige qu'il parle ainsi' (p 29).

3 The problem of the satiric intent of this play is fraught with difficulties. Hubert accepts Antoine Adam's contention that 'Molière definitely had in mind Madeleine de Scudéry and her coterie' (p 19) (an opinion advanced previously by Bray among others [p 185]). On the other hand, Francis Baumal, in his *Molière, auteur précieux* claims that 'pour les contemporains, à cette date de 1659, Madeleine de Scudéry était une de ces précieuses savantes [that is, 'les véritables précieuses' according to a distinction by Somaize cited on p 42] ... qui s'étaient mises au rang des meilleurs auteurs du siècle et qui jouissaient d'une estime indiscutée. Pour les contemporains encore, à cette même date, une distinction était à faire entre les précieuses véritables 'respectées autant que des princesses,' et leurs 'singesses,' pures façonnières, au parler gras, au jargon aussi obscur que maniéré. On ne voit pas pourquoi Molière n'aurait pas partagé cette façon de voir' (pp 44-5). Baumal, in his *Molière auteur précieux* claims that 'pour les contemporains, we accept his Preface at face value. By implication Adam accepts it in part as well when he asserts that certain *précieux* circles less affected in his view (that of la Comtesse de la Suze, for instance) escaped Molière's condemnation and when he admits that various 'cercles mondains et précieux de Paris' had the play performed privately without presumably taking offense. The essential difference lies in the attitude toward Mademoiselle de Scudéry. Bénichou seems the most convincing: 'toute [1'] époque [de Molière] blâmait sans doute avec lui une certaine affectation excessive et ridicule de bel-esprit, mais c'est une pure légende que celle d'une secte spéciale qui aurait fait de cette affectation sa loi propre' (p 183). In the final analysis, critics seem reluctant to face up to the fundamental ambiguity of the situation. If a literary form is presented in a ridiculous light, is the satire directed

against the form itself or against those whose stupidity prevents them from understanding the full dimension of the form? When the 'strange effects of literature on mediocre minds' are presented (Hubert 16), is literature itself the butt or the mediocrity that fails to comprehend it?

4 Hubert insists on the aggressiveness and cruelty of this play (p 21).

5 Lawrence analyses this work, in a rather different perspective, as 'a conventional farce turned inside out' (p 104).

6 See Lane Cooper's commentary on this treatise in *An Aristotelian Theory of Comedy* (Oxford 1924) 226.

7 Too much should not be made of Dandin's lucidity in this regard. As Gossman demonstrates, both Dandins are in the situation: 'At no time does George Dandin really see all of himself, and he remains comically blind to the — rather bitter — end' (p 162). As Helen Purkis argues, 'tout en se croyant lucide il est aveugle ... tout en croyant avoir raison, il a tort. Il croit que ses malheurs viennent de ce qu'il a épousé une jeune fille noble au lieu de se contenter d'une riche paysanne. En vérité, ils viennent de sa façon de traiter sa femme' ('Les Intermèdes musicaux de *George Dandin*,' *Baroque* 5 [1972] 66).

8 Hence she differs considerably from her namesake in *La Jalousie du barbouillé*, a farce traditionally attributed to Molière and based on premises similar to those of *George Dandin*. The girl of the farce and her *servante*, Cathau, continually insult the *barbouillé* who is little more than a ludicrous clown figure. She says nothing about having been forced to marry such a fool; the only remark on this subject is spoken by Cathau: 'Que maudite soit l'heure que vous avez choisi ce grigou!' (5).

This remark is probably directed at the parent, Gorgibus, but it could be meant for Angélique; in the latter case the position of the girl would be totally different from that of her counterpart in *George Dandin*.

9 Cf. Adam: 'Clitandre est un galant sans moralité qui ment sans scrupules et séduit à froid une petite sotte' (p 369).

10 Gossman too sees Clitandre as 'a new perspective from which the vanity and folly of the cloddish peasant and the equally cloddish nobleman Sotenville can be easily discerned' (p 151).

11 For Joan Crow, Dandin is simply uttering a wry quip ('Reflections on *George Dandin*,' *Molière: Stage and Study* 3-12). In any event, this sombre note is somewhat attenuated when we remember the final *intermède* which followed it in the original Court version of the play. A friend of Dandin's suggests that he drown his sorrows in wine, and a festive bacchanalian tone prevails. Yet, as Purkis points out, even this comic effect stands out in ironic contrast, as do all the interludes, with the main action: '[Dandin] donne en

effet raison à sa femme qui avait fait croire à ses parents qu'elle lui avait barré la porte de la maison parce qu'il était rentré ivre du village' (p 68).

12 Cf. Gossman's interesting application to this play of the Cartesian *malus genius* (p 2 and *passim*).

13 Gutwirth, for instance, sees in *Amphitryon* 'l'apothéose du mariage sur la scène' (p 96).

14 One senses with Guicharnaud 'un mépris de l'intrigue "bien faite" ' (*Aventure* 515).

15 Triumphant young love seems far away in this couple 'sans passions, sans surprises' (J. Mesnard, *'Le Misanthrope:* mise en question de l'art de plaire,' *RHLF* 72 [Sept.-Dec. 1972] 885).

16 Guicharnaud also notes an analogy with 'la princesse de tragédie galante' (*Aventure* 511).

17 Guicharnaud: '[Alceste] existe par son dialogue avec ce qu'il déteste' (*Aventure* 365); Gossman: 'Alceste craves the admiration and esteem of the very people whom he accuses of insincerity' (p 68).

18 I cannot share Guicharnaud's indulgence for this sonnet or put it on the level of the one in *La Comtesse d'Escarbagnas.* The latter is, as Guicharnaud himself states, 'la norme selon la pièce' (*Aventure* 380) set in contrast with the futile literary pretentions of the Comtesse's *salon.* In the scene with Oronte we see an ironic juxtaposition of two forms of mediocrity.

19 Adam maintains that Alceste is expressing in his song a 'vogue de la chanson populaire, une réaction contre les grands airs et la musique savante de la génération précédente' (p 345). Only a casual comment by d'Assoucy is adduced to support this contention, and no evidence is cited that the popular song established itself among the *honnêtes gens* of *salon* and Court. Still, Adam states flatly that 'Molière ne faisait pas de son Alceste un ridicule lorsqu'il mettait dans sa bouche l'éloge de la chanson' (*loc. cit.*). The rhapsodic commentary by Alceste and the enthusiastic reprise the song gets from him are completely ignored – Alceste is surely ridiculous for over-stating his tastes, if for nothing else. Cf. Guicharnaud: 'Philinte rit à cause du ton d'Alceste' (*Aventure* 387).

20 Gossman 75. See too Mauron, *Métaphores* 287.

21 Guicharnaud seems to condemn Célimène's compromise with a 'méchant' world: 'le personnage de Célimène, ici, tombe' (*Aventure* 486).

22 A view anticipated by Adam (p 354). Guicharnaud minimizes the question of Célimène's future.

23 Gossman also notes how sharply this martial language contrasts with the actual exploits referred to, and how the Don presents 'a debased and de-formed version of these heroic and adventurous existences' (p 52).

24 As Rousset puts it, 'inconstant, il l'est moins par l'entraînement heureux vers le plaisir, moins par le goût de la possession même furtive ... que par besoin d'affirmer sa supériorité conquérante, par curiosité des commencements' (*L'Intérieur et l'extérieur* 142).

25 Cf. Brody, '*Don Juan* and *Le Misanthrope*' 566.

26 Other commentators insist on the mediocrity of Don Juan's ideas (in opposition to the old-fashioned view that the hero is not only an accomplished *esprit fort*, but a spokesman for the *libertins* of the time and perhaps for Molière's own free thought): Guicharnaud: 'sur le plan de la pensée ... le plus élémentaire des êtres' (*Aventure* 253), and Hubert: 'one may even claim that he does not have any ideas whatever' (p 129).

27 'Une sorte de réciproque au genre comique proprement dit' (Guicharnaud, *Aventure* 522)

28 See Adam's discussion of Don Juan's good points (p 328).

29 Hubert also stresses the absence of reward as 'a major theme in this play' (p 121).

CONCLUSION

1 Gutkind proposes, at a cost of considerable over-simplification, an evolution through four periods with a partial return to the beginning (pp 165-83). Adam confines himself to noting an increased 'rosserie' in Molière's later plays. Finally, Mauron's thesis of three distinct phases in Molière's creative evolution (*Métaphores* 277-98), while ingeniously argued, does not stand up when the whole of the dramatist's canon is scrutinized.

2 Cf. Gouhier: 'Le dénouement réfléchit l'action entière' (*Théâtre et existence* 198).

3 Eustis provides an excellent account of this difficult problem (pp 181-93).

4 Cf. Guicharnaud's perceptive words: 'Ce que Molière exige de nous, c'est une reconnaissance répétée. Son univers est celle de la sécurité – une sécurité magique, semblable à celle que procurent les fées qui d'un coup de baguette amènent à l'existence précisément ce que nous voulons' (*Aventure* 82).

Chronological List of
Molière's Plays

To enable the reader to situate a given play in its chronological perspective, the following table is offered. The date and place shown refer to first performance. If a second date and place are indicated, they mark the first performance of a 'Court' play before '*La Ville.*'

Comédies-ballets are marked by an asterisk.[1] Plays not indicated otherwise are in verse. Generic distinctions are from Molière's text.

La Jalousie du barbouillé;
Le Médecin volant (prose)
  two farces traditionally found at the head of the Molière canon, although no convincing proof of attribution has been adduced.[2]

L'Etourdi ou Les Contre-temps	1655 (?); Lyon
Le Dépit amoureux	1656; Béziers
Les Précieuses ridicules (prose)	18 Nov. 1659; Théâtre du Petit Bourbon
Sganarelle ou Le Cocu imaginaire	28 May 1660; Théâtre du Petit Bourbon
Don Garcie de Navarre ou Le Prince jaloux ['comédie héroïque' in ed. of 1734]	4 Feb. 1661; Palais Royal
L'Ecole des maris	24 June 1661; Palais Royal
*Les Fâcheux**	Aug. 1661; Vaux
	4 Nov. 1661; Palais Royal
L'Ecole des femmes	26 Dec. 1662; Palais Royal
La Critique de L'Ecole des femmes (prose)	1 June 1663; Palais Royal
L'Impromptu de Versailles (prose)	14 Oct. 1663; Versailles
	4 Nov. 1663; Palais Royal

Le Mariage forcé *	29 Jan. 1664; Louvre
(prose)	15 Feb. 1664; Palais Royal
La Princesse d'Elide *	8 May 1664; Versailles
(verse and prose) 'comédie galante'	9 Nov. 1664; Palais Royal
Tartuffe ou L'Imposteur	12 May 1664; Versailles (three-act form)
	29 Nov. 1664; Château de Raincy (first five-act form)
(final five-act form) {	5 Aug. 1667 Palais Royal
	5 Feb. 1669
Don Juan ou le Festin	15 Feb. 1665; Palais Royal
de pierre (prose)	
L'Amour médecin * (prose)	15 Sept. 1665 (?); Versailles
	22 Sept. 1665; Palais Royal
Le Misanthrope	4 June 1666; Palais Royal
Le Médecin malgré lui (prose)	6 Aug. 1666; Palais Royal
Mélicerte * 'comédie-pastorale	2 Dec. 1666; Saint-Germain-en-Laye
héroïque' (incomplete)	('Ballet des muses')
Pastorale comique * (incomplete)	5 Jan. 1667; Saint-Germain-en-Laye
	('Ballet des muses')
Le Sicilien ou L'Amour peintre *	Feb. 1667; Saint-Germain-en-Laye
(prose)	(14th *entrée* of the 'Ballet des muses' — 'Turcs et Maures')
	10 June 1667; Palais Royal
Amphitryon	13 Jan. 1668; Palais Royal
George Dandin ou Le Mari confondu *	18 July 1668; Versailles
(prose)	9 Nov. 1668; Palais Royal
L'Avare (prose)	9 Sept. 1668; Palais Royal
Monsieur de Pourceaugnac *	Sept. 1669; Chambord
'comédie-ballet' (prose)	15 Nov. 1669; Palais Royal
Les Amants magnifiques *	Feb. 1670; Saint-Germain-en-Laye
Le Bourgeois gentilhomme *	Oct. 1670; Chambord
'comédie-ballet' (prose)	25 Nov. 1670; Palais Royal
Psyché 'tragédie-ballet'	1671; Tuileries
total design and part of text by Molière	24 July 1671; Palais Royal
Les Fourberies de Scapin (prose)	24 May 1671; Palais Royal
La Comtesse d'Escarbagnas	2 Dec. 1671; Saint-Germain-en-Laye
(frame for a ballet) (prose)	8 July 1672; Palais Royal
Les Femmes savantes	11 March 1672; Palais Royal
Le Malade imaginaire * (prose)	10 Feb. 1673; Palais Royal

NOTES

1 For a description of the ballet sequences in these plays (save *Le Malade imaginaire*), see M. F. Christout: *Le Ballet de cour de Louis XIV: 1643-1672, mises en scène* (Paris 1967).

2 The two farces were published for the first time by Viollet-le-Duc in 1819. In an attempt to refute Bray (without naming him), A. Adam argues very firmly that they are by Molière (pp 251-2) on the grounds that the titles appear in La Grange's *Registre* and that the biographers of 1682 attribute *Le Docteur amoureux* and other 'petites comédies' to him. Unfortunately, the same evidence could apply just as convincingly to the dozen or so lost farces listed in the *Registre*. One suspects that the real reason for this stubborn tradition of attribution is that we possess a text for the two farces in question. Bray's position is certainly no less plausible than Adam's: the two farces 'semblent être ... de méchants rapetissages opérés par quelque comédien ambulant sur les comédies que [Molière] avait tirées de ses premières farces' (p 170).

Archetypal Criticism
and *Structuralisme*

It was my intention, with respect to methodology, to provide for Molière's work the simplest possible conceptual framework on which to base what is essentially a work in practical criticism. Elaborate discussions of structuralist poetics would only have obfuscated my argument. However, for readers interested in questions of literary theory I provide in the following remarks a brief and necessarily provisional overview of the relationship between archetypal criticism and some aspects of *structuralisme*.

As in all such matters, the terminological problem is the first and most difficult to face, all the more since we are dealing here with what has become a cant word, a vague, fashionable antonym for 'literary history.' Jean Rousset offers a sound starting point with his definition of a literary structure as: 'des relations, des constantes, des champs associatifs dans un ensemble où tout est tenu pour solidaire et tirant son sens de cette solidarité, de cette dépendance au sein du système de cohérences concrètes qu'est une œuvre' ('Les Réalités formelles de l'œuvre,' in *Les Chemins actuels de la critique*, ed. G. Poulet [Paris 1968] 66). In an important note which states my own position, Rousset cautions us that 'la structure ... n'est qu'*une* des réalités formelles de l'œuvre.' Among other purely formal features he distinguishes 'les effets de la première, de la troisième et de la seconde personne, les positions respectives du récit, du dialogue et du monologue, le ou les points de vue pris par l'auteur ou concédés à ses personnages, etc.' (*ibid.* 67). In other words, *structuralisme* is a species of a larger entity we might call formalism, which, if one may extrapolate from the examples Rousset offers for prose narrative techniques, includes all intrinsic or internal study of literature. Point of view, for instance, is not structure, but form.

The special meaning of structure will become clearer if we imagine it as an outer manifestation of an inner pattern (to analogize from the useful distinction in German stylistics between inner and outer form – the form present in the creative imagination which is then projected upon the work). The 'système de cohérences concrètes' which is the work of literature is the projection of another structure with which that of the work itself corresponds. This inner pattern can be sought, of course, first within the psyche of the author; we recognize the basis for the techniques known in France as la psychocritique and whose best known practitioners are Mauron and J.-P. Weber. Here the search is for a 'mythe personnel' of which the structure of the work is a restatement. But the inner structure may be found as well in a hypothesized collective psyche, that of the readership-audience. This is the 'second manner,' so to speak, of la psycho-critique as exemplified in Mauron's study of the comic genre. Here the pheno-menon of recurrence leaves the domain of a single author's work to become truly archetypal; the 'mythe personnel' becomes the 'mythe générique' expres-sive of constant features in man's nature. Such is also the underlying premise of Roland Barthes' Sur Racine: the myth of the horde of which Racine's plays are seen as variants presumes a 'constante psychologique' in the spectator, not just of the seventeenth century but of any audience receptive to this theatre.[1]

The inner structure may be found in the social group of a particular time and place, in 'la sociologie structuraliste" which Doubrovsky defines as the attempt to place the writer 'dans l'ensemble qu'est le groupe social, et dont il n'est qu'un élément. Le concept "opératoire," qui relie de façon intelligible œuvre, individu et groupe et qui, pour Lucien Goldmann, constitue le fondement de toute interprétation culturelle, est la "vision du monde" ' (Pourquoi la nouvelle critique [Paris 1966] 130). Thus, quoting Goldmann's own words, Doubrovsky defines artistic activity in this sense as the 'création d'un monde dont la struc-ture est analogue à la structure essentielle de la réalité sociale au sein de laquelle l'œuvre a été écrite' (p 131).

The relevance of this mode of analysis to theatre is evident. A play is con-ceived to win over an audience of a particular time and place, and thus must reflect the Weltanschauung of that audience, even if, as today, it is a problematic one. I have thus had occasion to refer to Molière's own spectators and their dreams and aspirations as Molière gives them imaginative form. But as we are concerned in Goldmann with a concrete, historical reality, and not deep-seated, permanent universals in man's psyche, his structuralism is not, strictly speaking, archetypal.

In its broadest sense, structuralisme can endeavour to seek out in literature, as well as in any human creation, the enduring manifestations of man's own imagination as a structure of primordial images. The most ambitious synthesis of these modes of expression is Gilbert Durand's challenging Les Structures anthro-pologiques de l'imaginaire (Paris 1960). Durand has founded a Centre de

Recherches sur l'Imaginaire, an 'organisme centralisateur largement pluri-disciplinaire' as he defines it in *Circé* ([1969] 3). This very broad approach is, for our purposes, both a strength and a weakness. As the human imagination touches on every area of creative endeavour, Durand's wide-ranging investigations are diffuse and of comparatively limited usefulness. Very little is said, for instance, about comedy as a genre, except tangentially in terms of its underlying rites.[2]

The great French critic of whom Durand is an avowed disciple, Gaston Bachelard, had a more intuitive, personal, and literary programme. His stimulating research into element imagery takes us into true archetypal symbolism, and it is in this kind of activity that archetypal criticism has had the longest history in France. But there is much more to this sort of literary analysis than the themes of water and fire. In Genette's words, 'Bachelard nous a donné une typologie de l'imagination "matérielle": nul doute qu'il existe aussi, par exemple, une imagination des conduites, des situations, des relations humaines, une imagination *dramatique*, au sens large du terme, qui anime puissamment la production et la consommation des œuvres théâtrales et romanesques. La topique de cette imagination, les lois structurales de son fonctionnement importent de toute évidence, et au premier chef, à la critique littéraire' (*Figures* [I] [Paris 1966] 164). Genette's stress on 'conduites,' 'situations,' 'relations humaines' as functions of the human imagination leads us directly to the whole zone of archetypal features – motifs and characters in particular – which Frye codifies in his four *mythoi*. As Genette implies, they are most suited to narrative forms, theatre and the novel. But in French scholarship so far, the novel has received most attention by far in this kind of investigation.

We reach the most important facet of French *structuralisme* in terms of present-day activity: linguistic structuralism and its companion concept, semiotics. It is dangerous to generalize in such a complex domain into which so many currents of critical thought flow: Russian formalism, Anglo-Saxon rhetorical criticism, *stylistique*, and many others. One might say, however, that this sort of *structuralisme* tends to become *description* in Tzvetan Todorov's sense: 'la littérature n'y est pas considérée comme la manifestation de telle conception philosophique [a point of view Todorov later defines as 'traduction' and in which archetypal criticism obviously belongs], mais comme un discours qu'il faut connaître pour lui-même. Naturellement, l'œuvre littéraire est considérée dans ce cas plutôt comme une construction verbale que comme la représentation d'une réalité; et on cherche à expliquer ses particularités des relations qu'entretiennent ses éléments constitutifs' ('Poétique,' in *Qu'est-ce que le structuralisme?* [Paris 1968] 99-100). The two attitudes are more sharply – and less dispassionately – defined by Doubrovsky in a long rebuttal of Barthes' second manner, the Barthes who deserted 'traduction' for 'description,' or, in Doubrovsky's terms, 'la critique des significations' for 'la critique structuraliste' (*Nouvelle critique* 86); an existentialist critic concerned with the individual creative consciousness is bound to take issue with what Barthes calls 'la conscience syntagmatique' and defines as 'conscience des rapports qui unissent les signes entre eux au niveau du discours même' (cited *ibid*. 91). Echoing Rousset's warning against 'une interprétation réifiante' of literature, Doubrovsky argues vigorously that a literary work can never be studied as an autonomous system of signs distinct from the realities it conveys. 'Le signifiant ne peut jamais être coupé du signifié, et le littéraire de l'existentiel. Bref, *l'art n'est jamais un artisanat*. Et c'est pourquoi le critique n'est jamais placé en face d'une œuvre, comme le savant en face d'un objet, dans une position d'observateur; il interroge l'œuvre comme l'apparition d'un autrui, dans une relation de participant' (pp 90-1). In his stress on communication Doubrovsky is very much in the spirit of the archetypal approach: 'à travers de texte écrit ou la pièce jouée, à travers la beauté des mots ou la rigueur de la construction, *un homme parle de l'homme aux hommes*' (p 52).

Yet, Doubrovsky dismisses all too readily Barthes' 'critique structuraliste.' The article he condemns, 'L'Imagination des signes' in *Essais critiques* (Paris 1964) 206-12, is a straightforward restatement of now common Saussurean distinctions as enlarged upon by Jakobson (see Scholes 18-40). The syntagmatic axis – the linear alignment of words or elements in literary discourse – brings to the fore essential structuralist concepts of interrelationships and interdependence and does not imply the rejection of all externals. The referential fallacy does not apply to literary referents, only to real-life ones. Who Cassandre really was matters little to the structuralist critic; but he would never isolate her from the literary tradition she represents in Ronsard's ode. In short, archetypal criticism has obvious affinities with other structuralist approaches to poetry and narrative. It would have been possible to describe the comic story in the same functional detail as Lévi-Strauss analyzed myth or Propp the folk tale or as later scholars like Bremond and Greimas have scrutinized narrative prose. But the very elaborateness of these schemata points more toward poetics than practical criticism, and their descriptive empiricism seems to allow little room for the essential universal of archetypal criticism: the assumption of a psychological commonality in all mankind to which literature gives expression.

NOTES

1 Doubrovsky's attempt to differentiate radically between Barthes and Mauron results from an oversimplification. The structures described in *Sur Racine*, according to the author of *Pourquoi la nouvelle critique*, 'ne sont pas sociologiques, mais psychiques, elles devront être décrites en termes psychanalytiques (Père, Eros, etc.), étant bien entendu, à la différence de ce que prétend faire la psychocritique de Charles Mauron, qu'il s'agit uniquement de décrire les relations objectives de l'univers racinien telles qu'elles se manifestent dans les pièces, et non de les rattacher aux hypothétiques aventures de l'inconscient chez l'auteur' (p 12). Doubrovsky appears to neglect the wider aspect of Mauron's thought, for no attempt is made in *Psychocritique du genre comique* to find Molière in the structures of the comic myth as exemplified in his theatre; the 'constantes psychologiques' are sought in the audience. By the same token, Barthes' 'relations' are not 'objectives,' since in the final analysis they must correspond to the psychological structure of the reader-viewer.

2 Cf. his comment on the scapegoat: 'le sacrifice ... s'euphémise; et ce n'est plus qu'un simulacre que l'on maltraite et met à mort' (p 355), and on orgiastic ceremonies: 'la fête est à la fois moment négatif où les normes sont abolies, mais aussi joyeuse promesse à venir de l'ordre ressuscité' (p 359). While he thus alludes to the two ritual underpinnings of comedy, the expulsion of the *pharmakos* and the euphoric final festivity, he does not mention the genre itself.

Bibliography

Adam, Antoine *Histoire de la littérature française au XVIIe siècle* vol. III, Paris 1952

Attinger, Gustave *L'Esprit de la commedia dell'arte dans le théâtre français* Neuchâtel 1950

Aubouin, Elie *Les Genres du risible* Marseilles 1948

Barthes, Roland *Sur Racine* Paris 1963

Baumal, Francis *Molière auteur précieux* Paris nd [1925]

Bénichou, Paul *Morales du grand siècle* Paris 1948

Bidney, David 'Myth, Symbolism, and Truth,' *Myth: A Symposium*, ed. T.A. Sebeok, Philadelphia 1955, pp 1-14

Bodkin, Maud *Archetypal Patterns in Poetry* Oxford 1934, republished as a Vintage Book in 1958

Bordonove, Georges *Molière génial et familier* Paris 1967

Borgerhoff, E.B.O. 'Tartuffe,' *Esprit Créateur* 11, No. 2 (Summer 1971) 16-18

Bray, René *Molière homme de théâtre* Paris 1954

Brody, Jules 'Don Juan and Le Misanthrope, or The Esthetics of Individualism in Molière,' *PMLA* 84 (1969) 559-76

− 'Esthétique et société chez Molière,' *Dramaturgie et Société*, ed. J. Jacquot, Paris 1968, I, 307-26.

Cassirer, Ernest *Language and Myth*, trans. Susanne Langer, New York 1946
The Myth of the State New Haven 1950

Christout, Marie-Françoise *Le Ballet de cour de Louis XIV, 1643-1672, mises en scène* Paris 1967

Cornford, Francis *The Origin of Attic Comedy* London 1914

Cooper, Lane *An Aristotelian Theory of Comedy* Oxford 1924

Crow, Joan 'Reflections on George Dandin,' *Molière: Stage and Study: Essays in Honour of W.G. Moore*, ed. W.G. Howarth and M. Thomas, Oxford 1973, pp 3-12

Descotes, Maurice *La Fortune littéraire de Molière* Paris 1971
Descotes, Maurice 'Molière et le conflit des générations, *RHLF* 72 (Sept.-Dec. 1972) 786-99
Doubrovsky, Serge *Corneille et la dialectique du héros* Paris 1963
Pourquoi la nouvelle critique Paris 1966
Durand, Gilbert *Circé* Paris 1969
Les Structures anthropologiques de l'imaginaire Paris 1960
Eigeldinger, Marc *La Mythologie solaire dans l'œuvre de Racine* Neuchâtel 1969
Eliade, Mircea *Aspects du mythe* Paris 1963 Collection 'Idées'
Elliot, Revel *Mythe et légende dans le théâtre de Racine* Paris 1969
Eustis, A. *Molière as Ironic Contemplator* The Hague 1973
Fergusson, Francis *The Idea of a Theater* Princeton 1949
Fluchère, Henri 'Ploutos, Eros, Molière et les vieillards,' *Molière: Stage and Study: Essays in Honour of W.G. Moore*, ed. W.G. Howarth and M. Thomas, Oxford 1973, pp 117-31
Frye, Northrop *Anatomy of Criticism: Four Essays* Princeton 1957
Genette, Gérard *Figures* [I] Paris 1966 Collection 'Tel Quel'
Girard, R. *La Violence et le sacré* Paris, 1973
Gossman, Lionel *Men and Masks: A Study of Molière* Baltimore 1963
Gouhier, Henri *Théâtre et existence* Paris 1952
Guicharnaud, Jacques *Molière: une aventure théâtrale* Paris 1963
—'Les Trois Niveaux critiques des *Amants magnifiques*,' *Molière: Stage and Study: Essays in Honour of W.G. Moore*, ed. W.G. Howarth and M. Thomas, Oxford 1973, pp 21-42
Guichemerre, R. *La Comédie avant Molière, 1640-1660* Paris 1972
Gutkind, Curt *Molière und das Komische Drama* Halle 1928
Gutwirth, Marcel *Molière ou l'invention comique* Paris 1966
Hartman, G. 'Structuralism: The Anglo-American Adventure,' *Structuralism*, ed. J. Ehrmann, New York 1970, first published 1966
Herrick, M.T. *Comic Theory in the Sixteenth Century* Urbana 1950
Hope, Quentin 'Molière's Curtain Lines,' *French Studies* 26 (April 1972) 143-55
Hubert, Judd *Molière and the Comedy of Intellect* Berkeley 1962
Hyman, S.E. 'The Ritual View of Myth and the Mythic,' *Myth: A Symposium*, ed. T. Sebeok, Philadelphia 1955, pp 84-94
Jasinski, René *Molière* Paris 1969
Jouanny, Robert. See Molière.
Knapp, Bettina *Jean Racine: Mythos and Renewal in Modern Theater* University of Alabama 1971
Knutson, Harold C. *The Ironic Game: A Study of Rotrou's Comic Theater* Berkeley 1966

Langer, Susanne *Feeling and Form* New York 1953
Lapp, John 'Corneille's *Psyché* and the Metamorphosis of Love,' *French Studies* 26 (Oct. 1972) 395-403
Larthomas, Pierre *Le Language dramatique* Paris 1972
Lawrence, F.L. *Molière: The Comedy of Unreason.* New Orleans 1968 [Tulane Studies in Romance Languages and Literature, No. 2]
Lawton, N.W. *Handbook of French Renaissance Dramatic Theory* Manchester 1949
Leenhardt, Jacques 'Psychocritique et sociologie de la littérature,' *Les Chemins actuels de la critique*, ed. Georges Poulet, Paris 1968, pp 253-71
Mauron, Charles *Des métaphores obsédantes au mythe personnel* Paris 1962 *Psychocritique du genre comique* Paris 1964
Mesnard, J. '*Le Misanthrope*: mise en question de l'art de plaire,' *RHLF* 72 (Sept.-Dec. 1972) 863-89
Meyer, J. *Molière* Paris 1963
Michaut, Gustave *Les Débuts de Molière à Paris* Paris 1923
Molière *Oeuvres*, ed. Robert Jouanny. 2 vols. Paris 1962 Collection 'Classiques Garnier'
Moore, W.G. *Molière: A New Criticism* Oxford 1949
— 'Molière's Theory of Comedy,' *Esprit créateur* 6 (Fall 1966) 137-44
Northrop Frye in Modern Criticism, ed. M. Krieger, New York 1966
Poulet, Georges *Etudes sur le temps humain* Paris 1949
Purkis, Helen 'Les Intermèdes musicaux de *George Dandin*,' *Baroque* 5 (1972) 63-9
Rousset, Jean *Forme et signification* Paris 1962
L'Intérieur et l'extérieur Paris 1968
'Les Réalités formelles de l'œuvre,' *Les Chemins actuels de la critique*, ed. Georges Poulet, Paris 1968, pp 59-70
Sartre, J.-P. *Qu'est-ce que la littérature?* Paris 1948
Schérer, Jacques *La Dramaturgie classique en France* Paris nd [1951]
— 'Pour une sociologie des obstacles au mariage dans le théâtre français du XVIIe siècle, '*Dramaturgie et société*, ed. J. Jacquot, Paris 1968, I, pp 297-305
Scholes, R. *Structuralism in Literature: An Introduction* New Haven and London 1974
Sypher, Wylie *Comedy* [*An Essay on Comedy*, George Meredith; *Laughter*, Henri Bergson] New York 1956
Todorov, Tzvetan *Introduction à la littérature fantastique* Paris 1970
— 'Poétique,' *Qu'est-ce que le structuralisme?* Paris 1968, pp 99-166
Wheelwright, Philip *Metaphor and Reality* Indiana 1962

Index

Adam, A. 58, 72, 95, 157, 183-4n, 186n, 188-91n, 194n
Agon 25, 64, 65, 87, 90, 118, 120, 128, 171
Alazon 164, 166; the doctor as 53; *eiron-alazon* conflict: see *eiron; see also alazoneia.*
Alazoneia 66, 73, 80, 130, 154, 178; see also *alazon.*
Anagnorisis 7, 80, 155
Apuleius 142-3
Attinger, G. 25
Aubouin, E. 17
Auxiliaries 24-5, 33, 87, 98, 110; in romance 135-6; see also buffoon.

Bachelard, G. 197
Barbon 11, 14, 16, 44, 51, 53, 65, 69, 100, 111, 116, 121, 145, 156-7, 184n; see also *blondin*, father figure, scapegoat.
Barthes, R. 8, 25, 58, 62, 83, 196-8, 199n
Baudelaire, Ch. 17, 182n
Baumal, F. 9, 10, 174, 188n

Beaumarchais 11
Bénichou, P. 8, 20-1, 50, 70, 159, 170, 184-5n, 188n
Bergson, H. 17, 22, 43, 183n
Bidney, D. 12
Blocking character 11-12, 14-15 and passim; see also *barbon*, father figure, scapegoat.
Blondin ('le blondin berne le barbon') 11, 44, 111, 116, 121, 145
Bodkin, M. 4
Boileau 60, 183n
Bordonove, G. 180n
Borgerhoff, E. 183n
Bray, R. 21, 123, 173-4, 176, 180n, 188n, 194n
Bremond, C. 198
Brody, J. 9, 16, 18-19, 145, 164, 166, 170, 172, 179, 191n
Buffoon 26, 103, 147-8, 151; as symbolizing the pure sense of life 27-8; his role in M.'s theatre 28, 59; adaptability of 30-1; summary of M.'s buffoon plays 41-2; ironic counterpart of 162; see also auxiliaries.

Cambridge Hellenists 5, 180n
Cassirer, E. 3, 5-6, 11-12
Cervantes, M.: *Don Quixote* 168
La Chanson de Roland 131
Christout, M. 194n
Comedy (general): psychological basis of 4, 11-15; archetypal features of 4, 6, 8-10; as a *mythos* 7, 11, 15; ritual elements in 15-16; ternary form in 15-16, 76, 102, 132; social meaning of (in general) 17-19, 62, 174; dénouement of 19, 21-4, 174-5; fortuitous in 22-3; ironic phase of 76, 117, 157-8, 171-2; *see also* auxiliaries, dialectic of desire and repugnance, point of ritual death, the risible, spectacle.
Comedy (specific forms) Italian erudite 11; neo-classical 11, 43; social meaning of seventeenth-century French comedy 20-1; Shakespearian 26, 43; Elizabethan 43; *see also commedia dell'arte.*
Commedia dell'arte 11, 14, 50; the *zanni* in 25, 59, 123; *lazzi* in: 31; *see also* comedy.
Cooper, L. 189n
Copeau, J. 162
Corneille, P. 8, 11, 13, 161, 187n; *Nicomède* 87; *Le Cid* 120, 128, 187n; *Cinna* 120-1, 127
Cornford, F. 5, 15
Crow, J. 189n
Cuckoldry 44, 50-1, 62, 68, 72-3, 153, 157

Descotes, M. 180n, 185n
Dialectic of desire and repugnance 7, 9, 13-15, 43-4, 116-17, 144, 163-4; *see also* comedy.

Doctors: *see* medical profession.
Donatus 11
Double plot 24, 65, 110-11
Doubrovsky, S. 8, 188n, 196-8, 199n
Durand, G. 196-7, 199n

Eigeldinger, M. 181
Eiron 50, 58, 110; *eiron-alazon* conflict 25, 28, 55, 58, 65, 122, 146, 151, 171, 183n; *see alazon.*
Eliade, M. 16, 24, 186n
Elliot, R. 181n
Eustis, A. 45, 126, 180n, 187n, 191n

Father figure: as blocking character 24, 70, 95-6; *see barbon*, scapegoat; as good father 24, 68, 76, 88, 96, 110, 113, 148; in romance 121, 134, 139, 142-3
Fergusson, F. 187n
Figure-splitting 24; *see also* father figure, mother figure, son figure.
Fluchère, H. 181n
Frazer, J. 3, 5·
Freud, S. 3-4, 8, 12, 17, 182n
Frye, N. 4-5, 8-10, 13, 27, 50, 75-6, 177, 181n, 183n, 188n, 197; archetypal theory 3, 6-7; theory of *mythoi* 7, 174; *mythos* of comedy 11; social meaning of comedy 14, 174; ritual aspect of comedy 15-16; resolution of comic plot 18, 21-2, 174-5; *eiron-alazon* conflict 25; two ways of developing the comic plot 26, 43; the *mythos* of romance 118-20, 169; the fool in romance 135-6; theory of modes 139; the *mythos* of irony 144-6, 151, 173, 188n

Genette, G. 197

Girard, R. 181n
Goldmann, L. 196
Gossman, L.: 169, 176, 179, 180n, 185ꞧ, 189-90n
Gouhier, H.: 23, 191n
Greimas, A. 198
Guicharnaud, J. 9-10, 14, 22, 76, 82, 161-8, 171, 173-4, 176, 179, 180n, 183-7n, 190-1n
Guichemerre, R. 187n
Gutkind, C. 182n, 191n
Gutwirth, M. 9-10, 19, 28, 30, 49, 65, 103, 114, 132, 137, 163, 176, 180n, 186n, 190n

Hartman, G. 181n
Herrick, M. 183n
History play 132
Hobbes, T. 17
Hope, Q. 61, 90, 182n
Hubert, J. 29, 47, 55, 58, 69, 73, 99, 109, 132, 152, 155, 168, 177, 180n, 183-9n, 191n
Hyman, S. 180n

Irony: as a *mythos* 7, 144-6; dramatic 45, 48, 51-2, 56, 65-6, 75, 124, 141; of fate 75, 155

Jakobson, R. 198
La Jalousie du barbouillé (attributed to Molière) 189n
Jasinski, R. 180-1n
Jouanny, R. 29, 32, 34, 123-4, 126, 135-6, 153, 155-6, 184n, 186n
Jung, C. 3-5, 84

Kill-joy figure 30, 37, 57, 69, 80-1, 101, 113, 119, 163, 171, 175; the doctor as 53-4

Knapp, B. 181n
Knutson, H. 17, 187n

La Fayette, Mme de 19; *La Princesse de Clèves* 69, 186n
Langer, S. 6, 22-3, 26-9, 42, 132, 182n, 187n
Lapp, J. 141, 143, 187-8n
Larthomas, P. 182n
Lawrence, F. 10, 15, 99, 157, 174, 176-7, 180n, 184n, 189n
Lawton, H. 181n
Leenhardt, J. 182n
Lévi-Strauss, C. 198
Louis XIV 20, 43, 138, 143

Marivaux 11
Mauron, C. 4, 7-8, 11-13, 22-3, 37, 83, 103, 181n, 190n, 196, 199n
Le Médecin volant (attributed to Molière) 183n
Medical profession, the: 44, 52-3, 62; the archetypal significance of 53-4; as social misfits 104-5; satirized in *Le Malade imaginaire* 108-9
Meneur de jeu: buffoon as (Scapin) 34-5; (Mascarille) 38-40
Meredith, G. 183n
Mesnard, J. 190n
Meyer, J. 180n
Michaut, G. 184n
Molière: classification of plays by archetypal categories 25-6; romantic aspects of 174-5; plays in chronological order 192-3
Les Amants magnifiques 26, 43, 121, 133, **133-9**, 139-41, 152
L'Amour médecin 44, **51-4**, 57, 62, 122
Amphitryon 8, 20, 25, 140, 145, **158-61**, 168, 170, 190n

L'Avare 13-14, 21, 23-6, 28, 63-4, 68-9, 76-8, **95-102**, 103-6, 109, 111, 117, 175, 182n, 185-6n

Le Bourgeois gentilhomme 28, 43, 63-4, 102-4, 108, **110-16**, 117, 122, 139, 149, 176, 178, 186n

La Comtesse d'Escarbagnas **55-7**, 62, 149, 190n

La Critique de l'Ecole des femmes 25, 70, 75, **146-7**, 148, 178

Le Dépit amoureux 26, 64, **123-6**, 132, 142-3, 187n

Don Garcie de Navarre 26, 121, **127-32**, 136-7, 141, 143, 187n

Don Juan 8-9, 20, 25, 76, 145-6, 158, **167-72**, 177, 190-1n

L'Ecole des femmes 14-15, 18, 21, 24-5, 41-2, 45, 49, 51, 63, 68-9, **69-76**, 76-80, 93, 95-6, 98, 100-2, 107, 117, 121, 124, 145, 147, 155, 157, 162, 165-6, 175-8

L'Ecole des maris 28, 63, **64-9**, 70-5, 78, 100, 117, 153, 157, 163, 175-6, 178, 184n

L'Etourdi 26, **37-41**, 41-2, 44, 59, 64, 123, 132-3, 173, 178, 184n

Les Fâcheux 20, 44, **59-61**, 62, 184n

Les Femmes savantes 63, **83-95**, 101, 103-5, 108, 111-12, 117, 134, 175-6, 178, 185n

Les Fourberies de Scapin 28, **33-6**, 37-42, 133, 172-3, 182-3n

George Dandin 25, 41, 50, 122, 144, 146, **154-8**, 162, 166, 170-1, 189-90n

L'Impromptu de Versailles 25, 146, **147-8**, 149

Le Malade imaginaire 24, 28, 33, 54, 63-4, 83, 99, 102, **102-10**, 111-12, 114, 116, 122, 124, 147, 171, 176-8, 186n

Le Mariage forcé 24, 144-5, **151-4**, 156-7

Le Médecin malgré lui 28, **29-32**, 37, 41-2, 49, 54, 113, 149, 161, 172, 183n

Mélicerte 26, 119, 133

Le Misanthrope 9, 25, 41-2, 56, 68-9, 76, 86, 100-1, 145-6, 156, 158, **161-7**, 171, 173, 176-7, 190n

Monsieur de Pourceaugnac 15, 26, 28, 44, **57-9**, 62, 122, 184n

Pastorale comique 26, 133

Les Précieuses ridicules 25, 64, 145, **148-51**, 176, 188-9n

La Princesse d'Elide 10, 26, 43, 121, 125, **134-8**, 139-41, 152, 187n

Psyché 26, 121, **139-43**, 154, 158-9, 168

Sganarelle 44, **47-51**, 51, 57, 62, 64, 113, 149, 161, 184n

Le Sicilien 44, **44-7**, 52, 61, 66-7, 183-4n

Tartuffe 9-10, 14, 18-19, 21, 23-5, 43, 63, 69, **76-83**, 83-7, 89, 91, 95-7, 100, 103-5, 111-13, 121, 149, 163-4, 173, 175-9, 183n, 184-5n

Montfleury: *Ecole des cocus* 184n

Moore, W.G. 7, 14, 21, 79, 98, 164, 167-8, 174, 176-7, 180n, 182n

Moreto: *El Desdén con el desdén* 134

Mother figure: as evil force 24, 83-4; as good mother 24, 79, 83, 89, 113; in romance 134

Murray, G. 5

Narcissism 103, 106
Nobility: satire of provincial 55-9;
 satire of would-be 111-16
Novel: victorian 5; seventeenth-
 century 'grand roman' 118, 186n;
 pastoral 118-19, 150; see also La
 Fayette, Mme de.

Oedipus complex 4, 12-13, 96

Parody 88; of noble language 39, 44,
 50; of the comic reversal 40, 145-6,
 162, 172; of pastoral conventions
 137-8; in the ironic mythos 144-5,
 151, 154; of courtly love 150; of
 the comic myth 157, 171-2; of
 romance 146, 168-71, 188n
Pascal, B. 93-4
Pastoral 118-19, 121, 132-3, 150; see
 also novel.
Pensée magique 23, 32, 44, 69, 75-6,
 96; see also wish-fulfilment,
 pleasure principle.
Pharmakos 199n; see also scapegoat.
Plautus 98; Aulularia 99-100
Pleasure principle 55, 59, 68, 81-2,
 103, 116, 153, 171; see also pensée
 magique, wish-fulfilment.
Point of ritual death 23, 32, 36, 40,
 53, 75, 77-8, 89, 95, 110, 129, 142,
 148
Poulet, G. 182n
Propp, V. 198
Psychocritique 8, 11, 13, 196
Purkis, H. 189-90n

Rabelais: Abbaye de Thélème 20;
 mock epic 151

Racine 8, 13, 25, 162, 187n, 196;
 Britannicus 5, 83, 120, 131;
 Andromaque 120; Phèdre 131;
 Les Plaideurs 132
Raisonneur 86, 107, 175-7, 191n;
 archetypal meaning of 176
Risible, the 16-17; see also comedy.
Romance 7, 43, 117; definition as a
 mythos 118-21; romance and
 comedy 120-2; dialectic of 120-2;
 parody of 168-71; spectacle in: see
 spectacle.
Rotrou 11, 17, 161, 183n, 187n
Rousset, J. 159, 171, 191n, 195, 198
Sartre, J.P. 186n
Scaliger 183n
Scapegoat 5; in comedy 15-16, 21, 28,
 32, 52, 55, 57, 59, 63, 73, 79, 83,
 110, 116, 122, 125; in romance
 137, 142; in the ironic mythos
 145, 151, 160, 167
Scatology 29, 107
Schérer, J. 8-9
Scholes, R. 181n
Scudéry, Mademoiselle de, 119, 188n;
 Clélie 49, 118; Le Grand Cyrus
 118-19, 133
Semiotics 197
Senex 15-16, 65, 100-1; senex iratus
 100
Sévigné, Madame de 108
Son figure (splitting of good and bad)
 95-6
Sparagmos 107, 154, 160
Spectacle: in romance 121-2, 137-9,
 143; in comedy 122
Structuralism: 181n, 195-8, 199n;
 psychological 196; sociological
 (Marxist) 196; linguistic 197-8
Sypher, W. 25, 183n

Tirso de Molina: *El Burlador de Sevilla* 170
Todorov, T. 181n, 197
Tractatus Coislinianus 154
Tragedy 4-7, 9, 22; French classical 5, 119-20; as an image of fate 22-3
Tragi-comedy 87, 132

Urfé, Honoré d': *L'Astrée* 118-19

Weber, J.P. 196
Wheelwright, P. 180n
Wish-fulfilment 7, 9, 12-14, 51, 79, 91, 170; *see also pensée magique,* pleasure principle.

UNIVERSITY OF TORONTO ROMANCE SERIES

1 Guido Cavalcanti's Theory of Love
J.E. SHAW

2 Aspects of Racinian Tragedy
JOHN C. LAPP

3 The Idea of Decadence in French Literature, 1830-1900
A.E. CARTER

4 *Le Roman de Renart* dans la littérature française et dans les littératures
étrangères au moyen âge
JOHN FLINN

5 Henry Céard: Idéaliste détrompé
RONALD FRAZEE

6 La Chronique de Robert de Clari: Etude de la langue et du style
P.F. DEMBOWSKI

7 Zola before the *Rougon-Macquart*
JOHN C. LAPP

8 The Idea of Art as Propaganda in France, 1750-1759:
A Study in the History of Ideas
J.A. LEITH

9 Marivaux
E.J.H. GREENE

10 Sondages, 1830-1848: romanciers français secondaires
JOHN S. WOOD

11 The Sixth Sense: Individualism in French Poetry, 1686-1760
ROBERT FINCH

12 The Long Journey: Literary Themes of French Canada
JACK WARWICK

13 The Narreme in the Medieval Romance Epic:
An Introduction to Narrative Structures
EUGENE DORFMAN

14 Verlaine: A Study in Parallels
A.E. CARTER

15 An Index of Proper Names in French Arthurian Verse Romances, 1150-1300
G.D. WEST

16 Emery Bigot: Seventeenth-Century French Humanist
LEONARD E. DOUCETTE

17 Diderot the Satirist. An Analysis of *Le Neveu de Rameau* and Related Works
DONAL O'GORMAN

18 'Naturalisme pas mort': Lettres inédites de Paul Alexis à Emile Zola 1871-1900
B.H. BAKKER

19 Crispin Ier: La Vie et l'œuvre de Raymond Poisson, comédien-poète du XVIIe siècle
A. ROSS CURTIS

20 Tuscan and Etruscan: The Problem of Linguistic Substratum Influence in Central Italy
HERBERT J. IZZO

21 *Fécondité* d'Emile Zola: Roman à thèse, évangile, mythe
DAVID BAGULEY

22 Charles Baudelaire. Edgar Allan Poe: Sa Vie et ses ouvrages
W.T. BANDY

23 Paul Claudel's *Le Soulier de Satin:* A Stylistic, Structuralist, and Psychoanalytic Interpretation
JOAN FREILICH

24 Balzac's Recurring Characters
ANTHONY R. PUGH

25 Morality and Social Class in Eighteenth-Century French Literature and Painting
WARREN ROBERTS

26 The Imagination of Maurice Barrès
PHILIP OUSTON

27 La Cité idéale dans *Travail* d'Emile Zola
F.I. CASE

28 Critical Approaches to Rubén Dario
KEITH ELLIS

29 Universal Language Schemes in England and France 1600-1800
JAMES R. KNOWLSON

31 Science and the Human Comedy
HARCOURT BROWN

31 Molière: An Archetypal Approach
HAROLD C. KNUTSON